# TURBULENCE

A True Story of Survival

ANNETTE HERFKENS

**Regan Arts.**

NEW YORK

**Regan Arts.**

65 Bleecker Street
New York, NY 10012

First Regan Arts hardcover edition, October 2016

Library of Congress Control Number: 2016939706

ISBN 978-1-68245-042-0

Interior design by Nancy Singer
Cover design by Richard Ljoenes

All photos courtesy of the author unless otherwise noted.

Printed in the United States of America

10  9  8  7  6  5  4  3  2  1

For Jaime, Joosje, and Maxi

# CONTENTS

PART I

## THE ACCIDENT, 1979–1993
### 1

1   Lost  3

2   Found  67

3   After  111

PART II

## THE RETURN, 1993–2006
### 143

4   Moving On  145

5   Preparation  197

6   Back in Vietnam  217

7   My Mountain  241

Afterword  269

Acknowledgments  281

# PART I

―――――――

# THE ACCIDENT,

## 1979–1993

"The most beautiful thing we can experience
is the mysterious."

—*Albert Einstein*

# 1

## LOST

### VIETNAM, 1992

"*Wake up. Wake up!* It is five a.m.; we have to go! My driver is picking us up in half an hour."

*Five a.m.? Driver? What driver? What is he talking about?*

I wake up, disoriented and groggy, and take in my surroundings. I see Pasje standing at the end of the bed.

This is my first visit to Vietnam, to Pasje—that is what I call Willem, my boyfriend of thirteen years. He had moved there six months before to set up two branches for the ING Bank. As I wake up, I remember the night before—his driver, Mr. Hung, drove me to Pasje's hotel after I landed at the Ho Chi Minh City airport. Pasje introduced him as his "Mr. Fix-It-All."

Pasje then hands me a cup of coffee with an apologetic smile. He knows that I hate getting up early. Even more so with jet lag. But five a.m.? What is he thinking? I look at Pasje in his gray, plushy bathrobe. His mother had it embroidered. When he turns around, I see the words "Breda, Leiden, Santiago" on the back. No "Ho Chi Minh City" yet. *She'll likely hand-stitch that when she visits.* There is something about Pasje in his bathrobe. I love the relaxed laziness it exudes; it complements his slow preparation for the day. His ritual of coffee making. A cup for me in bed, a cup for him at the table. He likes getting to the airport on time. He hates my tight planning when he visits me. He likes to get ready

3

slowly and thoroughly. I prefer fast and sloppy. Especially if it gives me
an extra half hour of sleep. But I love him. And the coffee.

I take my time sipping it, which leaves me about eight minutes to
shower and get dressed. Pasje tries to hide his irritation. Once we leave
the room—on time—he kisses me gently.

"Well done," he says.

We are off to a romantic vacation in Nha Trang, a beautiful resort
on the South China Sea. That's all I know. Pasje wants it to be a surprise.

When we get to the lobby, Mr. Hung is dutifully waiting. He gives us a
sneaky smile. There's something about him that makes me uncomfortable.
But Willem slaps him on the shoulder in his warm manner. It is strange
to see how at ease Pasje looks in this foreign environment. He obviously
feels at home, and it makes me feel out of place. *Am I jealous?*

It is still dark outside, as it was last night when we drove into town.
Again we pass crowds of people on bikes wearing triangular straw hats
and printed handkerchiefs covering their mouths. A Vietnam War
movie meets a Western. Our headlights illuminate their pajama-style
outfits, one by one. Or rather, five by five. Whole families seem to travel
together, sometimes several of them crowded onto one bike.

Though there are fewer people in the streets than the previous night,
there are still more than we would see during rush hour when we lived
in Amsterdam.

As Hung drops us off at the airport, Pasje gives him a list of things
to do in his absence. Off we go, finally. We walk into the 1960s-style
airport, with its retro chairs, counters, and lamps; it all resembles an old
movie. As always, Pasje takes care of the formalities of checking in, first
parking me in a little coffee shop. I feel more at ease once Pasje and I
are on the go. This is what we are used to doing. I look around and try
to appreciate the different culture. Next to me, a man is noisily slurping
a large bowl of soup, just like the Chinese traders do when we have
breakfast in New York's Chinatown.

Pasje returns with our boarding passes in hand. "We have to walk
over to the plane," he says. "No buses here." I follow him down the stairs
onto the tarmac. We pass a few army jets, lined up as if ready for combat. *I
have never seen that before!* When we finally stop in front of our plane, my
heart sinks. I cannot believe how small it is—I am very claustrophobic.

"I am not going on that!" I exclaim in terror. "There is no way I can do that. You know I can't!"

Pasje is obviously prepared for this. "I know, I know. But I am sure you can do it. This is the only way to get there."

"What do you mean the only way? Can't we take a car?"

"The jungle is very dense, and the road is horrible. It would take days. By the time we get there, we would have to leave again. Please?"

"I'll try," I say with effort. I force myself to climb the steps leading to the rear entrance of the plane. I step inside. My head almost touches the ceiling. I immediately turn around. "Let me out of here!" I beg. Pasje steps in front of the exit. "Please, Pasje, I can't do this." I panic and start beating his chest with both my fists. Pasje takes them in a tight grip and forces me to look into his eyes.

"You can do it; I know you can. You just have to. For me, for us. It is only twenty minutes."

With my heart pounding in my throat, I follow him to the third row. Out of fifteen, I count. I sit down in the aisle seat. I could easily touch the passenger across the aisle if I wanted to. I can touch the ceiling without even straightening my arm. My knees are touching the blue seat in front of me. Pasje puts on his seat belt. It goes across his chest, like the ones they use in a car. I shrug off mine. I feel restrained enough as it is. The stewardess, a tiny, pretty Vietnamese girl, lets me off the hook. She continues with her emergency routine. I try to focus, but I can only think of plotting my exit. I recite things in my head to distract myself, anything I can think of. Homer: "Oh, Muse, tell me about the man who has traveled the seas." Or something like that. OK, "The Lorelei": "*Ich weiß nicht, was soll es bedeuten, daß ich so traurig bin.*" "I don't know why I am so blue" is the only poetry I know by heart. It was my German teacher's favorite punishment. "*Ein Märchen aus uralten Zeiten, das kommt mich nicht aus dem Sinn.*" "I can't get my mind off a very old tale." We are taking off. At least we are moving.

I keep my eyes fixed on Pasje's watch, the 1940 Rolex I bought him in Washington, DC last year when I turned thirty. He had told me he wanted to get married by the time I turned thirty, which made me very anxious. But when my actual birthday came, he just laughed it all off. I was so relieved that I splurged on that Rolex as a gift for him. I had seen the way he admired it in a store.

I try to focus on that US trip. There was a wedding in New York. Pasje flew in from Chile, where he was working at the time, and I from Madrid. My parents were there too. And my older sister, who lives in DC. Turns out the deadline was her idea. Having no children of her own, she had wanted nieces and nephews. I was not ready to be a parent, and ate myself up with worry after Pasje's proposal: I lost ten pounds, trying to come up with a "Yes, now!" But it didn't make sense. Yet. We were both doing so well. Careers and money still had to be made before we could settle in the same place. We were a done deal anyway.

My thoughts come back to the plane. Time is creeping by. When I have made it through twenty minutes, there is still no evidence of a descent.

"Why are we not landing?" I ask the stewardess.

"Because the flight is fifty-five minutes," she answers with a smile. I turn to Pasje, who is now avoiding eye contact.

"I knew it was the only way," he says guiltily.

I want to stand up and break free, but realize I will only bump my head. There is nowhere to go, except the even tinier bathroom. I look at the watch. My heart is thumping in my ears. Pasje strokes my arm, but I shake him off.

"How could you do that to me?" I hiss between my teeth. "You tricked me!" I turn my focus back to the watch. And the roaring engines. Forty-nine minutes. Six to go. I keep looking at the watch. Then all of a sudden, we drop. A tremendous drop.

Now Pasje looks straight at me. "This I don't like," he says nervously.

"Of course a shitty little toy plane drops like this!" I reply. "It's just an air pocket; don't worry," I add softly, when I see the fear in his eyes. We drop again. Farther this time. Someone screams. Pasje grabs my hand; I reach for his.

Pitch-black.


## The Yak

The Yak, short for Yakovlev Yak-40, is a small, three-engine airliner. Often called the first regional jet transport aircraft, it was introduced in September 1968 by Aeroflot, the Russian airline. It is comparable to a

Boeing 727. Its maximum cruising speed is 341 miles per hour.

Our flight VN 474 was carrying twenty-four passengers, three stewardesses, two pilots, and an engineer. On its descent to the coastal resort of Nha Trang, the aircraft somehow deviated from its assigned flight path. It was descending more steeply than the crew appeared to realize. The pilot is believed to have made a navigational error, estimating the distance to the coast at twelve miles, whereas it was probably twenty-six miles.

According to the descent profile provided by Vietnam Airlines, the weather on the morning of November 14, 1992, took a sudden turn, causing extreme turbulence. The pilot is believed to have struggled to control the aircraft.

VN 474 was flying at a speed of around 300 miles per hour when it struck the ridge of a mountain. The force of impact was tempered by the fact that the plane only lost one wing and kept flying. But a plane that loses its wings turns into a missile (or in our case, half a missile). So when the plane finally crashed into the neighboring mountain, the impact was even greater.

I was sitting in what was said to be the least safe part of the cabin—in front of the wing—with the lowest survival rates. But where I sat turned out to be irrelevant. I wasn't wearing my seat belt. Everyone else was. The seat belt is designed to withstand 3,000 pounds of force—that is 17 g for a typical 170-pound man. Experts say that people can survive this kind of force if they are restrained well. They were. I wasn't. I went flying. I survived. They didn't.

Pasje was killed—his ribs got crushed into his lungs from the impact, whereas I took off from my seat. I don't remember, but I must have tumbled around in the cabin like a lonely piece of laundry in a dryer, hitting my head and limbs against the ceiling, baggage lockers, and chairs. At some point I must have landed and slipped under a seat, legs first, and gotten stuck. This might have kept me in place for the second, bigger impact, which caused the plane to break into three pieces: the cockpit, the remaining wing, and the fuselage.

We were nineteen miles from Nha Trang, our destination, and ten miles from the nearest village.

# THE HAGUE, 1979

"It is as if you were born for good luck," my old classmate said when I interviewed him recently about our high school days. "I know you had that terrible accident," he continued, "but if you asked me if I ever thought you were doomed somehow, I would say no, on the contrary. Everything about you seemed happy-go-lucky. You were always cheerful. You had those older brothers, so you felt easy around the big boys. You looked good, were successful at school, sports, music, even drawing and painting. You were the leader of your group of friends, yet you moved around easily among other groups. What more can I say?"

Was I lucky, or what? Lucky and privileged. I grew up in a beautiful green neighborhood, with a large extended family. We were quite protected, yet with many Dutch freedoms. With my bike, I could go wherever I wanted. All I had to do was tell my parents where I was. Our mother was warm, open, inclusive: our house was always open to anyone. My father was a lenient parent who kept us grounded—for I kept my judgments in check and never felt superior to others. After school, I would play in one

Elementary school, The Hague, 1970

of the lovely old parks in our area, or cycle to the tennis club and hang out between games. In my teens, I joined a sports club and played competitive field hockey and tennis. My life was all about these clubs, where we would hang out to watch the others play or dance at club parties.

As a teenager, I would go out with my friends to the small cafés in the old center of town, or sing in the Roaring Twenties bar. I would drink a bit, but not too much. I didn't have to. My brothers and sister were there or had been there and done that. That made all the difference.

After school, I went to study law at Leiden University, the oldest university in the Netherlands. In 1575, William I, Prince of Orange, gave this beautiful old town the right to found the university as a reward for Leiden's brave resistance against the Spaniards in the Eighty Years' War. More than my studies, the student society—which was also the country's first—defined my college days. It was a members-only association with influential alumni, located in a grand building with libraries, bars, a restaurant, and even a disco. The society had some rather feudal and eccentric subsocieties. The choice to become a society member was a natural one for many. The tradition was passed on from generation to generation. Everyone could join, but only some did. It was a system based on self-selection, rather than rejection.

Life as a society member was a bit of a survival game, which, if survived well, would guarantee a post-graduation job in the "old boys'" network of companies and law firms. There were endless, intricate, uncontested rules of behavior. I can't say they all suited me, but I had a great time nonetheless.

Nightlife revolved around the club. We entered the building at five p.m. and left twelve hours later. Once inside, everything revolved around conversations—either superficial or deep, and often with male friends. For me, conversation only, not sex. Back then, sex would under-mine a girl's image.

The "popular" girls lived in "popular" sorority houses, and the "popular" boys lived in "popular" frat houses in the town center, along the beautiful canals of Leiden. Coed houses were frowned upon. There was only one more or less accepted coed house: the one I lived in. The one where Willem van der Pas—or Pasje, as everyone called him—also lived.

# WAKING UP

I wake up to the strange sounds of the jungle. I see wild vegetation through an enormous gap in the front of the plane's fuselage. The cockpit has broken off. It is both eerily still and strangely noisy.

I am still inside the plane—stuck under a seat, weighted down by a dead body. I try to push it off me. I can't. I yank my legs from underneath the seat, ripping them open in the process. Then I see Pasje across the aisle. He is lying in his seat, which has somehow flipped backward. He has a smile on his lips. A sweet little smile. He is dead.

I must have gone into shock, because suddenly I am sitting outside the cabin, on the ground, on countless little twigs. In the middle of the jungle. Everything hurts. I can't move. I look down at my bare legs. My wraparound skirt is gone. On my left knee there is a large, gaping wound. My right foot is covered in blood; the skin on my ankle seems to have been torn off. But the worst sight is my shin: I can see four inches of bluish bone sticking out through layers of flesh. Like a picture from a biology book. I make a startled, jerky move, and feel an excruciating pain in my hips. I try to sit up, but the pain in my chest stops me. My breath feels thin and shallow. Thoughts are coming all at once: *What has happened? Where am I?*

I look around. I am sitting on a mountain slope, under the trees, in dense undergrowth. Pieces of wreckage are everywhere. The plane has lost its wings. The cockpit has broken off. A weird, unreal reality. Everything is green. And those jungle sounds! The more I listen to them, the louder they seem to become.

There are a few people lying on the mountain slope, beneath the wreckage.

And I can still hear some of the passengers moaning from inside the plane. About ten feet to my right, a Vietnamese girl is groaning loudly. A bit farther away lies the lifeless body of a man. Then I realize I am sitting right next to someone, a Vietnamese man. Alive. He speaks to me.

"Don't worry. They will come for us," he says, pronouncing his Rs like Ls. Just like Numachi, my Japanese colleague. I am suddenly aware that I am sitting in my panties. I look shamefully down my legs at my bluish bone proudly sticking out of my flesh. The man sitting next to me opens a little square suitcase he is holding on to for dear life. He hands me a pair of trousers. They are part of a suit. *Polyester*, I cannot help thinking, but I thank him profusely. It hurts like hell to pull the trouser legs over my wounds.

When I get to my hips, I realize something is terribly wrong. An unbelievable pain cuts off my breath. The bones in my bottom feel crushed. Still my manners get the better of me. I grind my teeth and slowly, painfully force the pants over my hips. I quickly close the zipper and thank the man again. He smiles. "I am a very important man," he says. "They will come for me."

"They better!" I answer. *I certainly hope so,* I think, but I feel comforted by his words. By his presence. We both retreat into our injuries. Over the following few hours, we speak a few times, all initiated by me. Bugging him. I ask when he thinks the rescue workers will come. I can see he is getting weaker. "Please don't die," I beg him. "Let's try to locate some water."

"I already had something to drink," he answers, ever so faintly.

*Well, that's nice!* I think. My mouth is so dry. It tastes foul and sticky. "Will you give me some?" I ask. He closes his eyes, in a more definite manner, it seems. I beg and plead: "Please don't die; please don't leave me!" He does not answer. "Please don't leave me here on my own!" I almost scream.

But he has difficulty breathing. I see the life go out of him. He takes his last breath. He is gone. There are no more sounds coming from the Vietnamese girl. There are no sounds, no movements from any of the other passengers.

Everyone else is dead.

Pasje also studied law in Leiden, and we were initiated into our student club in the same year. His friends were all the cool and conservative guys in our club, known as the "Best Boys." But Pasje was different. Not just older, he was a man in both demeanor and looks. Broad-shouldered, stocky, with curly, brown hair and a manly but friendly face, he had soft, brown eyes, a five-o'clock shadow, and hair on his chest. He was unlike most Dutch boys, who were mostly tall, thin, blue-eyed, and hairless. Moreover, he had his own ideas, not his father's. Very different, well-informed, articulate ideas about religion, politics, and the world. He called himself an autonomous thinker—an anarchist when he was drunk—and he defied conformity. Yet, his warmth and tolerance made him much liked by everyone.

At first I only eyed him as a prospective housemate. When a male housemate graduated, we needed to replace him, and wanted another "Best Boy." I approached Pasje in our club's discotheque. He flirted, which I ignored. I made a big plea for our house, emphasizing its fantastic location on the Rapenburg canal, at the center of social and academic life. He moved in a month later.

He had a bit of a southern accent—I had to overcome my own northern prejudice. Then we became great friends. Real buddies. We studied, shopped for food, made dinner, and watched TV together. At night, we went to the society together. That is where we each went our own way. He said I only had eyes for the older boys. It was true. I knew many because they were my brother's friends, and I had my heart set on one of them. After a night at the society, I would discuss my progress with Pasje the next day. All the ups and downs of the relationship, which ended in a breakup before it had really begun. Pasje's broad shoulders were always there to cry on.

We both said it was the other who started our romance. One evening, we ended up alone in his room. We were having a conversation. I said I had no fears, that I dared everything. He looked me in the eyes, and suddenly, the tension was palpable. "I know something you wouldn't dare," he said, his dark eyes gleaming with anticipation. So I dared . . .

He was my first. Few people would have believed that, because I had a big mouth and moved around in a self-possessed way. "Unaware," I would call it today. I was fully focused on the outside world, rather than how that world perceived me. I was also used to hanging out with boys. Pasje knew all that and more. Looking back, I now realize how wise and insightful he was.

We had hit the jackpot. Our love was real. At first, we had to keep it a secret because of the coed house rules. To be alone, we would casually stroll across the Rapenburg bridge to the Academy Building and climb over the walls of the Hortus Botanicus botanical garden with a bottle of wine. Weekends, when he would go back home, were endless and full of anticipation. On Sunday night he would show me the poems he had written during our separation.

For our first joint vacation we went to Paris. He proudly showed me the city he knew very well, thanks to an ex-girlfriend who had lived there. From Paris, we hitchhiked to his parents' country house in Normandy. Both the area and the house were deserted. It felt like a true honeymoon.

Paris, 1981

Costume party, Leiden, 1983

After we went public with our relationship, Pasje had to move out; romantic liaisons were not permitted in our house. He chose to move to the biggest frat house in Leiden. It was big enough to allow him to go his own way. He had both the character and the time to play house with me and still be one of the guys. He never gave in to peer pressure, whether it concerned me, his taste in music, or his political views—all three radical.

There was an enormous intimacy and a total lack of shame between us. He called me a dolphin, or sometimes Flipper, "because of that smile with the little teeth." I called him a seal, because of his eyes—the sweet brown eyes I kissed immediately when we woke up every time we were together, for thirteen years. I would sign every note with a little drawing of a mouth, an arrow, and an eye.

Yet, I had a longing for the world in the same deep way other girls can long for love, or the idea of love. I liked the idea of seeing the world. Maybe because I already had love, maybe because of my programming or my destiny. Two years after I took Pasje's dare, when most of our friends were eyeing management jobs at the student club, my focus turned to getting out of there, to Latin America. Preferably with Pasje, but otherwise, for the time being, without.

# DAY ONE

*Everyone is dead.* I am sitting here. In a jungle. Alone. I move my eyes. I see the leaves, the broken plane parts, the bodies. I listen to my breath. It sounds as labored as it feels; my chest hurts so much! But I am breathing. Loud and clear!

Again, I observe: the sounds, the jungle, the leaves, the plane, the bodies. And myself, lying on a bed of twigs. Sharp little twigs. They hurt. I move a bit. It hurts. My hips hurt. Everything hurts. *Help me, dear Lord. Help me!*

My forehead feels as if somebody is pounding on it with a hammer. I cannot move my legs. They seem both cramped and lifeless. I stay on my back and look at my arms. They are covered with blood. There are two gaping wounds near my right elbow. They feel tender. When I graze my fingers over them, I nearly scream.

I go outside myself again. I focus on the leaves. On the broken plane parts. On the bodies. The Vietnamese girl died with her fist clenched. The man next to me looks both peacefully asleep and dead. Like Pasje, with his sweet smile . . . *Don't think of Pasje. Don't think of Pasje.* I look back at the man. He is not scary, just dead. I know what the dead look like. I have seen corpses. I think of the ones I have seen. Mr. Bongaerts. My grandmother. Manuel in Chile. You only have to see one to know that dead is dead. And that they are not scary, that there is nothing to fear. I check the man's watch: ten o'clock. Ironic how that keeps going.

I look at the sky through the trees. There are clouds, but they don't seem to hold rain. *Isn't it rainy season?* I wish I had read up on my travels! I have no idea of where I am. I just know the jungles are endless. And I don't see any planes. *Where is the next plane? The next plane will surely see us.* We seem high up the mountain. Who knows how far from where. I have not even looked at the map! I have no idea what direction we are flying. Pasje is my compass. *Don't think of Pasje!*

I look at the sun coming through the leaves. The palette of light and shade is beautiful. The leaves are radiant. My mother would appreciate it. My mother always says she does not worry about me when I am with Pasje. She thinks I am safe because I am with Pasje. Pasje who is . . . *Don't think. Don't think of Pasje! Think of mammie.* She'd be happy to know I got my shots. How smart of her to make me get those. Even tetanus! All arranged against my will, with Jaime, my business partner, as her accomplice. They made sure I had them administered at Schiphol airport. Before my flight to Tokyo. "What for?" I had asked her. "We're not going to the jungle." *Right!*

I look at my feet sticking out of the borrowed pants. They are swollen, really swollen. My favorite shoes—gray-blue woven crocodile leather moccasins from El Corte Inglés—are cutting into bluish flesh that does not seem like mine.

I grab my purse. *How strange that I still have it on me.* I check the contents: very basic travel supplies. No wallet. Pasje has the money. No watch. Pasje has the watch. *Don't think of Pasje!* No cell phone. I always have a cell phone. To call Jaime. I think of Jaime. *What would he say if he knew where I am?* These are going to be the first two business days since we have been working together that I am unable to call him. Since we began at Banco Santander, I always called him. With those big cell phones. Everyone looked at me in the beginning. Sometimes they would point at me in the street in Madrid. In Holland, they would scream that I am a show-off with my phone. No phone now. Can't call Jaime now.

Not until Wednesday. On Wednesday, Pasje and I are scheduled to return to Ho Chi Minh City. Jaime expects me to call immediately when I get back to the hotel. I always call him, from wherever I am. To talk about the markets, to make decisions. If he doesn't hear from me by Thursday, he will definitely make noise. Lots of noise, knowing him.

I continue checking my purse. There is a makeup pouch, a camera, three packages of Philip Morris Super Lights cigarettes, and a Bic lighter. The makeup pouch is from Loewe. Beautiful, soft Spanish leather, evidence of my recent "upgrade" at Banco Santander. No use for it now. The camera I bought with Numachi in Tokyo. Patient Numachi. How my dead neighbor reminds me of him: the way he spoke, or rather, the way he didn't. And the careful way in which he had handed me his trousers. Thank God for those; they protect me somewhat from these horrible insects! I hope he was right, that they might come for him soon. Nobody will miss me until Wednesday. It's Saturday now. Saturday, Sunday, Monday, Tuesday. Four days until Wednesday.

It does not occur to me to take pictures. Nor does it cross my mind to open the man's suitcase. And I don't make my way back to the main part of the plane, where the bodies are, to search for food or drinks. I don't even dare to look over my shoulder. I just stay there, looking down the mountain, telling myself this is real, this is where I am. I have no water. *Dear Lord, help me get through this.* My mouth is dry. So dry. I contemplate smoking, but with nothing to eat or drink, I decide this might as well be the moment to finally stop. Pasje would have been proud. He wouldn't have believed it. *Don't think of Pasje! Look at the sun coming through the leaves. Wow! How pretty!* I am normally not really into the woods. I prefer the sun on the water. But this is beautiful!

The sun is setting. Somewhere. I can't see through the trees. It gets dark fast. Very fast. I look at the watch: six o'clock. *Time to go to bed?* I may as well. I am not scared. I wonder why. I have never been so completely alone.

# CHILE, 1983

While most of my friends were still fully immersed in college life, I had my heart set on an internship in Chile. The South American country seemed to represent everything I wanted to make up my mind about, economically and politically, with a dictatorship to seal the deal. With an iron hand, Augusto Pinochet was dictating free markets to reign. With my combative, socialist older sister in one ear and my conservative friends in the other, I felt it was time to find out where I stood.

I liked the idea of Latin America. I loved the music and the stories. I was born in Venezuela; my father worked for Shell, a Dutch oil company. My family left when I was a baby, but, as siblings do, my older sister and brothers endlessly reminisced about those days. They wove into their stories that I had been switched as a baby, that the real Annette was still living in Maracaibo. In a slum, my left-wing sister added, "wondering whether she will get anything to eat that day." I, on the contrary, got a good education, clean water, and went on skiing holidays. I had believed the story for years, so wasn't it logical that I wanted to go back to my roots?

My major was international law, with an emphasis on economics. I knew there was one professor who could help me get into the United Nations in Chile. He had made an appeal in an economics magazine for a synthesis of economic theories: from the tightfisted Milton Friedman to the easy-spending Maynard Keynes. I sweated the whole summer, working out his suggestions in a paper. Then I made an appointment to see him. To my relief, he liked the paper, or the fact that I had written about him, and got me my dream internship, at the Santiago offices of the International Labor Organization, an agency of the United Nations. Luckily, Pasje decided to come along and do research for his graduation thesis on the Andean Pact.

We made a point of getting contacts on "the other side," those who opposed the government: we got acquainted with a Chilean exile in Amsterdam, Noemi Baeza, who, after the military coup in 1973, had been rounded up with many of her left-wing friends. She had been at the infamous stadium in Santiago, and was later sent to a camp where she was tortured so badly she could never have children. Her husband was exiled to a different country, where he married a woman who could. Despite all this, Noemi was a warm and open person, and we became very close. By the time Pasje and I left, she trusted us with the addresses of her underground friends in Chile.

We left Amsterdam in September, after an elaborate good-bye from our college friends. My housemates went undercover, a flippant reminder that I was going to a police state. Big trips were still special back then. My sorority even composed a song for the occasion, titled "Missing Herf." In Santiago, Pasje and I began playing house. We learned Spanish, and we made a wide variety of friends. We spent our time both uptown in trendy restaurants and downtown at demonstrations against Pinochet.

The building that housed the United Nations Economic Commission for Latin America and the Caribbean (ECLAC), where we both worked, was beautiful. A kind of big version of the Guggenheim, with a reflecting pond. It was located in a wealthy uptown neighborhood at the foot of the *cordillera*, the mountain chain that spans the continent from Venezuela to Chile's south. In the afternoon, the mountains would turn a rosé pink. It made a wonderful backdrop for the stunning architecture of our workplace.

Saying goodbye to our parents, Schiphol Airport, September 1983

Pasje used the library to write his final thesis. I took a course on employment, organized by the regional labor program for Latin America and the Caribbean, which, contrary to Pinochet's policies, advocated a big role for the public sector in creating jobs. My classmates were about twenty economists from around the continent, all government employees. The course did not convince me. I believed the one thing the government should leave to the private sector was creating employment. But I cherished the opportunity to get to know people from all over Latin America. At night we would visit the *peñas*, the Chilean music cafés. Everyone from my class would request songs from their home countries, and we would sing them together.

When the course ended, Pasje and I traveled north, through South America's longest desert to Peru, intending to walk the Inca Trail. We managed to walk all the way to the top of Machu Picchu. It was beautiful, majestic, and overwhelmingly peaceful; the raw spirituality touched both of us deeply. However, I got so sick after eating an omelette a local acquaintance had offered that we had to cut the hike short.

Back in Chile, Pasje, who was four years older than I, decided it was time to go home and finish his studies. I was going to stay in Santiago for another six months on my own.

In the following year, I was given my own office in the United Nations building to write a report as part of my apprenticeship. That report would also serve as my final college thesis. Every morning at ten thirty, the *funcionarios* would all have coffee around a big table and discuss the state of the world. Most conversations were about the high exchange rate of the dollar. Of course, this greatly impacted Latin American countries because they had to cope with interest payments on large debts owed to the US. The eagerness to check the dollar exchange rate in the newspapers also had to do with the fact that *funcionario* salaries were denominated in US dollars. A higher dollar gave them more purchasing power in the local peso. It made me realize that in Latin America, like everywhere else, money was everything. A bit of a turnoff, actually: a revolutionary dream in a cesspool of tax-free BMWs.

Sometimes after work, I would play tennis with my colleagues, and wine and dine in uptown restaurants, but more often, I would take

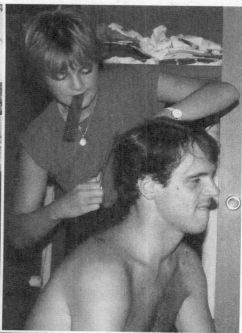

Playing house, Santiago, Chile,
September 1983 *(top left)*
Cutting hair, Santiago, Chile,
1983 *(top right)*

Peru, December 1983

Opening St. Nicholas presents
from our families, Santiago,
Chile, December 5, 1983

the subway downtown. I had become close with Noemi's friends, and they regularly took me to protests against Pinochet. I relished the atmosphere.

*"El pueblo unido jamás será vencido! El pueblo unido jamás será vencido!"* Which means "The people united will never be defeated!" Standing in a chanting crowd at a protest downtown, I would look at the heated faces around me in awe. I had never felt that strongly about anything. Their cause seemed so much more immediate to me than the lack of housing in Amsterdam or US nuclear warheads in Europe. Between the rousing speeches, they sang songs that went straight to my heart. After the demonstrations we would go to the *taller* to eat. (*Taller* is Spanish for "studio," and Taller Amistad doubled as the house and studio of Pablo Madero, a warm and round-faced communist painter.)

His work was Picasso-style with bright blues, reds, and yellows. He had a golden heart, though he had several left-wing Dutch acquaintances whom he knew how to play for subsidies. He seemed to treat me differently, as one of his own. Perhaps he recognized the opportunist in me. He would say that I was more Latino than Dutch. It was true, if it meant that I easily forgot the time, and myself. I loved being part of the demonstrations, the late dining, singing, and talking. I enjoyed discussing politics and economics with Manuel, Pablo's brother-in-law, who was the most educated of the pack. I often ended up staying over on the little couch in the hall and taking an ice-cold shower before making it back to the office uptown. I cared about my hosts as individuals. And how could I not understand their cause as I listened to their stories about life in the slums?

I learned how unconditional Chileans could be in their friendship, whether they lived uptown or downtown. They gave and did things for each other without keeping score.

My thesis was on the Chilean forestry sector. The Pinochet government prided itself on its laissez-faire credentials. Yet, contrary to its principles, it was subsidizing the forestry sector, and the sector was flourishing. I hoped to use this contradiction to make the government look bad, not only on human rights but also on economic policies. So for research purposes, I planned a trip to a work site deep in the forests of the south.

I knew that in order to make supply meet demand perfectly, workers were hired on short-term contracts. My work would consist of interviewing the workers. Reaching their work site would require a ten-hour drive south, plus two hours on a dirt track into the woods. I was going to carpool and hitchhike. My colleagues wondered why I did not rent a car. The fact was I didn't know how to drive.

The first leg of the trip, down to Valparaiso, I traveled piled into the back of a Fiat with three "lefty" engineers. We stayed overnight in a desperately poor mining town. It had no electricity and many miserable stories to tell. From there, I continued on my own, hitching rides from truck drivers on their way to the woodcutting sites. I knew I might be taking a risk traveling into the woods like that on my own, but I trusted my instincts. And there was nothing to worry about. The drivers and their companions were friendly and almost falling over each other to be able to share how badly their lives had been affected by Pinochet's economic policies.

One of the laborers at the site took me to his home on a tractor, to interview his wife. He proudly showed me his two chickens, his goat, and five very cute young children. He explained how he extracted charcoal to heat his house, which was made of clay. It was still freezing inside. He was only paid three months a year. The other nine months he had to live off the woods, the chickens, and the goat.

Back in my uptown office, I could not muster up the focus to produce a written report. I was too involved in local reality and too busy living a double life. So I decided to go back to Holland, where, within the cold and damp university walls of ancient Leiden, I produced my ambiguous conclusions. Although the government subsidies had indeed strengthened the foresting sector, the Chilean economy as a whole had become more sensitive to the ups and downs of the world economy. This turned out to be a good thing, however, as the world economy was on its way up at the time.

As grateful as I was for the internship, I decided not to pursue a career at the United Nations.

# DAY TWO

The sun is shining when I wake up. And I open my eyes to the strangest reality: the thick growth of plants all around me. The creepy, crawly insects. The sounds! The thirst. The all-encompassing, overwhelming thirst. I see dead "Numachi" next to me, his eyes half open. I move. It hurts. I try to sit up, but I fall back. My hips are on fire. Oh, those twigs! I check his watch: six-thirty.

Further to the right I see the body of the Vietnamese girl. Her hair shines in the sun. I move my eyes. Farther down is a wing of the plane. It all comes back to me. I am in Vietnam. On vacation. With Pasje. *Where is Pasje? No, I can't think of Pasje. Pasje is dead. Pasje is dead. My Pasje is dead! I saw him. Dead. . . . And then? What did I do? How did I get out?* I don't remember. But I do remember Pasje. *Dead. Strapped in his seat. With a smile. Like a sweet mummy.* I panic. *Help! Help me!*

A pain in my chest stops me. I can hardly breathe. I have to calm myself. *Don't think of Pasje. Breathe slowly. Don't think of Pasje. Don't cry. Crying will make you thirsty. Don't look back over your shoulder. Look at the leaves.*

I rest my head and stare at the leaves. I feel the pain come and go in waves. I squint. I play with the sunlight through my eyelashes. How pretty. That filtered sunlight lighting up the dew on the leaves.

I tune in to the sounds. A cacophony, each sound competing with the others. The sounds of the jungle. I try to single them out. *Are those screaming monkeys? What the . . . ?*

I keep telling myself this is real. *This is not a sound box. Or a movie. A movie about Vietnam. I have seen so many. The last one was* Platoon. *Where did I see it? A long time ago. When I was living in New York. At the Yale Club, with that Yalie who wanted to date me. Imagine those young American soldiers crossing here, packed with artillery, waiting for a Vietnamese soldier to jump on them at any moment from behind a tree. So many trees.*

*No one is looking for me. I am all alone. Ridiculously alone.* I remember how Pasje and I used to climb over the wall of the botanical gardens in

Leiden to be "alone." Once, we got caught by my friend Jet, but she didn't know what we were up to. "I know what you are doing!" she screamed. "You are smoking pot!" Ha ha. We never did! We were just hiding the bottle of wine. She had no clue we were a couple. No more "we"! No more Pasje. Alone, alone. *Don't think! I am here. Alive. In the jungle. In the jungle, not a botanical garden. Isn't it supposed to be muggy and hot? Why am I so cold?*

I look at my hands. *What are those black, round things? Scabs? Oh, my God, they are leeches!* I rub the back of my hands together to get them off. They won't come off. *Don't look at them!*

I look at the leaves again. I can almost sense them. I remember how I always liked to stare at leaves, though in more urban settings, through windows. So different from the ones I see now.

Too many leaves remind me of hiking. Hiking makes me hungry and long for food. Not now, though. I am just thirsty, so thirsty.

Then suddenly it rains. And how! It is that kind of hard rain that punches you. It strikes my wounds, and it hurts my face when I look up with my mouth open. I almost gag, happily: so much water I get to swallow! The sun comes out as suddenly as the rain started. My T-shirt is drenched. I suck out some water. What a relief! I warm myself in the feeble sun rays that reach me through the leaves. I am cold. So cold.

I look at my belongings. Neatly lined up next to me. Soaking wet. The camera. The makeup pouch. The Bic lighter. *Lighter? Of course! The lighter! I can make a fire! Like Robinson Crusoe.* I try to light it. Nothing happens. It does not even spark. It won't. Ever. It is too wet. So are the twigs. It is too damp. I have made enough fires to know that. *What do I need a fire for, anyway? To prepare food? There is no food.* I can't walk. Can't even sit up straight. All I can see is grass, bushes, and plants. *Make smoke signals? Like Hiawatha.* This is what Pasje called me when I got those green boots, after the Native American girl: "My Minnehaha." *Don't think of Pasje.*

Instead I think of the bond markets. Where would MYDFA, Brazil, be? But it is the weekend; there are no markets. I think of Jaime. *What is he doing now?* He is probably with his sons. Playing games in an arcade. Or playing "Who can pee the farthest?" It makes me smile. Silly

Jaime. He'll seriously wonder what's up if he hasn't heard from me by Wednesday afternoon. *He'll raise hell by Thursday morning. I'll give him a few extra days to find me.* I relax. *Jaime.* I check the watch again and again. I wait and wait. I focus on the leaves.

My dead neighbor has a fifty-dollar bill sticking out of his breast pocket. *I might need that. To bribe someone to help me.* Not yet. Though I reckon he will soon become too unpleasant to sit next to, that I will have to move away somehow. I muse that he does not arouse my appetite, unlike that rugby team that crashed in the Andes and ate each other. I am thirsty, but not bloodthirsty.

*I'll give them a week. I'll need real water by then. And food. Otherwise I'll die. Just like the others, just like Pasje. Don't think of Pasje. Think of everyone else who loves us. How strange. So many people care so much about us, yet none of them know.*

I think of my brother Bernard. *What is he doing now? Probably flying somewhere.* I try to picture him in his air force uniform. I smile. Wherever he goes, he is the life of the party. *What would he say if he were here? Give me some sound advice?* He has helped me with social jungles. Always told me to keep my mouth shut, or at least use my brain before opening it. "Don't talk about your travels when you come back home. People are not interested; they don't want to know." *If only I make it home this time.*

*I'll crawl into the jungle if no one has come by Saturday.* That is my plan! To survive until Saturday. Six more days.

# LEIDEN, 1984

By the time I came back from Chile, I had seniority in our student house and got the biggest room. It looked out over the Rapenburg, Leiden's best-known canal. My window faced the Academy Building of Leiden University. Alas, my mind could not have been farther away from Holland and its orange history.

Ever since my return from Chile, Chilean protest music had been blaring from my stereo. I was "Chile-sick." But I also had a real fever, a high one. So high that I stayed at home by myself while Pasje and the rest were out celebrating the 170th anniversary of our student club.

The fever got worse, and when I went to our kitchen to fetch a drink of water, I got so dizzy I passed out. Next thing I knew, Pasje was lifting me up and putting me into a car. He took me to my parents' house. They were away for the weekend. He put me in their bed and said he was going out to get dinner. McDonald's.

I ate a Big Mac and later threw it up in an ambulance. I passed out again soon after. This time I woke up in a hospital room with three other patients, old ladies, chorusing: "Child, you scared us with all that screaming you did! All night long, in Spanish and in Dutch. Child, you really did scare us. You were yelling something like, 'I am not telling anything, even if you pull my nails out!' What was that all about?"

They treated me for malaria. Unsuccessfully. I got sicker and sicker and ended up in intensive care. I had a cocktail of diseases I had somehow suppressed for months: typhoid, amoebas, and hepatitis. I was quickly separated from the old ladies and put in a room by myself. Friends visited daily from Leiden, and my mother brought me homemade food. I got stronger bit by bit. Pasje was always by my side. How much I loved him.

After three weeks I was finally wheeled out of the hospital. I took another three weeks to recover . . . *almost* recover. I remained vulnerable. In the following years, I kept passing out when things got too tough, physically or mentally. For a couple of minutes, my eyes would roll backward into Nowhereland. I might have returned to college too soon.

I didn't get much studying done. The letters were dancing before my eyes. I tried to return to an active social life, probably more than I should have. I was just happy to be back with Pasje. It seemed as if I had never been away.

That is, until I found a letter in my mailbox with a plane ticket. My wealthier friends in Chile had taken up a collection. They all thought I should go back to fully recuperate. "The clear air and the warm climate will be better for you than the cold, rainy college life in Holland," they wrote.

Back in Santiago, I found the climate very different indeed. Pinochet was cutting down many of the newly gained liberties to stifle the various political movements that were rumbling underground. Parties from the left to the center-right had been organizing themselves in anticipation of the democratic future they believed to be near, but despite his earlier promise to reform, Pinochet had a change of heart. He was not quite ready to give up his absolute power. It would take another six years.

My friend Noemi had been given permission to return to her country. But after thirteen years of exile in Amsterdam, longing to be among her old friends in Santiago, she found it hard to reconnect with some of them. They resented her for the economic affluence she had enjoyed in Holland. They had been struggling to survive Pinochet's economic measures that favored the rich and had left them even poorer than before.

Noemi was also very afraid—constantly looking over her shoulder, lowering her voice, seemingly at random. She warned me that many of the people I had befriended were in danger. Among them was Manuel Guerrero, the college professor I had spent much time with at the Taller Amistad. When he spoke at an underground protest at a university, we met up briefly and embraced. It was the last time we saw him.

A week later, Noemi was on the phone, crying hysterically. Manuel was missing. They had taken him from his lecture room two days before. There was no news. She did not dare stay at her house, afraid they would come after her again. She asked whether she could please stay with me. She couldn't. My Chilean host was too scared. An old colleague from the United Nations offered his guest room. We both moved there.

After a week of anxiety and terror, Manuel's body and those of two other *subversivos* were found by the road to the airport. Their throats had been slit.

We went to see Manuel's body at his family's home. It was spooky. A thick layer of makeup covered his face. He had a white bandage around his neck. We were walking around the coffin, when I noticed his nails were missing. The tops of his fingers, which were crossed over his chest in the customary manner, were bloody and blue. They had pulled out his nails.

I didn't have time to process it. His family told me it was a comfort that there was a foreigner to bear witness. To see what had been done to their son, husband, father. They slipped me a videotape. Surely I would tell the world.

In the funeral procession, I walked right behind the coffin. The cemetery was all the way on the other side of town. I walked next to the family, at the front of the large crowd, which got bigger and bigger. I could see for miles ahead, as I was so much taller than everyone else—literally sticking out. From a funeral, it turned into a march, from a march into a mass protest. It was truly impressive. By the time we reached the wide lane leading up to the cemetery, there were thousands marching with us.

I was in a haze. I couldn't believe that this pain was intentionally inflicted by a government! A military government that considered itself so civil.

We entered the gates of the cemetery. There were people everywhere. I expected to see graves, but we moved toward a wall. Everyone began screaming: "Manuel! Manuel! Manuel!" Many, many hands shoved his coffin into one of the openings in the wall. I had never seen anything like it. People were crying; people were screaming. It was getting dark. Then, suddenly, the cemetery was surrounded by buses full of soldiers. The crowd quickly dispersed. *Better get out of here!* Noemi grabbed my hand, and—reluctantly but hastily—we made our way to the nearest subway station.

Manuel's sister went on a hunger strike in a church in the center of Santiago. With two other sympathizers, I went to pay my respects. That's what one did to show solidarity. The atmosphere was awkward. There

Demonstration, Santiago, Chile, 1984

were all these educated people, civilized people, watched by an army of policemen (*pacos*), who, wearing their guns visibly and holding their bats in their hands, were ready to jump in. Where does a government like that draw the line? At what moment do they decide to intervene? I would soon find out.

There was also a bunch of young men loitering in the church. Many looked like Che Guevara: beards and longish hair, the bourgeoisie's idea of the "bad guy." There were more of them outside, making noise with banners and slogans. They were living their cause. I gave some water to Manuel's sister and hugged his family. When I was about to leave the churchyard, a military bus pulled up in front of the gates. Five pacos jumped out and surrounded the protesters. They started pushing them toward the bus. The pacos had rubber sticks and looked like they would not hesitate to use them. The protesters were screaming, but they all obeyed. They let themselves be herded into the bus like cattle.

I was nailed to the spot, watching in awe, when suddenly one paco singled me out, grabbed my arm, and dragged me away. At first I was too flabbergasted to react and I let him push me toward the bus. I was already on the first step when I asked him in Spanish: "Can't you see that I am a foreigner?"

"Señorita, we know exactly who you are," he answered, and pushed me even harder. His eyes told me there was no room for reasoning. Instinctively, I shoved him aside as hard as I could and began running. I saw his stunned face when I looked over my shoulder. I ran as I had never run before. For my life, just in case. I ran for at least fifteen minutes through the busiest part of town. To the Vicaria, the Catholic church, which was sympathetic to the democratic cause. I caught my breath and reported to the priest what I had seen.

My heart, too, was with the cause, but it was not my path to follow. The least I could do, though, was carry the videotape out of the country. Manuel's family had asked me to take it back home to Amsterdam, and give it to the Chilean movement. My heart was pounding in my throat when I passed the uniformed customs agents, but I got through.

# DAY THREE

When I wake up, it is morning again. It is raining! I am so thirsty. I stick out my tongue. That helps a bit. I open my mouth as wide as possible. I savor every little drop that I manage to catch. Then the sun comes out. That is good news to a Dutch person, under any circumstance.

I look at my surroundings again and again. Everything is green. So green it almost absorbs me. Pine, thick grass, moss, and plants all over.

It is Monday. Jaime is on his way back from New York to Madrid. *He'll arrive to the office late, straight from the airport. Where would the markets be?* I am not supposed to care. Not until Wednesday. *Then Jaime will surely move mountains. He will.* I trust him to. And Helen. *She will help him.* She is my buddy. I think of Helen, small and smart. She does not let those dandy equity guys tell her anything. She tells them what to do. And she takes care of me. Makes sure I eat well.

I look at the watch. It is seven a.m. I look at the man—not deliberately; he is just there, right next to me. *Hey! What is that little white cord coming out of the corner of his eye? Is that a white worm? Of course! He has already started to decay! In this hot, wet place bodies decompose more quickly. Decomposition?* Oh, my God. I glance back, and then I see them: maggots. All over his body. That is what that smell is. Decay! That horrible smell I then suddenly become fully aware of. That sickly, rotten smell! I move away with a jerk. Pain erupts in my hips. I check out my hands: no maggots. Just leeches feasting on my blood. *Calm down. Don't look.*

I take a deep breath. It makes sense. This is a greenhouse. Like a giant womb for all its species. This is natural. Nature. Birth and rebirth. The circle of life. The beauty of life. *Don't look at the maggots. Look at the beauty!* I look at the trees, the plants, the leaves. As if I can, I inhale them and not the ferocious smell. This helps. I calm down.

I decide it is time to move away from the man. I quickly snatch the fifty-dollar bill out of his pocket. I look at the watch. *Can I take it?* I'd have to grab his cold arm, maggots and all, and undo the strap. I can't. I read a Dutch book as a teenager about a farm boy who spots a floating body in the river. He looks at the floater's watch and says: "Go away or I'll take you!" and then he grabs it anyway. Not me. I also remember the scene from *Les Misérables* in which the innkeeper ends up stealing from dead bodies in the catacombs of Paris. I saw that musical both on Broadway and in Covent Garden. *Oh, different worlds!*

I move on my elbows. I have a huge open wound on my right elbow, so with every move I feel the twigs and dirt rubbing against my flesh. I have no choice: my hips feel unhinged, and my legs are broken. I have to pull my body along with my arms. I move past the dead man, past the dead girl, her fist no longer clenched. She holds a linen bag. I guess no circumstances are horrifying enough to let go of one's bag. We all held on to ours: me, the girl, the man next to me. What does this say about us? I decide to take the bag. I put it around my shoulder and move downhill, toward the loose wing of the plane. Everything hurts like hell. Hell! *Don't look back. Don't think of Pasje.* I settle down next to the wing. This is my new spot.

I look around. I have a more open view here. The scenery is just as pretty. Many new things to look at. I can see a huge mountain on my right. The plane has left a swath of shattered trees. It has also made a kind of clearing. With the tops of the trees gone, the sun can get all the way down to the ground. I warm myself contentedly in its rays.

I open the girl's bag. It looks like those linen bags they give out at Barnes & Noble. It contains a Vietnamese grammar book and a blue rain cape. The cape has a pointy hood and a long front. I recognize the design. It is meant to be worn while biking, with the front of the cape over the handlebars. In Holland, the newspaper boys and girls wear them a lot. I put the cape over my head. *Maybe it will help me stay dry and warm.*

I stay put. Still cold. So cold. Shivering. Exhausted, I put my head down.

The moon rises next to the mountain. It is almost full. There are some clouds. The setting resembles a Disney movie. Real nature, only moonlight. I am such a city girl! *Bedtime, go to sleep.* I dream about the office, about my boss, Ana Botín, Helen, Jaime, the markets . . .

# AMSTERDAM, 1986

After we finished our studies, Pasje and I moved to Amsterdam. My brother-in-law had just become mayor of the city. My sister was a member of parliament in The Hague. She didn't have the time or enthusiasm to play the part of a mayor's wife. I did, so off I went to official receptions, concerts, football matches, and award ceremonies. Pasje would often come along. We had just finished our studies, and our only job was to apply for one.

Like my sister and her husband, Pasje and I were living apart. He shared a house with some of our good friends, while I lived "anti-squat" with two other friends. In the 1980s, Amsterdam's empty houses on the market were at risk of being taken over by squatters. Housesitting was one of the solutions. We would live short-term in these houses, at the owner's request. The houses were often beautiful, in the best locations. Once the house was sold, we would move on to the next one. By sheer coincidence, I lived right next door to the mayor—and sometimes my sister—for six months.

Pasje and I spent most of our time together at his place, which was better furnished. He did not move all the time. It was also on a lovely canal right next to the red-light district. We did our shopping at the same local supermarket as the professional ladies. We regularly exchanged jokes and small talk with them—all very Amsterdam.

When Amsterdam made its Olympic bid, we helped my brother-in-law entertain the International Olympic Committee. On one of the outings, a canal tour on the city's official boat, we passed one of the smaller canals in the district. One of our new prostitute acquaintances was just locking her red-lit door. When she looked up to see who was on the official boat, her face lit up and she yelled, "Hey, Willem!" Everyone looked at me.

I got a job at ING Bank, for they were known for asset trading: Latin American debt swaps. Pasje ended up there too, though at the domestic division. He was considered too old to be part of the management trainee program at the foreign division. But he turned out to be the real banker. He fit in; I did not.

Perhaps the disdain I encountered from my all-male colleagues during my first year of banking had to do not only with the fact that I was the first female executive trainee, but also with their intuition—right enough—that I was in the wrong place. I needed a whole different set of skills if I was going to survive there as the first woman.

The first six months of my traineeship I worked at a local branch of the bank in the north of Holland. So did Pasje. We took the train there together. It was more of a culture shock for me than working in Chile had been. The people of the north were reserved and old-fashioned. I was a strange bird from the big city. Too worldly, too irreverent, too . . . something.

I had to spend time in each department, beginning as a cashier and ending at credit analysis, the core business. On my first day there, the department head bluntly told me he would try to teach me the business, but he had little hope of getting a woman to analyze anything at all.

All day long I had to crunch numbers, describe them in a page or two, and fill out an accompanying form. My crunching and writing weren't great, but it was the forms that really got me. I was too sloppy with the details, and had to redo them time after time.

At first, I was not allowed to see any clients—that was the privilege of the senior executives and the branch manager—but then something unusual happened. The branch's largest client singled me out and wanted me to be his account manager. Until that moment, he had not talked to anyone other than the general manager. Although quite socially awkward, he was the kind of Dutchman who had made Holland a trading power: thrifty, no-nonsense, with not much regard for appearances, but full of good common sense. He somehow always managed to invest large amounts of money in the right up-and-coming company. My colleagues were piqued when he asked me along to a cocktail reception for a local businesswoman who was getting an award. "It must be because you're a chick," they joked. Perhaps, although the man was in his late fifties, still lived with his mother, and did not flirt with me at all. He did, however, give me very good advice: "Always follow your instincts."

When my time at the branch was up, I moved on to the larger credits department at the head office in Amsterdam. I was put on the construction industry desk. Was I sent here on purpose, to find out whether I could handle the testosterone? The office consisted of a huge, open floor plan with blocks of desks put together. All men. My only distraction was a walk to the coffee machine. I could feel people looking at me. I was their distraction.

It was boring to analyze one annual report after another. I was supposed to give my opinion about whether loans should be approved or declined. There was no real wiggle room, because the advice was really supposed to be positive, for these were mostly renewals of existing loans. Then one day, I was looking at a credit application and going over some press cuttings of a certain company, when something did not feel quite right. I didn't know why, but there was something about the company's CEO that I just didn't like. The company was located in Eindhoven, so I picked up the phone and called my cousin who worked for Philips and was well connected in that town. Everyone was listening in on my conversation. "Are you working for a detective agency now?" they asked when I hung up. My cousin called me back to tell me the CEO gambled on horse races. I stamped "Negative" on the application. Later the general manager came over to my desk and asked whether I could provide more detail regarding my decision. He was going to defend it to the board.

After work, Pasje and I went to Hoppe, a popular bankers' pub in Amsterdam, to celebrate my first success in credits. Later that evening, as we sat down for dinner at his house, Pasje got a phone call from Hoppe's friendly bartender. I had left my briefcase in the pub. With the very confidential file in it.

Once a month, the management trainees—seven guys and I—would meet at the head office to discuss our progress. Afterward, John, who managed the trainees, would take us for a drink at Hoppe. He was always looking for new ways to develop the program and discuss his latest ideas. We were his guinea pigs, if not his laboratory rats.

At the pub, John told us that AMRO Bank had just sent its management trainees on a survival course in the Ardennes. "Rafting down the river, being dropped in the woods at night, and so on. Do you think we should send you guys?" John asked.

The boys immediately loved the idea. Great way to discover your skills. Real character-building stuff. But John, who always visibly enjoyed governing by dividing us, said the aim of the course was to find out who the natural leaders were. Then he looked at me sardonically. "What does the lady think?" he asked.

I purposely shrugged my shoulders. "Be my guest! You might be surprised. I might very well survive—be one of the fittest." I looked at my co-rats and added: "But that does not necessarily make me a good banker."

We didn't go rafting, but as time went by, our traineeship did become more and more competitive. Two-thirds of the way into the program we were going to hear what our first foreign posting would be, and everyone was scurrying to get into position. The most sought-after spot was New York. I—and everyone else—was well aware that if I survived the program, I would be the first female executive trainee ever to be sent abroad by a Dutch bank. I don't believe I deserved it, but I got New York.

# DAY FOUR

I wake up in my new spot. No more dead neighbors. No watch either, but it seems early. I look at the sun. The mountain on my right sticks out like a giant cone. The ravine that separates me from that mountain is full of wild vegetation. Like Tarzan's jungle. *Me Jane. Yeah, right.*

About ten feet below my feet, the clearing created by the plane ended and the jungle became jungle again. I must be pretty high up my mountain. *It is going to be quite a hike if I have to get out of here by myself.* I hope I don't have to. According to the plan, I still have four more days of waiting. I flip through the girl's German-Vietnamese grammar book and read one page of declensions. I never liked German. Maybe I can use the Vietnamese. I can't concentrate. My head is light. It seems as if a blanket of clouds is covering my brain. *Forget it!* I turn back into myself. I wait.

I enjoy the open view there at my new spot. I miss the detail of the leaves, but I can look farther down the ravine on my right, where the jungle seems so dense, like a giant green wall. *And, hey, I can see the search planes when they come! And they can see me!*

Suddenly I realize how important it is just to be there, alive and conscious. My mind becomes both hazy and determined at the same time. *Water! I must have water. I need water.* My perceptions have both sharpened and narrowed. I look at the airplane's broken wing and see that the insulation material is made out of paper or foam. I get an idea: the insulation could work like a sponge, to soak up the rain! *I have to get to it!* I somehow force myself to stand up slowly on my broken legs. I reach for the broken wing. I feel an excruciating pain in my hips. I can't reach. I move closer. I try again. I feel a stab in my chest, but I put all my life into my effort to get to the wing. Finally, I can reach right into the insulation material. I grab little pieces and drop them onto the ground next to me. When I think I have enough, I even more painfully get back to the ground. "*Aaahhhhh!*" I scream out in pain. When I am lying down again, I collect the pieces of foam. I mold seven little balls. I line them up and wait for it to rain. So thirsty, oh-so-thirsty. I am awfully tired. The standing has drained me. I rest my head.

I wake up because it is raining. It pours! So much that I hold up the rain cape with two arms to catch the water, and I literally slurp it up. *Oh, vintage Veuve Clicquot!*

I watch contentedly as the insulation balls soak up the water. I congratulate myself. I did it! This will keep me going for the remaining days!

The sun is setting. *Go to sleep*, I tell myself. *Don't think, just sleep.* Because my new spot is brighter, I sleep even lighter. I clearly see my friend Helen emerging from the mountain. Helen grew up in New Jersey as the second of four children, and has a habit of "feeding" me in Madrid. Now she offers to bring me a Lipton Iced Tea, one of those American drinks of hers. But then I see her moving back toward the mountain.

*"Hey! Don't leave!"* I scream. I know I am sleeping and I know she could not even walk over there, but I want Helen to come back. I scream and scream her name. *I want my iced tea!*

"I am going to make you cry," the head of least developed countries (LDC) trading told me when I was transferred to his department in New York. "I make everyone cry. Lap cried only an hour ago." He was referring to one of the junior traders, a smart Chinese-American.

I looked at him with incredulity. I had made it through two years of traineeship without crying. This could not possibly be any worse. I was finally where I wanted to be. In the temple of LDC trading. This was why I had chosen ING Bank in the first place. It was small, but it was at the very heart of the young market.

The department head didn't bite, but he had quite a powerful bark. Rightly so. He was brilliant in his enthusiasm. The LDC trading department was run by young, bright people driven by the fun of seeking solutions to the debt crisis rather than the money.

In the liquid 1970s, the world had been flooded by petrol dollars. Chasing their margins, bankers had raced to lend the excess dollars to less-developed countries, nowadays called emerging markets. In the early 1980s, the interest rates more than doubled because of the oil crisis. This led to a massive default by less-developed countries. They had no more money to pay off the loans. A secondary market was born—an exotic, brand-new, sexy market.

It went like this: We would buy a defaulted US loan to Brazil from, say, a bank in Germany at a discount. We would sell that loan to a company that needed local Brazilian currency for an investment. The Central Bank in Brazil—the debtor—would provide the local currency to the company, again, at a discounted rate. It was a win-win situation. We all profited. The German bank was already provisioned for more than the discount and got a free fall; the company made a cheaper investment; Brazil had less foreign debt; and we made a nice commission.

With all these transactions in the pipeline, we began buying the debt for our own account. Then we were traders, taking positions in third world debt.

I loved it. And I cried so little that I was sent back to Amsterdam to continue at the European least-developed countries trading desk.

In Amsterdam, our market was the baby of the charismatic and visionary vice chairman, Mr. T, as we called him. Everyone in our head office was hoping to please him, and looking for brilliant ideas of how and where to cancel debt. Debt for hotels, debt for ships, debt for this, and debt for that. The most imaginative debt-canceling transactions would make the news. Like the article with the headline DEBT FOR SOCCER PLAYER, which detailed the Brazilian soccer player Romário being bought by the Philips soccer club PSV (Philips Sport Vereniging).

We felt like we were an elite team within the bank. We were more corporate than traders. We looked and acted corporate. We were educated. We were not sitting in trading rooms with suspenders on, though I was still the only one wearing a skirt. We had normal desks in real offices. We were visible.

Prices were still quoted over the phone; we did not yet have trading screens. We had to constantly call around to see who was doing what at what price. If we were dealing with New York, we had to stay late or rush home and continue working there. The cell phone hadn't become popular yet.

Young, urban, and professional, we did it all. We made the calls to the banks to convince them to swap or sell their loans. We gave them ideas on how to structure both the deals and their portfolios. We structured every single transaction and prepared the endless loan documents. We stayed overnight to sit next to slow fax machines, cutting long rolls of fax paper into normal pages. Then we went to the closings in the lawyers' offices.

I felt like a kid in a candy store. It was so up my alley. All my interests seemed to converge: global economy, foreign debt, chatting on the phone, and taking risks. What's more, I got to live in Amsterdam with Pasje.

After less than a year, however, the bank decided to move our department to London. I was told there was no way they would send me there. The bank did not want me to become a specialist in one area. They had not invested in my training "to have me buy at fifty and sell at fifty and a quarter." I had been trained to become a manager in one of the foreign offices, not a debt trader.

But that happened to be my calling. I was prepared to leave ING, and was already interviewing with other banks when our LDC trader in London, Hernán, suddenly died.

Hernán had been a young, upward-moving Argentinean with a beautiful wife, Fabiana. They were as handsome a couple as they come. "Too perfect for this world," an English secretary had said after they died. They had moved from Buenos Aires to London five months earlier. The couple had decided at the last minute to fly via New York before going home for Christmas. They flew Pan Am, and their lives were cut short over Lockerbie. Hernán's terrible fate became my good luck. Ironically, my professional career took off because of a plane crash.

I was promoted and would be sent to London. The final deal took a lot of meetings and negotiations; ING Amsterdam did not want to let me go. I packed, unpacked, and packed again, waiting for the final decision. Pasje watched me do this, changing his plans along with mine with his usual good humor. In the end, I was sent under a special short contract. I was paid an allowance in addition to my Dutch salary. I got to repay all my student loans at once. Even better, Pasje and I were allowed to visit each other every other weekend, all expenses paid; for ING, we had the same status as a married couple. And I got to keep my flat in Amsterdam.

Not only was I given Hernán's job and contacts, but also moved into his expensive house. It was right at the intersection of Knightsbridge, Chelsea, and South Kensington. The London high life! From Chanel to Joseph. From bowler hats to foreigners. From Brits in Aston Martins to Latin playboys in Porsches, casually having brunch at the brasserie. But in the ancient grocery shop on Walton Street they would still ask me: "What will it be today, love?"

To get to the office in the city, I had to take the very crowded tube, the world's first underground train. Being claustrophobic, and feeling quite panicky so far down, I was impressed with the ultracool demeanor of the Brits. They would fold their *Financial Times* into a minuscule strip, respecting their neighbor's five square inches of private space. And they wouldn't flinch—or talk—when the tube stalled, not even after half an hour. When it was hot in the summer, sweat pouring down their stoic faces, they would rather leave their jackets on than reveal the damp patches on their tailored shirts.

Our general manager was a caricature, an Oxford-educated stiff upper lip in a tailored, striped suit. When talking to me, he would often lift one eyebrow. Once, in great stress, I ran into his office to ask him for an immediate increase in my trading line. I apologized for not knocking and stated that I needed his approval. Self-consciously, I added I knew I had runs in my "panty" (Dutch for "stockings"), but had had no time to change. I was totally unaware that in British English I had just stated I had diarrhea in my underpants. About this, he lifted both eyebrows.

I loved my job and my independent life in London. After work, I went to the pubs with the other traders. There, over beers, we traded jokes and information, all in a competitive, but friendly manner.

Emerging markets trading desk,
London, January 1989

My forte lay in my dealings with the Eastern European debtors. They trusted me. They trusted me because they could. They were not yet savvy with the markets, and I really had their interest at heart—more so than our bigmouthed traders in New York who wanted ever-bigger margins. It was easy to fake it and take a huge percentage. I made what I considered a reasonable profit, and that was still more than enough in those early days.

As our market took off, so did our bonuses. We were feeling more and more entitled to the best restaurants, wines, and hotels. Our parties became more lavish. We all became wine connoisseurs, in the sense that we knew how to order the 500 quid Pomerol or Château d'Yquemn.

With Jaime, second from left, in *Hello* magazine, June 1991

# Perspectives

**MARK, MY CO-TRADER:** We had a great time working together in what was still—in the early 1990s—a pretty innocent market. Everyone knew everyone and we spent as much time socializing with other market participants as trading with them.

There was a very warm and friendly atmosphere in our small office, and I remember the kindness that I received. For example, Annette used to cover for me when I was late. If our boss had a meeting, he would often leave the office before I arrived. If I still wasn't there when he returned, Annette would put cigarette stubs in my ashtray as if I'd been in but had gone out for a minute.

Annette was a charming and elegant colleague—popular, intelligent, and always laughing. Behind that carefree façade, she had a profound knowledge of our countries and securities—as well as a great feel for markets. On a number of occasions, that strong intuition got us out of trouble when things didn't go our way.

A few years later, I was intently watching my Bloomberg screen when Willem came out of his office to tell us that Annette's plane had crashed. Everyone was quiet for a few seconds and then people began crying. It was very emotional.

**HELEN, MY BUDDY:** Before I ever met Annette, the one person we had a common connection with was Numachi. I worked under Numachi at my first real post-college job at Mitsui Bank. He taught me about the LDC debt market, and we traded debt instruments on behalf of the bank, with counterparts from large US and foreign banks. After completing my MBA, Numachi was working at Santander Tokyo and helped get me a job at Santander in Madrid.

I arrived in Madrid in early 1992. One of the first people I met in the investment banking division was Annette. She stood out in the trading room not just because of her striking looks and heavily Dutch-accented Spanish, but her *strong* personality. She carried herself with such confidence and pride—in the macho Spanish financial world. We became dear friends. We spent our free time exploring shops and tapas bars all over Madrid, many times with her trading partner Jaime.

In the fall of 1992, Annette was off to Vietnam to celebrate her fiancé's opening of ING's office. I remember Annette was not looking forward to the long flight, but couldn't wait to see him and go on vacation afterward.

I will never forget the Reuters headlines—scrolling in red letters—on November 14: "Vietnam Air Crash in Mountains and Plane is Missing." At first I did not think it could be Annette's flight. Jaime always had his eyes glued to that Reuters screen, and when that headline hit, he came over to my desk to tell me it was *the* flight. We were all in shock! I looked at macho Jaime, and had never seen him that scared and vulnerable. We all felt helpless. What were we to do then? Think *positive*! Have *hope*!

That's what we did, especially Jaime. He had the most hope; he had no choice. Annette was his trading partner, his best friend, and his whole world at the time.

The next days in and out of the office were very tense. Everyone wanted to keep believing Annette and her plane would be found. Jaime, Gary, and I went to Annette's apartment one day to gather some of her precious things—jewelry, antique watches—that Jaime could bring to her parents. It was so eerie being in Annette's big apartment without knowing where she could be. All three of us could not help feeling upset, nor could we face the possibility we would not see Annette again. But no one dared express it out loud. As tough as Jaime was in the office, I could see the deep sadness in his eyes and actions. As the days passed without much news, some coworkers began to talk about Annette in the past tense. Jaime would not stand for it, and got very angry.

# DAY FIVE

I look at the sun's position. *What time is it?* I can't rely on my Girl Scout knowledge, but I think I can figure out when enough hours have passed to deserve a sip of water. To have one of those sponge balls. Every three hours, I have promised myself. I have an intuitive feel for numbers, anyway.

*Let's go.* I suck out some water, and savor every drop. Two or three hours pass, I think. I squeeze out another sponge ball. The water tastes fantastic, worth the wait. I enjoy the routine.

I look at my hands. My beautiful hands—the only part of my body I am really vain about. They are enormous. So puffy and swollen that Pasje's little ring is cutting into my finger. We had bought that golden band for twenty-five guilders in Haarlemmerstraat in Leiden thirteen years before. Still, it gives me comfort.

I study my hands. *Those bloody leeches are having a ball!* My feet are also twice their normal size. *Hey! I am only wearing one shoe. When did that happen?* The shoeless foot is full of wounds. My toes are black, as if they were frostbitten! *Ha, I do have something in common with those cannibal survivors in the Andes.* I remember seeing the pictures of their blackened toes in that trashy Dutch magazine *Panorama.* I was reading it in the coffee bar next to my sorority house in Leiden while I was having a *koffie verkeerd,* what the Dutch call "café au lait"—lots of milk, little coffee. *Was Pasje there? Don't think of Pasje. Don't look at the little golden band.*

I wait. I calculate the time and I wait. *I have waited so long already! What patience!* I laugh at myself. Of all things and all people! Claustrophobic and no patience! No patience for anything. I think of the tanning beds in Madrid, how I never manage to stay the whole half hour.

Always jumping out after twenty minutes, too long already. I never have my hair blown dry when I go to have a haircut. Takes too long. No patience. And here I am, condemned to wait and stay still, so patiently.

My claustrophobia must have something to do with my impatience.

I just need to keep moving. I hate planes of any size if they don't move when they are supposed to, when they sit on the runway. When that happened in DC, Pasje had to strike a deal with the cabin crew that I could go into the cockpit. I had to get out. Same with elevators, boats, and ski lifts. Cars even. When they don't move, I panic. And stuck, yet not panicking. Just waiting.

I tune in to the sounds. A cacophony. The droning insects, the chirping crickets, the chattering birds. They sound familiar. They remind me of *The Hidden Force,* a drama series on Dutch TV. *How old was I when I saw that? Twelve?* The series was based on a classic Dutch novel, about Java, Indonesia. Where papa grew up. When it was still a colony. The Dutch Indies, they called it. There was a dark, mystical undertone to the story. Now I understand. It is in the air. In the sounds . . . It must have been quite a culture shock for Dutch men and women arriving from the cold and rational Netherlands to this mystical environment. Like my grandmother, who married by proxy. She traveled across the globe by boat for a life with a man she only knew from dance class. My grandfather-to-be. He had been working in the Dutch Indies for an oil company.

Papa was born in the Dutch Indies. His father was a teacher. We got our union blood from him: he made all his Dutch students pay one cent to facilitate education for the local people. It made my father more aware, and allowed him to identify with the Indonesian people. He also used to tell us scary stories about the evil eye and the white hajji who could enter through locked doors—a joke, but with serious undertones. I used to pass them on to my cousin when she came to stay, and she would be hysterical with fear. A bit mean. I wasn't scared at all. Nor am I now. So what if there is more here than meets the eye? It makes me less lonely.

# CHILE, LONDON, MADRID, 1989

"I have a surprise for you," Pasje said. It was a Friday night, and I was back in Amsterdam for the weekend. We were having a drink on our favorite terrace. In suits. With attaché cases. Both bankers then. "I have arranged to become an expatriate."

I gave him a blank look. "What?"

"I have been thinking about a move for some time. If we really want to have a future together, I have to become more international. So I have just closed a deal with the international division." I was speechless. "Not just any move," Pasje continued; "a two-year assignment to Chile." I couldn't believe it. Pasje was moving. To the other side of the world. To Chile. My Chile. Our Chile. "It will be good," he said. "Trust me."

He left in September. I went to see him in December for three weeks. It was good to be back in Chile. It was as if our love for each other was sealed by that country all over again. By its music, its language, its hospitality, its paradoxes. By its mountains, its raw countryside, and its wild ocean—its very nature.

Our friend Noemi had been adjusting very well. She worked with poor children in the slums and organized radio workshops for a radio program about the UN's International Rights for Children effort. She and all our friends were thrilled by Pinochet's defeat in the 1988 plebiscite. Now Chile was truly "civilized."

Pasje had also invited my brother, sister, and brother-in-law. My brother had just survived a series of cancer treatments. There wasn't much left of him, physically or mentally. We took him along on our romantic journey to the seaside, where he visibly recuperated. Apparently it was then that Pasje asked him to be his best man.

I noticed more than once Pasje attempted to pop the question to me. "Don't you dare!" I joked time after time. "We are in it together, and we will, for sure . . . eventually!"

. . .

Back in London I got a call. It was the assistant of Jaime Lupa, the big, swinging Mexican head trader of Citibank New York. "Mr. Jaime Lupa is coming to London next week to visit his counterparts. He would like to have dinner with you. Alone." Dinner? Alone? I knew he disliked my boss, but that was not how it worked. Boss should meet boss.

I knew Jaime well, if only by phone. Like ING, Citi was one of the biggest players in our market. I was the first one he called every morning when New York started its day, to find out what the European banks were doing, and what I had heard the night before from the other traders in the pub. Information was power, and power was information. He enjoyed talking to me. I liked his voice, his accent, his sense of humor, as well as his power. He was one of the very first traders in our market. A real trader, savoring liquidity over investment, prudence over politics, cash over corporate. The "money talks; bullshit walks" kind. So I happily accepted the dinner invitation. As I put down the phone, Jaime called me on the other line to "talk about the markets."

"Why so formal?" I asked. "Why have your assistant call me when you were going to call me anyway?"

"Because that's how we do things at Citibank," he answered, proudly. OK, I got it. Selective conservatism and loyalties. Whatever. But I still was nervous to meet him.

It was always strange to meet people who worked in the market in person for the first time, after having discussed vacations and weekend plans on the phone at length for months. With Jaime the conversations had even more intimacy, probably because they were forbidden, something we both enjoyed. When he wanted information he was *supposed* to call our New York office, as Jaime was in New York and the counterparties were geographically divided between our offices. He refused to do so. "Why should I, if *she* calls the shots in Eastern Europe?" he asked. And I was supposed to call my New York brothers for information on Latin American debt and US banks, but they traded away my information for their own gain, and Jaime would give me Citibank's information directly. We spoke in Spanish, which nobody else in my office understood.

People you have spoken to but have never met often look very different from what you imagine. Apparently the general opinion was that I sounded like a rather heavy, short brunette. I am the opposite. When Jaime warned me last minute that he had long hair, I imagined a sleek, clean ponytail. The reality was a shock when he walked into the office. No sleekness—all bushy instead. His shoulder-length hair was cut Farrah Fawcett-style (some would say Hells Angels-style). On top of that, he had a big mustache. And he was hairy, very hairy. My boss maneuvered him quickly into a conference room while I was still sitting behind my desk with my mouth open. "No way will I have dinner with *that*!" I said to my chuckling colleagues. They reminded me that I was due in the conference room. I reluctantly went in and sat down next to him. Then I recognized his voice. I calmed down. By the time he was snatching cigarettes from my packet I was grinning, as I was throughout dinner that night.

Jaime told me he had just divorced. "Kicked out," he said, "with reason." He looked guilty but quickly added, "I never cheated."

"Oh," I said. What did I know about these things? *Pictures in the wallet*, I thought. Yep, there they were: his two boys, each cute as a button.

He looked vulnerable. Not the great macho Jaime I had anticipated. The one everyone talked about and had warned me about. The ruthless, smart head trader from Citibank who "takes no prisoners."

He put the pictures back, tenderly and carefully, behind his credit cards. "They are the best thing that came out of it," he said.

Some weeks later Jaime called me from New York. "Have you ever been to Madrid?" he asked.

"No, why?"

"You know Ana Botín, the daughter of the owner of Santander Bank? She has invited me over for an interview. She wants me to put Santander on the map."

"Nice," I answered absentmindedly, while filling out a deal sheet.

"I've told her I will not come on my own, that I have to pick someone up in London," he said.

Suddenly I was all ears. "You did?"

We went to Madrid and were hired on the spot. The offer was just too good to refuse. Ana Botín would give us carte blanche. We could do whatever it took to put her bank in the emerging markets top ten. I would develop the nonexistent Eastern European side all by myself, corporate and trading. Jaime would show her traders what could be done in Latin America. We would be more or less equals, which was a giant step up for me.

Jaime and I knew each other from talking daily on the phone. He knew I had a boyfriend, that I am Dutch. Though I had seemed genuinely friendly, he also knew I could be quite competitive. We had gone "partners" in big deals; when packages of loans were too large, we would split them. More than once I had threatened to purchase a package all by myself if he would not sharpen his pricing.

Office life was exciting and all-consuming. From our Madrid base we were covering the markets in both London and New York. From ten a.m. to eleven p.m. we worked our socks off, but we did well. We didn't have to deal with any red tape to get what we needed, and in just six months of trading we had landed Santander in several top fives in *Euromoney*. The Eastern European central bankers had happily switched banks with me, and I continued to arrange buybacks for them.

The Spanish authority-driven way of working was quite different from the Dutch consensus model, but I was relieved that I didn't see any

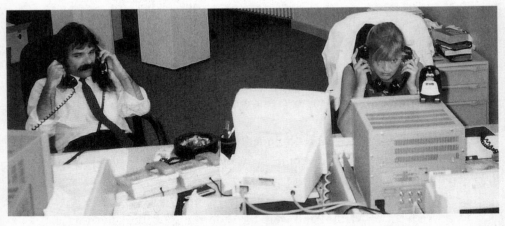

Emerging markets trading desk with Jaime Lupa, Madrid, 1989

evidence of Spanish machismo. Contrary to ING, many women held key positions on our floor. Our boss was the daughter of the chairman and owner. Her husband also worked on our floor and played Frisbee with us. Or any other game we had lying around: darts, putting, you name it.

After work, at eleven or even midnight, Jaime and I would go out for dinner. I got so thin, I suggested eating at my house at nine and putting the brokers in New York on speakerphone. In our business we were kept informed by brokers who would receive one-eighth on any resulting transaction. The eat/work arrangement worked well. I had purchased a fryer, and a whole new section at the Spanish supermarket had opened up to me. We could do business and make our own mayonnaise at the same time. In good team spirit, Jaime stirred while I poured the oil, with the brokers on the speaker commenting on the ingredients.

Office life equaled private life. All our friends were from the office too. We organized barbecues on my terrace, and watched TV and original movies Jaime brought back from New York—since all movies in Spain were dubbed in Spanish. We played Super Mario Brothers on the Nintendo and saved the princess in the wee hours of the morning.

# DAY SIX

I have to go to the bathroom. To excrete, to be precise.

"Eeeew!" Helen would say. She never goes to the bathroom in front of her boyfriend. I do.

*How am I going to do this?* First I have to move away from my spot, away from my sacred foam balls. I drag myself uphill on my back, just using my elbows. *Ouch, ouch, ouch.* I hope it will be easier and less painful to come back down afterward. Now I have to lower the borrowed pants. I open the zipper. I start pulling them down. That hurts! So much! I can't believe the pain in my hips. I want to stop but, oh, sense of decorum! I can't just do it in my pants! No matter what! I pull the pants down slowly, lifting up my hips a bit. *What pain!* I see in my underpants that I got my period. Of course! When it rains it pours. Just when you think you had it all!

I do what I have to do, though the pain is almost unbearable. Oh those twigs! I use leaves to wipe my bottom. Civilized at a most agonizing price! *Well done!* I move back down to my spot. On my back, on my elbows. I am exhausted.

I wonder what my parents are doing. My brothers, my sister, my friends. Are they sleeping in their warm beds? Taking a shower? Eating at a table? How easy for them to drink water, to just open the tap.

A centipede crawls over my legs. I just stay still. We share this space. He is one part of the jungle; I am another.

The rest of the day becomes one big blur. My mind goes still. I am no longer thinking not to think of Pasje. I am just hanging in there; I have become one with my surroundings. It is as if I am living through the trees. The more I have been looking at them, the more beautiful they have become. It is as if I am inhaling them. My belabored breath seems to expand my hurting chest with an energy that makes me light-headed. In a good way. A liberating way. It helps me escape the pain. As if I am out of my body. Whereas I was first forcing myself to focus on the beauty, then I am in it. I am one with everything around me. With the beauty. With the dead. With the process of decay, death, and rebirth. It is wonderful. Before I had to recite the names of my family members and friends to recall their love for me, my love for them. Now it just feels like I am in a bed of love. Or some kind of love frequency is in the air. Or rather, I am in that frequency, on that wavelength, moving within it. Back and forth to an even higher state of mind, in some kind of perfect harmony with my surroundings. It is a beautiful, pleasant frequency, which I would not mind staying in forever.

# MADRID, CHILE, VIETNAM, 1987–1992

Pasje was thrilled about my move to Madrid. He liked trading. The idea of me trading. He would understand when I said, "Oh, I'm in the middle of something; I'll call you back," and then forgot to do so. He would call again. Always. "You're just like Joe," he would laugh, a reference to his best friend who was a stock trader. He would sound proud of me. Very proud.

He also loved the money and the freedom that came with the new job. I could easily combine business trips with visits to Chile. Or we would meet halfway across the globe in New York.

We became very good at sharing our lives over the phone. We would talk at length at least twice a day. With the five-hour time difference, I would wake him up. I would whisper tender words in Dutch from behind the trading desk, or say them more loudly if I had managed to find an empty conference room. In turn he would talk me to sleep from his office. Often we would chat between six and seven p.m., when his lunch at his desk coincided with my dinner at my desk. And we spent all our vacations together. I knew his life. He knew mine.

Pasje's assignment in Chile was meant to last two more years. After that we were going to make a serious effort to get stationed in the same place. London or New York seemed most feasible. My new boss often hinted that she could transfer me wherever I wanted, when the time was right.

We were not in a hurry. A life together was only a matter of time. Didn't we have our whole lives in front of us?

"Flipper, they offered me Vietnam," Pasje said on the phone. "To set up two local branches. I get to build them from scratch. I might even become the general manager if I do well." He sounded excited. "It is a huge promotion. I have always been interested in that region. And Vietnam is such virgin territory. It's a great challenge."

And so our future together took another detour.

# DAY SEVEN

Days have passed. I don't think I am losing track; I just have to add the nights! So it is the sixth or seventh day?

My head is light. The plants around me are radiant. I do not feel the pain any longer. I am both out of my body and close to my body. I have left, but I am present. When I open my eyes, I see the plants shining in the sunlight. When I close them, I see golden lights and a golden center. A big glowing ball, like a late-afternoon sun setting. But this ball has no setting. It is all-encompassing. Both dark and light, and all colors. One big mixture of colors. Yet I can distinguish every single color. They have a golden overtone. Darkness is mixed with brightness, the day with the night, everything with nothing. I feel as protected as I possibly can be. I have surrendered myself completely. To the trees, the leaves, the crickets, the ants, the centipedes, life. Or is it to death I have surrendered?

The jungle cacophony has become a symphony. Of silence. I belong without past or future. I am within the moment. A timeless moment of ecstatic freedom. A moment that gives me peace, unity, and joy. A moment within something greater than my own life. I am the moment. I belong to life itself! To the universe. To God. I feel connected in a miraculous and unified and beautiful way. No divisions, boundaries, or separation, but innate unity. I am seeing the secret. I am the secret.

But then, suddenly, I hear the sound of cracking wood. I see something move in my peripheral view. I turn my head slightly and try to focus my eyes. It is a man. *A man? Am I dead?* Is he the one taking me? Some version of Peter? No, he is real! He is here! I put more effort into sharpening my vision. It *is* a man! On the other side of the ravine. I can clearly see his face. He wears an orange hood. He is dressed in orange. He is staring at me. I shake off my altered state of mind as much as I can, trying to come back to practical, rational awareness. I try to find my voice. It comes out soft and croaky: "Hello? Can you help me?"

I try again. It comes out stronger now, I think. I hope. "*Hello?* Can you help me?" He doesn't move, just stares at me. Louder now: "Hey there!

Help me! *Help me!*" I scream louder and louder, but he stays motionless. "Can't you see I need help?" I am getting angry now. "Do something!" I plunge right out of my pleasant wavelength, right back to earth. Literally back to earth, as I become aware of the ground I am sitting on, the painful little twigs. *I have to get out of here!* This man can help me. He should help me. I scream and I scream. I start cursing in all languages I can think of: *pendejo, Schweinhund, eikel, salot!* He won't move a muscle. He just stands there, staring at me, without even blinking, for hours.

*Who is he? What does he want? To watch me die?*

Then he is gone. As phantomlike as he appeared. Was he a phantom? Did I make him up? But then, why should I have? I was happily minding my own business before I saw him. Too happily perhaps. Slowly drifting away to another world. Now I feel the pain all over again. And the discomfort. Oh hell, what a discomfort it is! I focus on the jungle again. When dusk comes I force myself to go to sleep. Clear my mind of thoughts about the man. Perhaps I was just hallucinating.

# VIETNAM, SUMMER 1992

Pasje moved to Ho Chi Minh City in April 1992. He was one of the first to set up offices for a foreign bank in Vietnam, a communist country that was still trying to find its way out of perpetual war. Only a year earlier there had been armed conflict at the Cambodian border. Pasje had turned into a pioneer.

He was assigned a helper by the government to inform him about the dos and don'ts. And also to check up on him. Mr. Hung was his driver, adviser, and go-between, all in one. But Mr. Hung had clear priorities: he was a government watchdog, and the government came first. Mr. Hung himself came second, Pasje third. Pasje understood that was the cost of doing business in Vietnam and remained on friendly terms with Mr. Hung, even when it meant having to rent an office away from the center, a property owned by a relative of Mr. Hung's. With the help of only a young trainee named Carola, he managed to get both offices in Ho Chi Minh City and Hanoi up and running by October, just before a delegation from the head office was due to visit.

His days were chaotic, and often the phone lines were down. He would send me faxes, though. Sweet and loving, asking me to please be patient. Saying that he was busy fighting bureaucracies, both in Vietnam and within his own bank.

We saw each other in Holland for just a week in late June. We spent most of our time with our friends cheering the Dutch soccer team in the European championship. Our summer vacation was yet to come, so we thought.

Pasje was still negotiating his contract with the head office in Amsterdam. They were suddenly making waves. We were treated as a couple while I was in London, but we had to be legally married for them to pay costs such as plane tickets for us to visit each other. That was no problem; we wanted to take care of that. But we had to be physically together to tie the knot. Moreover, in Holland there was a six-week waiting period to get married, so Pasje would have to be there twice. But because Pasje had not yet signed the contract, he would not be allowed to participate in the general managers meeting in August in Holland. He was over his ears in work, so we decided he would stay in Vietnam and I would visit him in September instead. Then one of my best friends in Holland decided to get married in September. She was pregnant and happy, and asked me to be in her wedding party. How could I say no? Now Pasje and I were looking at October—but in October Pasje would be busy hosting the delegation from head office. I didn't want to be in the way. So we finally settled on November. Five months to go. The longest we had been apart in thirteen years.

How I missed him that long summer, as it turned into fall. At the wedding his absence was palpable. When it was time for the bride to throw her bouquet, she came over to me and placed the flowers in my hands. I made a face. Everyone applauded. It was evident I was going to be next.

At my friend's wedding, Amsterdam, September 1992

# DAY EIGHT

I am woken up by the sun rays on my face. Is it day seven or eight? I might have lost count. Is it Saturday? I think I am supposed to move into the jungle today! I have been distracted by the orange man. Where is he? I immediately look to my right. There he is again! Standing some fifty yards away from me, framed by the jungle growth. Or is he squatting?

I decide to study him first, before making a fool of myself again by screaming into a void. I try to make out his face. It is a beautiful face. Definitely human. Native, I believe. Medium-dark skin, brown eyes, straight black hair. Staring at me, emotionless it seems. He is dressed in orange again. Bright orange. Official orange, like those plastic things on the road. Those cones they use when they do construction. His hat is pointy. Like Paddington Bear's. An orange Paddington Bear. Pasje bought me that bear in London, a small one. That was five years before . . . *Pasje?* By now every part of my mind is groggy. I decide again that I must be hallucinating, making up an imaginary friend. But I do scream at him anyway: "Hello!" It actually helps to scream and focus on the man. Hallucination or not. He pulls me back into the real world, out of my dreamy one.

I think a few hours have passed when I notice he has disappeared again, just like the day before. Gone. Disappeared into thin air. Thick air, I should say! I revert to my tranquil state of mind. My beautiful wavelength. *Hang in there.*

It seems there is a golden veil over my brain. I am overwhelmed with warm energy. My every cell seems filled with it, yet each cell has no boundary. I am aware of every single cell as well as its endlessness. My eyes seem to have moved behind my brain. My brain seems no longer relevant by itself. It is connected, plugged into this giant glowing ball of energy. And love. Big, effortless love, without any object.

# THE HAGUE, TOKYO, HONG KONG, VIETNAM, 1992

Saturday, November 9, 1992: Jaime and I flew together from Madrid to Amsterdam. The next day he was going to New York to visit his sons, as he did every two weeks. I was going on to Tokyo to call on our Japanese clients before visiting Pasje in Vietnam. Finally. For the very first time since his move there in April.

We went out with my brother in The Hague and stayed at my parents'. It was only the second time Jaime had met them. My mother was her usual warm hostess self; my father loved to pick Jaime's extensive brain, on subjects ranging from religion to food and politics. Jaime stayed in my former room on the top floor, which was unused since all my siblings and I had left home. I slept on the first floor, in a little room near my parents. It was cozy to be close to them.

At the breakfast table my mother confessed she had not quite trusted Pasje's advice that I wouldn't need any shots for Vietnam. She had consulted our family doctor and had arranged injections for me at the airport. "Just go to the first-aid office. They know your name," she said.

"What do you mean they know my name?" I answered. "I don't need injections! We'll only be in the city and on the beach!"

"It's a cocktail," my mother continued, patiently. "It includes tetanus." Aha, tetanus, my mother's hobbyhorse. "We'll take you to the airport early tomorrow; then you cannot use your usual excuse that you are running late."

I protested: "But I don't need them! We are going to a beach! We are not going to go hiking in the jungle or anything."

But my mother got her way as Jaime made me go to the nurse's office at the airport.

I had been in Tokyo before, but I still felt out of place. Even though there were more signs in English now, something in the collectiveness of the Japanese made me feel excluded.

My sense of alienation was not at all due to Numachi, the head of our Japanese investment bank. Tommy, as I called him, went out of his way to accommodate me. He consulted me constantly. What did I want to see, what did I like to eat, and what did I need to buy?

We had developed this special relationship over the three years we had worked together. He would wake me up regularly by calling between two and three in the morning, asking me to price packages of loans the Japanese banks were selling. My accent was probably as incomprehensible to him as his English was to me. We had managed to overcome many misunderstandings, a quite costly confusion of tongues. And we both had learned to survive in Spanish, in a culture so different from our own. It had created a bond. I could even make Tommy laugh, not just giggle.

Compared with my open, lighthearted, freethinking attitude, Tommy was serious and timid, keeping everything close to his chest. He worked harder than anyone I had ever met. He worked nonstop, and he did not really need to. He came from an affluent family. "We Japanese Buddhists believe in hard work," he said, "In Japan we work our way to enlightenment."

I tried to read up on Buddhism at my hotel. I had found *The Teaching of Buddha* in my nightstand. On top of the Bible. Each page was printed

With Numachi, Tokyo, November 1992

in Japanese and English. It looked really interesting. *For later*, I thought, and sneaked the book into my luggage, breaking the eighth commandment in the book underneath it.

Tommy watched over my itinerary, from morning till night. Minute by minute. When I went missing, he sent Jaime a fax describing my last actions before leaving Japan. Step by step. Seven pages long. As if he was warding off my death by revisiting every move I had made while I was still alive.

From Tokyo I flew to Hong Kong for two days, to visit just a couple banks. I had dinner with an ex-colleague from ING Bank. We had plenty to talk about: we had both studied in Leiden, he used to live in Willem's frat house, and he had gone through the same management trainee program I had.

The next day, Thursday, November 12, I would be flying to Ho Chi Minh City at five p.m. I only had a breakfast meeting, so I would have the rest of the day to myself in Hong Kong to shop—what else?

I took the crowded ferry to the Stanley Market. It struck me how loudly the Chinese spoke on their mobile phones, even in a confined space. And how many mobiles there were to begin with! In Spain my mobile was still a novelty; people looked on in admiration. The Dutch would often disapprove when I used it. They should see and hear this crowd, screaming into their phones all at the same time.

I really liked Stanley Market the few times I had been there before. Now it was enough to buy a couple of the white silk T-shirts I wore daily to the office. I wanted to return to the hotel, pick up my bags, and go straight to the airport. I wanted to fly to my Pasje. So I took the ferry back and checked out of the Mandarin three hours early. I had never done that in my whole life. On the contrary, I usually made many last-minute shopping detours, even in the taxi on the way to the airport. Often I was so late I had to run to the gate to make the plane. Not now. I was going to see my Pasje after five months. The longest I had not seen him ever.

When I got to the check-in counter and handed my ticket to the attendant, she became flustered.

"We have been trying to contact you all day! The flight is leaving four hours earlier," she said, checking her watch. "*Now*, in fact."

She frantically got on the phone. When she hung up she told me to put my luggage on the belt. "You are lucky. They will wait for you." She handed me the boarding pass. "Please hurry! There is no flight tomorrow. You are so lucky!"

I hurried through immigration and ran toward the gate. From the corner of my eye I regretfully took note of Hong Kong International Airport's shopping facility.

I plopped down in the luxurious airplane seat. The stewardess handed me a wet towel and a glass of champagne. I raised my glass: I was on my way to see the love of my life.

It was night by the time I arrived in Vietnam. Pasje was waiting at the airport. As always. Standing strong, solid, open, warm, and full of expectation. I rushed into his arms.

• • •

The next morning I was unpacking and repacking my suitcase on the bed in the hotel suite that Pasje was calling his home for now. We would leave on a short beach holiday the next day at seven a.m.

"Why do you always do that to me?" I asked.

"What?" Pasje answered.

"Booking the earliest possible plane only one day after I arrive. I just got here."

I was putting my beach clothes in a pile, all ready for the flight to the coast.

"I *just* got here," I repeated grumpily, stuffing the remaining clothes in the drawers and hiding my watch, necklace, and bracelet at the bottom. I showed Pasje a fancy hairpin I had bought in Tokyo.

He smiled. "You know you'll never wear that."

He was right, and I put it in the drawer.

"Pack one smarter dress for the hotel," Pasje said, looking over my shoulder. "It is kind of old and grand. That is all I can tell you. It's a surprise." I softened and let go of my irritation. He was so proud to finally show me his new life. What he had built in only six months by working nonstop: two offices, a new circle of friends, and large stepping stones for our future. I turned around and threw my arms around his neck. I kissed his mouth: familiar, determined, sweet. We took a break from packing.

Later we walked over to his country club at the river. Making our way through the swarms of cyclists, we passed several markets. The merchants, taking a chance that we were American, were offering us military dog tags. With real names, of real people. It made me uncomfortable. I stopped, feeling a sense of responsibility. *Shouldn't we send those to their loved ones?* Pasje moved me away. "It's the tip of the iceberg," he said.

Pasje was on full alert for pickpockets. He told me you could trust no one. A month earlier two friendly old ladies had sandwiched him in and emptied his pockets. He must have felt so defeated after all that alertness he had acquired on our travels. I was surprised as well. Strong Pasje mugged by two old women? I was on guard.

We spent the day at the club's swimming pool, full of pink expatriates. It was Pasje's first relaxing day in months. He turned such a painful shade of red he could barely sit through our romantic dinner that evening.

The night was way too short, as we had to get up at five the next morning to catch our flight to the coast. It was Friday, November 14.

Last picture of Pasje (taken with the camera that survived), Ho Chi Min City,
November 14, 1992

# 2

# FOUND

## THE RESCUE

Suddenly, in late afternoon, I hear ruffling leaves and loud male voices—a group of Vietnamese men appears from the bushes. They are carrying big black bags. I can't believe my eyes. They seem to move in a purposeful way. A man in his twenties comes toward me. He is holding a piece of paper. He leans forward and shows it to me. It is a passenger list. He gestures. He wants me to point out my name. I oblige and point at "Annette Henriet"—my first and middle names. He smiles and rewards me with a sip of water. From a square, light blue plastic bottle. No words can ever describe the taste of that one little sip. That bottle will forever be etched in my memory.

More men approach. They move me onto a canvas. Then they bind both ends to a big stick. Two men carry me, each with one end of the stick over his shoulder. I can't believe what is happening. The men have started to move; I am hanging between them. We pass the dead girl. We pass "Numachi." They are both badly decomposed and are being put in the black bags. The men zip up bags. Now I am suddenly terrified! *But what about Pasje? What about my man?* I don't want to leave him! This is the first time I truly panic. They are taking me away! Away from my Pasje, away from my mountain, away from where I feel protected! I beg for water. They give me a little sip. It works like a Valium.

The men start moving right into the jungle. I see the leaves up close again; the afternoon sun lights up the raindrops. I relax. I am still hanging between the men's shoulders. They tread lightly, almost like slow running, up and down little hills. Then my sense of humor comes back: *who would be so privileged as to be carried like this?* We come to a deep crevasse, which we have to cross. The men form a line and pass me from one to another. They make an obvious effort not to hurt me, but I scream with pain every time I am transferred. After that the men who are carrying me take off their shoes, one by one. They are treading even more lightly now. I smile at them gratefully. Dusk sets. The men stop. To camp? They make a fire. They put me near the fire, hanging my canvas between two sticks, like a roasting pig. I beg for water, but they shake their heads. I beg for more, feeling furious. Like an addict: "Give me more of that crystal liquid!" Meanwhile they are boiling something on the fire. It is rice. After a while they let me drink hot rice water. Finally! It tastes OK. Way better than nothing, but I so crave those earlier sips of pure cold water!

I fall in and out of sleep. The men, all six of them, are talking around the fire. In loud Vietnamese. Very loud. Some are smoking. Whenever one of them is near me, I gesture for more to drink. They sometimes oblige by giving me little sips of the rice water. But when I make a smoking sign with my two fingers on my lips, they laugh as if I am making the biggest joke. I am not, but I smile back and shrug my shoulders. I guess they have a point. I like them. Then they start to move around, disappear into their tents. I panic. I beg them, "Please leave some light on." All those days alone in the jungle without fear, and now suddenly I panic about everything. They strap their lantern onto yet another stick and throw more wood on the fire. They then withdraw into their tent. I sleep outside, hanging between the two sticks. Like a roasting pig.

# Perspectives

**MY MOTHER:** I woke up on Saturday night from an awful dream. Something had happened to one of my daughters! I did not know which one. I told my husband the next morning when we were walking in the woods. We were spending the weekend at a cottage in the country.

In the dream, I had to clean up an apartment. I was terribly sad. Sitting on the floor, surrounded by CDs. There were so many, and I had to sort them out. "Well, that's obvious," my husband said. "All those CDs, they must have been Annette's. It is just a dream," he added when he saw my worried face.

Their plane had crashed around one a.m. Dutch time.

**MY SISTER, EVELINE:** I woke up early that Sunday morning in DC. I had spent the day before hiking and enjoying an outdoor barbecue in the Blue Ridge mountain range. I was looking forward to a quiet day of work-related reading. At that time I was a board member of the World Bank. Life was perfect. Then the phone rang. It had to be from Europe. A male voice. Dutch. Someone from ING. Taking care of Dutch interests was part of my job, but bothering me on a Sunday morning, that early?

It had nothing to do with my job. He apologized for calling me, but he needed the contact details of Willem's parents. ING did not have them on file. He paused for a moment and then broke the news. Willem had taken a domestic flight in Vietnam. There had been a storm or something, and the plane was missing. And yes, my sister was on board too. And they had to contact Willem's family. No, no further information was available, but when did I think I could get back to them with those phone numbers? I told them to check the phone directory for the city of Breda . . . I hung up.

This couldn't be possible. My little sister! And dear Pasje. Both conquering the world, such a beautiful couple. A plane crash? That should have happened to me! All those dubious South American airlines I had flown. And lately various Yaks, parts from Aeroflot appropriated by the former Soviet republics—those kept crashing. But there was no time to think or feel anything. My parents had to be told, my brothers. I booked the next plane to Amsterdam. But that wouldn't land until Monday morning. That would be too late. Freek, my eldest brother, had to be told *now*—and he had to tell our parents. Freek's wife, Marije, answered the phone. I started crying the moment I heard her voice.

**MY BROTHER FREEK:** I decided to get in the car right away. It was the second time I had to bring bad news—the first time was when our brother had cancer—but this was even worse. Both of them gone! Annette, the youngest, was much closer to our parents than the rest of us. They were much more involved in her life, her friends. And, of course, Pasje, whom they loved as a son.

It was early evening by the time I got there. They had just finished dinner. They immediately sensed that something was wrong. It was not like me to come unannounced. The only time I had done that had been two years before, when I had to tell them my younger brother had cancer. The oldest child, as well as a radiologist, I was the bearer of bad news in our cancerous family. I told them to sit down. "I might have terrible news," I said.

**JAIME:** I walked into the office late Monday morning, straight from the airport. Everyone jumped up when I came in, as if they had been waiting for me. Anita, our secretary, told me to go straight into the boss's office. I noticed that she was looking very pale.

When Ana told me the news, I could not believe it. I immediately walked over to the screens on my desks and checked at Reuters whether it was on the news. It was. Something to the effect that the plane had not made it to its destination. I sat down. On automatic pilot, I unlocked my desk, took my handset out of the drawer, cleaned it, connected it, and stared at the screen, waiting. All my colleagues tiptoed over to share their dismay, to give their condolences. But every time someone referred to Annette in the past tense, I would bark at them. "She *is*. She *has*. She is not dead."

That evening I went over to Annette's apartment with her friend

Helen, to check if everything was OK and collect some things her family had asked for. Photo albums and valuables. Helen picked up a few pieces of jewelry. I was too scared, too shaken to go through her things. I just took her hairbrush from the bathroom. "She might need it," I said.

Then I picked up a picture of Annette and went out onto the terrace. There I had a private conversation with God. I looked at the picture. "I will bring you back," I said out loud.

**MY MOTHER:** When Freek left, my husband started drinking. After a lot of Dutch gin, he even managed to fall asleep. I wondered how he could. I did not even bother going to bed that night. The next day Freek drove us to our house in The Hague, where visitors took over. My family, our friends, Annette's friends and cousins, all camping out to commiserate. Every time the phone rang, we all jumped up—for news that didn't come.

Annette's boss called. She was sweet and supportive. She said not to spare any costs in the effort to find Annette. She would pay for everything. Airplane tickets to Vietnam, hotels, anything and everything. I thanked her politely.

I just kept on moving. Between the living room, the kitchen, and the hall. As if waiting for a messenger. I think I attended to my guests. My sister prepared sandwich after sandwich. The phone was ringing all the time, with condolences. There were flowers everywhere. I hated them. I wanted to throw them out of my house!

When it all became too much, I went upstairs. I was chilled to the bone. Psychological, I guess. It consoled me to put on Annette's coat. The sheepskin coat she had bought in Hungary. She always brought us presents, from all those places she went to for work. So thoughtful. Oh, those stopovers! We loved having her with us, even if it was just for a day or two. How I hated taking her back to the airport. Time and again. And now . . . I sat down on her bed. *Now I will never have a granddaughter.*

# THE VILLAGE

The pain wakes me up. Overwhelming pain. Nothing like I have ever felt before. Everything hurts, everywhere. As if my makeshift hammock is crushing me. It is still early; the campsite is purple with the light of dawn. The men look packed and ready to go. When they see I am awake, they start speaking loudly in Vietnamese, like the day before. They give me a sip of rice water and put me back between their shoulders. Again they handle me with the utmost care. Again they take off their shoes, to walk more smoothly. They are checking all the time to see if I am all right. I try to be brave, try not to show how much pain I am in. I can only hope my tortured smile communicates how grateful I am.

We go down the mountain, dense with trees. Thousands of them. It is very steep. Twigs are sweeping against my face. I close my eyes. Dizzy. *Can't see the forest for the trees,* I think. We continue downhill for hours. Then suddenly civilization of some sort. I see a few wooden huts scattered around. An authoritarian-looking man appears and takes charge. He is dressed in army clothes. I take an instant dislike to him. He can speak English but doesn't show any interest in talking to me. He just says, "I have to make a phone call." *Hey! So do I!* The men put me in the back of a minivan; only one of them gets in and sits next to me. I wave at the rest of the crew almost nostalgically. I put my hands together in front of my chest and bow my head. A thank-you nod I am used to making when dealing with the Japanese. They smile widely, showing crooked teeth. My saviors.

We drive for about half an hour. I try to communicate with the military man, who is sitting next to the driver, but he ignores me. He doesn't seem to see me as a person. In contrast, the man next to me responds each time with a smile.

We stop at a village. "Hospital," the man sitting next to me says. They lift me up and bring me into a small building across a little square. They leave me in a windowless room, on a stone platform built into the wall like a box bed. Two friendly Vietnamese girls are there to watch over me. They smile a lot. They dab my wounds gently with a cloth. Just my arms and feet. They do not take off my clothes; they just work around them. There is no light, no electricity. I am amazed by how primitive it is. "How did you ever manage to beat the Americans?" I ask. They just smile. Don't they understand English, or is my broken jaw flapping too much? I do like them, though.

I fall in and out of sleep on my bed of stone, without even bothering to define what all this means for me. I patiently take things as they come.

## 1.16.    Interviews

## 1.16.1.    Interviewing Mr. Mau Quoc Tan

Question:  Do you work for the local authority of the Son Trung Commune? What is your job?

Answer:    I am the head of village militia Unit and a member of the Communist Party Cell of the Commune.

Question:  Tell us about the Vietnam Airlines' aircraft crash in Son Trung Commune, Khanh Son District, Khanh Hoa Province.

Answer:    I was informed by the Khanh Son militia Unit on 15 November, 1994 that there might be a Vietnam Airlines' aircraft crash in Khanh Hoa District; the District militia Unit ordered the village militia Unit to start searching. In the afternoon of 15 November, 1992 the Search and Rescue team of the CAAV led by Mr. Le Hai arrived. Our Commune formed two search teams working from 16 to 18 November, 1992 but failed to spot the scene except one air sickness bag and 2 foreign language-written papers that we handed over to the district militia Unit and the Search and Rescue team. The SAR team spotted a burnt tree on 19 November, 1992 at the top of Mount Manhan, near Mountain Sanh where we had collected the above mentioned bag and papers. The SAR team and district militia Unit suspected that the aircraft had crashed in Manhan Mountain so they directed us to search this area.
In the morning of 20 November, 1992, our Commune formed one team led by myself together with following five members:

1.    Bo Bo Thanh Lan
2.    Cao Thang
3.    Mau Hoa
4.    Mau Thieu
5.    Mau Chuyen

Six of us set off early in the morning and found the aircraft at about 10 o'clock at the top of Mount Manhan. After having spotted the crash scene, we broke for lunch. Four of us looked after the scene while Mau Chuyen and I ran all the way through the forest back to the District Militia Unit and reported our findings to them and the SAR team. I came back to the District Militia Unit at 1630 hours on 20 November, 1994. On 21 November, 1994 I myself took the SAR team led by Mr. Le Hai

Eyewitness' perspective (first page), Hon Ba Mountain, Vietnam, December, 1992 to Mount Manhan where the aircraft crashed. At about 1400 hours the same day, the team arrived at the scene and found one female survivor - a foreign woman passenger with blond hair.

Question: How many places with aircraft wreckage did you see?

Answer: By the time we spotted the aircraft, we saw only one place with wreckage, but when we took the SAR team there we found that the aircraft had been broken into many pieces in three main places:

1. the place where we first spotted was the one with one wing;
2. one place with the tail and the other wing;
3. one place with the cockpit and the fuselage where there were many corpses.

Question: Which duties have you been assigned since the aircraft was spotted and what have you been doing for the SAR team?

Answer: I have remained at the scene since then to help the team with the following works:

- keeping watch on the scene;
- paving the way to the scene;
- assisting the SAR team.

The report was finished in the same day and read to Mr Mau Quoc Tan for his confirmation and his signature.

Witness                         Report maker
Mau Quoc Tan (signed)           Nguyen Thanh Hai(signed)

                Inspector
                Ha Thanh Lam(signed)


1.16.2.  A witness -- Mrs. Mau Thi Nam in Mo O Village of Son Trung Commune stated that:

On 14 November, 1994 while she was digging maniocs in the field near her house, it was raining heavily, she heard a loud aircraft noise. Looking up toward the sky, she saw an aircraft overflying a high tree, over passing a jackfruit tree and coming toward Che Stream flashing, heading for Che Mountain and then she heard 2 loud explosions. When the aircraft was flying over her head, she could see that the aircraft wings was rolling.

Witness Mau Thi Nam signed.

Listeners: Messrs Bui Vo and Nguyen Ngoc Trung signed.

Eyewitness' perspective (second page), Hon Ba Mountain, Vietnam, December, 1992

# Perspectives

**MY FATHER:** By Tuesday the story of the accident was all over the news. In the newspapers, on television. But in fact there was no news. No updates, no connections. The phone kept ringing and ringing, but they were just calls from friends and journalists. With questions. No answers. Vietnam was sealed off. Impenetrable. No phone lines, no Internet. Just rumors, lots of rumors. That they had been lost at sea. That they had crashed into a mountain. We could only speculate. It was monsoon season in Vietnam; the weather could have played a role. The only facts were the planned route and the make of the plane: a Yak-40. Anyone with any knowledge about aircraft was quick to talk about the poor performance record of these planes. That they didn't have radar. That the Russians no longer sent maintenance crews to check the mechanics.

What hope was left? With my operational research background, I calculated the chance that anyone would have survived this: point zero. My wife is a natural realist. We were just waiting for the final confirmation.

We stayed in constant contact with Willem's family. His parents came to The Hague, and we all decided to organize a joint service in a week's time, in the nondenominational St. Peter's Church in Leiden, a historic landmark, just behind the house where Willem and Annette had spent their early years together. We also decided we should put some kind of notice in the paper. People had to be informed. "Missing since November 14, our dear Annette, 31 years old, and Willem, 36. They loved each other for thirteen years."

Willem's uncles and aunts also placed a notice. A real death notice: "Our dear cousin and nephew, Willem van der Pas, who loved life and all people, has died in an airplane accident in Vietnam, together with his girlfriend."

**MY FRIEND CHRISTINA IN LONDON:** I arrived at Banco do Brasil early on Monday morning, as usual, to get a sense of the market before it started heating up. Mid-morning Ria from ING Bank phoned.

Unusual, I thought. Then she gave me the news: Annette had not arrived at her holiday destination in Vietnam. They didn't know where the plane was, maybe in the sea. They just didn't know yet.

I couldn't believe it. I just could not believe it. We had spent such a beautiful long weekend together in Madrid before Annette traveled to Hong Kong and then to Vietnam to meet Willem for a holiday. We had enjoyed ourselves in the bright sunshine, and had talked and talked as we often did when together, enjoying the free time as young free spirits without worries. Annette had even put her little rubber pool out on the terrace. I was shocked. I just couldn't accept that Annette had died. No one could.

The news went around fast. Everyone in the market hoped that Annette was still out there somewhere, alive and feisty. "Negotiating herself out of there," someone said. I tried to figure out how to talk to Jaime, to Annette's parents, but I couldn't do it. Not that Monday.

On Tuesday I finally picked up the phone and called her parents, with a heavy heart. I knew them and liked them so much. Annette's mum came to the phone. We had the strangest conversation. I talked as if Annette was alive, and her mother talked as if she was dead. So difficult. I didn't want to add more pain and tell them that I was still hopeful. I understood that, having waited for news since Sunday morning, they were accepting the fact that the worst had happened.

A bit later I phoned Jaime and asked him how I could help. He told me he just needed a visa to go to Vietnam, to find Annette. He was sure she was still alive. The problem was that he was a Mexican citizen with an American green card and could not easily get a visa. I told Jaime I would ask around and get back to him. I phoned the Brazilian ambassador in London and asked him for a big favor.

"Is Annette Brazilian?" he asked.

"No, Ambassador, but she is one of the biggest traders in Brazilian external debt, and everyone knows her."

"No problem. I will make the necessary inquiries and phone you back." He did. Jaime could pick up his visa in Switzerland. The Vietnamese ambassador in Geneva had arranged it for him. I was delighted to phone Jaime back and give him the good news. He could arrange his journey now. The journey to get Annette back.

**JAIME:** On Thursday morning I took a taxi to Annette's house. I had arrived in The Hague the night before from Geneva, where I had picked up my visa to Vietnam. Ana had told me the same thing she had told Annette's mom: "Save no expense. Do what you have to do." At the office they had been relieved to see me go. They did not know whether to admire me for my persistence or to think I was crazy. But I was adamant. Our secretary had obtained Annette's dental records and had put them on my desk. I had picked them up, looked at the envelope, and returned them to her, saying, "I am not going to need those."

From Geneva I had flown to Holland and checked into Hotel Des Indes in The Hague, an old, colonial hotel overlooking the pond with the medieval buildings that housed the Dutch parliament.

Annette's family and friends did not know what to expect. They were sitting at the window when I arrived in a taxi. I took my time. Paying the driver, waiting for a receipt. I put the receipt in my wallet, put the wallet in my backpack, zipped up the backpack, and put it around my shoulder. I got out slowly. Jeans, white T-shirt, shoulder-length hair. Not quite the look of the neighborhood, I presumed.

Her family received me warmly, hungry for news, for any information. But her friends obviously wondered what my story was. Later they told Annette that they regarded me with a mixture of curiosity, admiration, even envy. Those friends had known her for so many years. They had written her parents letters, sent them flowers, or paid them a visit or two; now they felt they were just sitting around, waiting, while I, the stranger, was taking the initiative. "Look at this odd-looking guy. He's a colleague, flying all over the place for her. Shouldn't we be doing that?" But they didn't show it at the time. They took me out to a restaurant. When everyone was seated, I showed them the letter that Numachi had sent me: a seven-page fax describing Annette's very last steps. Step by little step.

**MY SISTER, EVELINE:** Nothing had ever hit me this hard. My little sister. I had waited nine years for her to be born. A sister I could take to play in the garden, feed the ducks with, read stories to. After I had left home, she would come over and stay with me in my sorority house.

When she was finally a student herself, she spent her holidays in my little cottage in the country, to prepare for exams and write papers. And Pasje—always together with Pasje. The long bike rides, the endless games of Acquire. They were such a beautiful couple. Not just in looks, although I did love to take pictures of them. They were so perfectly made for each other. It had just taken my sister rather long to realize that. . . . Oh, we had had such great times together, in Chile and, just the month before, in DC. My little sister. Accompanying me to grand World Bank receptions. Good-looking, smart, well-dressed. How proud I was. Always showing her off. I had given up hope that she might have survived—but if she had, what kind of animals lived in the Vietnamese jungle?

Yes, all of us had given up hope. Completely. My father had, on the basis of the statistical evidence. And the rest of us? Perhaps the uncertainty, the emotional roller coaster of not knowing, was more challenging to cope with than bracing ourselves for the final verdict.

My parents' home was overflowing with friends and relatives, providing distraction and forcing us to keep up appearances. But late in the evenings, when we were finally left by ourselves, it would hit. It would hurt. My mother would weep and weep, quietly. My youngest brother Bernard was beside himself.

The secretary general of foreign affairs had phoned, on behalf of the minister. They were doing everything they could to help. But of course the Dutch government had closed its embassy in Hanoi, so they had to work through the Belgians. A World Bank vice president also had approached the Vietnamese authorities. He insisted his influence would be pivotal in Annette's rescue. Who knows? Personally, I felt the Vietnamese might prefer it if there were no survivors. So they could kill a story that could damage their promising tourism sector. And then there was ING Bank, Willem's employer. I knew the chairman personally, but ING was anxiously keeping communications limited to Willem's family. They seemed powerless anyway, leaving it all up to Willem's assistant.

All those contacts of mine, all those connections to power centers in the Netherlands and Washington, were totally useless when it came to doing something about a plane that had crashed in the Vietnamese jungle. With my only sister on it.

Aan het begin van hun vakantie
zijn op 14 november 1992
na een vliegtuigongeluk in Vietnam
vermist

onze lieve

**ANNETTE HERFKENS, 31 jaar**

**en**

**WILLEM VAN DER PAS, 36 jaar**

Zij hielden 12 jaar van elkaar

| | |
|---|---|
| Den Haag, | Breda, |
| Ruychrocklaan 68 | Valkenierslaan 307 |
| | |
| B.D. Herfkens | A.F. van der Pas |
| L. Herfkens-van der Staay | T.A.M. van der Pas-de Jong |
| Freek en Marije | Miebeth en Eric-Jaap |
| Eveline | Jasper en Sandra |
| Bernard en Marijke | |

Aan het begin van hun vakantie zijn op 14 november 1992 na een vliegtuigongeluk in Vietnam vermist

onze lieve

**ANNETTE HERFKENS**
31 jaar

en

**WILLEM VAN DER PAS**
36 jaar

Zij hielden 12 jaar van elkaar

Den Haag,
Ruychrocklaan 68

Breda,
Valkenierslaan 307

B. D. HERFKENS
L. HERFKENS-VAN DER STAAY
FREEK EN MARIJE
EVELINE
BERNARD EN MARIJKE

A. F. VAN DER PAS
T. A. M. VAN DER PAS-DE JONG
MIEBETH EN ERIC-JAAP
JASPER EN SANDRA

Onze lieve neef

**WILLEM VAN DER PAS**

die zo van het leven hield en van mensen
en van de wereld, is samen met zijn vrien-
din omgekomen bij een vliegtuigongeluk in
Vietnam.

Riet van der Pas
Ans Hurkens-van der Pas en Frans Voncke
Jasper en Femy van der Pas-Weterman
Jos en Fieke van der Pas-Swinkels
Alice van der Pas en Ann Colt

"Lost" notices in Dutch newspapers that we had gone missing and had died,
November 17, 1992

## Morgan Grenfell & Co. Limited
*Member of The Securities and Futures Authority*

Debt Arbitrage and Trading

| | | |
|---|---|---|
| Total pages | 1 | (including this header) |
| Date | 16th November 1992 | |
| To | Banco Santander, Madrid | |
| | Attn: Anna Botín, Jaime Lupa, Gary Cressman | |
| Fax No. | 010 341 581 4165 | |
| From | Morgan Grenfell Debt Arbitrage and Trading | |
| Extension | 71 826 7953 | |

# MORGAN GRENFELL

If you do not receive all the pages, please telephone or telex immediately

Message

Dear Anna, Jaime and Gary,

We were all shocked to hear of the tragic news about Annette. She was well-liked here at Morgan Grenfell and we will miss her sense of humour and vivacious approach to all aspects of life. We would be grateful if you could pass on our heart-felt condolences to all her friends and relatives, she will leave a big gap in the market generally.

It will be difficult for us to imagine Banco Santander without Annette but please rest assured that you all have our full support in these sad circumstances. We hope we will see you all again soon at one or other of the year-end gatherings.

est regards

MORGAN GRENFELL DEBT ARBITRAGE AND TRADING

Authorised by

| 1 | 2 | Cost Centre | Expenses A/c |
|---|---|---|---|
| | | | Tel. Code |

Condolence letter to my boss from other traders, November 16, 1992

**JAIME:** I left the bereaved Herfkens household on Saturday morning. One week had passed, and my determination seemed more and more delusional. Annette's father got angry when I promised him before I left: "I will bring back your daughter alive." "You are an idiot," he snapped. "Get real!" But he was very grateful too that I offered to go. In his mind I was going to do his dirty work: identifying the body if and when it were found.

I left for the airport with Jasper and Miebeth, Willem's brother and sister. They believed, like everyone else, that they were going there to face the daunting task of identifying the bodies once they had been found. They did bring dental records. I brought Annette's hairbrush.

I took good care of Jasper and Miebeth. I got the royal treatment from KLM airlines and arranged to have them upgraded. They thought I was quite the hero. I liked them; we were bonding.

We got off in Singapore and from there we flew Garuda Indonesia to Ho Chi Minh City. The Indonesian stewardess offered little porcelain statues as a first-class token. Jasper and Miebeth each chose one for themselves. I picked two—one for Annette.

# CAGED MONKEY

The next morning they put me back in the old minivan, my ambulance. On my own this time, without my friendly companion. The military man is still there, next to the driver. He doesn't bother to tell me where we are going. Every movement makes my injuries hurt. I am uncomfortable and claustrophobic. I am constantly begging for water. The men are engaged in conversation. They do not seem to listen or care.

We drive through endless green hills. Suddenly, without any explanation, we stop. At least twenty children are peeping into the van through all the windows. All wearing those iconic conical hats. They are climbing over each other to get a glimpse of me. Unable to move, I feel like a caged monkey.

We drive on, through what seems to me the kind of nowhere that could be anywhere. I must have fallen asleep, because the next thing I know, I am looking at a face. A white face with light eyes. A young woman with straw-blond hair is bending over me, looking very worried. And speaking Dutch!

# Perspectives

**PASJE'S ASSISTANT, CAROLA:** The time of the accident made a profound impression on all of us who were involved. I was in my twenties when I started working in Vietnam, a strange country with a completely different culture. When Willem went on his short holiday with Annette, I had only worked for him for two months, but I had enjoyed every minute of it. I loved his warmth, his sense of humor, and his quiet guidance in dealing with the Vietnamese and doing business over there. After the accident, I was all of a sudden left to my own devices.

On Sunday morning the hotel in Nha Trang called and told Hung that Willem and Annette had not yet arrived. Hung was Willem's "assistant," appointed by the government as our watchdog. He had made the hotel reservation for Willem. Hung called Vietnam Airlines. They said something was wrong with the flight that Willem and Annette were on, that we had to come to the airport to look at the passenger list, as their names were unclear. I was shocked. The day before, Saturday morning, I had flown back from Hanoi to Ho Chi Minh City, and when we flew over Nha Trang I had this strong sense of Willem and Annette. It had felt strange, but I had not paid any further attention to it.

At the office of Vietnam Airlines we were told that they were extremely worried indeed. That the plane had gone missing at sea, and that they were searching for the wreckage. They told us that the chance of anyone surviving was nil. The names of Willem and Annette were on the list—spelled incorrectly but unmistakably their names.

I called ING Hong Kong to inform them and discuss the situation. They had a close relationship with ING Vietnam and with Willem. They called the families of Willem and Annette, and then the families called me. The calls were very emotional. They were so sad. So sad. But always warm at the same time.

The number of people who called grew every day. Other family members of Willem and Annette, their friends, people from several ING and Banco Santander offices, people in Vietnam who knew Willem. All offering their help to search, to make money available, to fly over, to be there. There was one person who called twice every day, in the morning and in the evening, asking whether Annette had been found yet: Jaime. He said that he was Annette's closest colleague, with whom she worked those long hours. Jaime did not believe that Annette was dead. He was convinced that she was alive, walking through the jungle, looking for a phone booth, worrying about Santander's portfolios. He wanted to come over and go looking for her.

The week passed and the plane still had not been found. I was asked to go to Willem's hotel room to pack his and Annette's belongings. I had never met Annette, but through Willem's stories, my telephone calls with her family, and the daily conversations with Jaime, I had a picture of a very strong woman. Willem was always jokingly calling her a woman of the world. Successful, making lots of money, always traveling first class. And very independent. He told me that he had often proposed to her. "I think I have finally got her," he had said, with a twinkle in his eye, just before her visit. In a strange way, her stuff confirmed everything. Stylish clothes, brands from all over the world, small sizes (*arrrghh*).

Then, on Saturday morning, a week after the crash, we got a phone call from Vietnam Airlines. They had found the plane in the region of Khánh So'n. There was only one survivor, and it was Annette. They said she was doing really well. She had a few scratches, a broken tooth, nothing else. They were going to send a helicopter with doctors from Nha Trang to fetch her. They said I could come along if I could get to Nha Trang on time. They had a plane leaving in one hour.

I called Chris, the "local" Dutchman. He had lived in Vietnam for many years. He knew Willem and had offered to help several times that week. Chris knew everyone, and everyone knew Chris. I asked Chris to help me with all the things that had to be done: informing the families, informing ING, setting everything in motion to get her out of the country, and opening our office on Monday if I was not back in time. I rushed to the airport. My flight to Nha Trang was not delayed, but when I finally got there I heard that the helicopter had taken off without me and had subsequently crashed in the same jungle! There had been six doctors on board. All dead. I was flabbergasted that they had taken off without me. I felt angry and at the same time very grateful that I had missed them. The accident was never made public. The Vietnamese authorities kept it out of the press.

There was no other helicopter available in the country, so I was told that Annette would be transported by jeep. I asked again how she was: "Fine, just a few scratches." I went to a hotel in Nha Trang to wait for her, assuming that she would arrive the same day. That evening a Vietnam Airlines official told me they had been informed that Annette had to stay in the jungle. In a hospital, he assured me. She was too weak for further transportation and needed rest. What? Too weak? I panicked. She couldn't die now! I protested, to no avail.

The next morning I was informed that Annette was on her way. They had to drive the jeep very slowly because of her condition. I flipped. My God! Were they mad? Didn't their army have a helicopter? The French consul arrived. He was there to identify the body of the French passenger. He was kept in the dark by the same people and was also furious. We joined forces and threatened to call the international press if they didn't handle this matter with more professionalism. The atmosphere changed.

From then on, government officials kept us continuously informed. Annette remained in the jeep, though. The only helicopter they could get would have to come from the north, and that would take too long.

I had no idea what to expect. After eight days in that jungle, Willem dead, what sort of state would she be in? I only knew her from stories and, bizarrely, from the contents of the suitcase of her belongings that I had packed. A woman of the world.

She was so very different when I finally met her. Like a fragile little bird. Totally dependent on other people. Her jaw was hanging at an angle; she could hardly talk. Her face and arms were full of wounds and insect bites. Some parts were swollen. She was almost dead. And in pain, in such terrible pain. A stretcher had been arranged to get her on the plane. When they tried to put her on it, she screamed with pain. *Oh, my God, she is going to break*, I thought. I wasn't the only one, and someone was sent to the market to buy a mattress, to put that on the stretcher. That worked better. It turned out later that she was really broken in pieces. Except her eyes. Those feisty blue eyes. Those were constantly busy registering everything around her. They registered me too. "Who are you? What are you doing here?" When I said I would fly back with her to Ho Chi Minh City, they became even feistier. *No way*, they told me. "No way," she said. "I am not going on any plane."

She simply refused to go. "Not again," she kept saying. I told her that she had to. In order to live. That she had no choice. Eventually she gave in. She pulled herself together with her last bit of strength. Once we were on the plane, she even made conversation. Although her jaw was broken, what she said was quite coherent. She said, wearily, that this should have been her honeymoon. She complained that the insect bites were itching. She told me that she had stopped smoking.

We landed and Annette was raced off to a hospital. Chris was there and went along in the ambulance. I waited at the airport for Annette's parents to arrive. The next person I saw was Jaime. He hugged me and just said, "I told you so." Then he jumped into a taxi to the hospital. He didn't have the patience to wait for the rest.

# HO CHI MINH CITY HOSPITAL

I am in the Cho Ray Hospital in Ho Chi Minh City. They put me on the floor among other victims of what turns out to be a bus accident. They are all moaning noisily. Two European men approach me. One is talking loudly on his cell phone, in French. He seems agitated. He introduces himself as a doctor and then quickly returns to his phone call. The other man is Chris, a local Dutchman Pasje has befriended. He is calmness personified. He tells me Willem's brother and sister have come to Vietnam and that my parents are on their way. I can hardly believe it. "We are going to get you out of here," he says, in a soothing voice. "You just have to hold on a bit longer." Two male nurses pick me up from the floor. I feel faint and only vaguely register the chaos and noise, people everywhere, camping out in the corridors. The nurses carry me up the stairs to a semiprivate room.

And there he is! Jaime. As always, in his white T-shirt and blue jeans. Looking at me full of relief, fear, expectation. I can't believe my eyes. *How is that possible?* I worry about our trading positions. The first thing I say is "What the fuck are you doing here? Who is minding the business? Where is MYDFA, Brazil?" He looks perplexed.

Jaime tells me how he left the Netherlands with Willem's brother and sister two days earlier, not yet knowing what had happened to the plane. He was told by Chris when he arrived in Vietnam that Willem was dead and I was alive. Chris convinced him to stay put, not to try to go to Nha Trang. Although I am happy to see Jaime, I know Jasper and Miebeth are waiting. I want to tell them how Pasje died. Despite everything, I still feel responsible and very much in control. Miebeth comes in alone. We look at each other. "Willem is dead," I say. "He had a little smile on his face." She bends over my bed and hugs me.

We are interrupted by two nurses, who take me away for X-rays. It feels like torture. They put my broken hips on thick metal plates. When they walk out of the room to take the pictures, I scream in pain and fear.

Fear of being left alone, without water. How feeble is my psychological state! So different from the one in the jungle.

Meanwhile my parents and my sister have arrived in Vietnam. My mother enters the room. When I see her face, I just let go. I finally cry. "Did you come all the way here for me? Pasje is dead." I do not remember anything after that.

# Perspectives

**MY BROTHER FREEK:** At four o'clock in the morning I was woken up by the phone. It was the manager of ING Hong Kong telling me there were indications that Annette might still be alive. He was waiting to receive confirmation. I did not quite know how to react. "Why don't you call me when you have it," I suggested, and went back to sleep, not daring to believe it was true.

At ten a.m. the confirmation came. Again I drove over to my parents' house. Again I asked if I could talk to them alone. The house was full of visitors, so I asked my parents to follow me upstairs. "No!" my mother said. "I am not going to. I can't hear any more bad news! Has something happened to Marije? The boys? I won't hear it!"

"Well, then I won't tell you!" I said, irritably. The constant presence of "strangers" was getting on my nerves. To me they seemed like the suitors in Odysseus's palace.

They did follow me up the stairs, to their bedroom, and sat down. Trembling. When I told them the news, my father broke down. He fell into my mother's arms, sobbing, "Now you might get your granddaughter after all."

**JAIME:** It was Sunday evening when I finally arrived in Vietnam. Chris had sent two cars to the airport: one for Jasper and Miebeth, one for me. Once I was in the car by myself, the driver told me, in broken English: "I am not supposed to say anything, but you are going to hear very good news." I felt confirmed in my confidence. I focused on getting used to being in a real developing country. I had not been in one since I had left my own: Mexico. I preferred traveling within the developed world.

Chris was waiting in the restaurant of the hotel. He introduced himself quickly and asked the three of us to sit down. He did not beat about the bush. "Willem is dead," he said to Jasper and Miebeth. Then he turned to me and said, "Annette is alive." It was as if I had been awarded some morbid prize. I exchanged horrified looks with Jasper. Miebeth smiled at me through tears.

I turned to Chris. "Where is she? I want to see her."

"I knew you were going to say that," Chris answered. "We have been warned about you!" Then his tone became more urgent. "You cannot see her now, and I strongly advise you to accept that. This is a communist country. You will have to stay put until she comes to Ho Chi Minh City. Tomorrow morning she'll be flown here on the first flight from Nha Trang. You will be able to see her then."

I was taken aback. "How is she?" I wanted to know.

"There are different reports," Chris answered. "From just a scratch to serious injuries. I am afraid we'll just have to wait and see. You will not get permission to travel."

I first made a round of phone calls and then I stayed up the whole night with Jasper. I told him that was my specialty. Jasper talked about his sorrow. His truth. His version of his brother. I listened.

**MY FRIEND HELEN:** After a week passed, I too had started to lose hope. Then literally on the eighth day, in the middle of the night, the

With Helen on vacation, Morocco, July 1992

phone right by my bed rang. I had no idea who would be calling at that time—maybe a broker who had forgotten about the time difference. On the other end of the phone was Jaime's voice—quivering but loud—shouting, "She's alive! She's alive!" I could not believe my ears and cried for joy. Unbelievable. Jaime's and our wish came true. He shared what information he knew, and said he was planning to go and see her as soon as possible. "Rescue her," he said. If anyone could survive eight days in the jungle, it was my dear friend Annette. I still can't believe she did it.

**MIEBETH:** For me, that time was traumatic in more ways than one. The first thing, of course, was the sudden loss of my oldest brother. We had been close as kids, and with his amiable personality, he had played a central role in our family. How central only became clear when he was gone. My relationship with my mother had always been difficult. It originated from her relationship with her own mother, who she said had been extremely tough on her. In contrast, the sun rose and set on Willem. Literally—when he was gone she continued living only in the shrine she had built around his memory.

That trip to Vietnam with Jasper and Jaime was surreal. We were suddenly drawn into this world that had nothing to do with our daily lives. It started with the journey from Amsterdam with Jaime. I had never met anyone like him: He looked like a rock star and acted like a businessman. On top of that, he was oozing charm and charisma.

Once we were in Vietnam, I gradually realized that Willem had made this strange country his own. The office he had built and the kind of employer he had been to his staff showed us a side of him that we had never known. It doubled the culture shock that I was feeling.

When I heard from Chris that Annette was still alive, I responded according to my own plan. I had considered what I would do if she survived and Willem didn't, and I had decided that I would open my heart for her. That Annette would be the closest thing I had to Willem. He adored her, and she had been with him for thirteen years. They were a great couple. And I liked her, for her tolerance, her fashion sense, her nonconformism. She made me laugh.

When I arrived at the hospital, I was nervous that I would react differently, that I would not be so bighearted after all. That I would be resentful. Of course the thought *Why her and not Willem?* had crossed my mind. Or worse: *Why Willem and not her?* But then I saw her, among the rats and cockroaches, a miserable heap of bones. And she still wanted to tell me how Willem had died. "He had a little smile on his face," she said. I hugged her bony shoulders, and then I saw something moving inside her chin. She had this big open wound, and a giant maggot was crawling around in it. I screamed, "Nurse!" The nurse was not startled at all. She just pulled the thing out with a cloth so dirty I wouldn't use it to clean my kitchen floor.

I looked at Annette and couldn't believe how brave she was being. All that dirt and those creatures inside and around her. It was then that I took her in my heart forever.

We still had an awful job to do: identifying Willem. Jasper and I went with Carola to a hangar on the outskirts of Ho Chi Minh City. This was where the bodies of the plane crash victims were being kept. A Vietnamese official directed us inside. It was not refrigerated; the smell almost made me choke. Carola handed me a handkerchief sprayed with perfume: Chanel N°5. Another "fragrance" I will never forget. It only helped a bit.

There were many people walking around, both Vietnamese and European. I recognized the Swedes from the hotel. They had told us that they had been in Vietnam the whole week waiting for news and that they were worried about their dwindling finances.

The bodies were not covered. I hardly dared look, nearly closing my eyes. But through my eyelashes they did not seem recognizable at all. They all looked alike, faces without eyebrows. Even their skin tone had turned the same shade of gray. It was not scary, it was just . . . nothing.

But then, suddenly, I saw these big calves. Unmistakably Willem's "football calves," as he proudly used to call them. "That is him," I said. I was still two yards away from the body. "That *must* be him."

"You stay here," Carola said. She looked. She nodded. "It does look like Willem's build," she said. I turned around and ran for the exit, retching. Carola caught up with me, and on our way out we met the Swedish and English families, with whom I exchanged condolences. We were in the same sickening boat.

**MY MOTHER:** As soon as I heard the incredible news, I started packing our suitcases. *She's alive, she's alive, she's alive*, I kept saying to myself.

Willem's employer arranged seats on the first flight to Vietnam for my husband and me. We decided that our other daughter, Eveline, should come as well. She had a lot of experience in dealing with developing countries. At the airport and throughout the flight, the airline's personnel shared our joy. Actually, it felt as if the whole country did, as Annette's survival had already been on the news. My husband happily drank the champagne and dug into the caviar that the cabin crew kept offering. The latest update we had was that Annette was completely unharmed. That she was only missing a few teeth. I had already made an appointment for her with my dentist, but I hardly dared believe that she had no other injuries. It seemed too good to be true. Anyhow, any happy thoughts I had were overshadowed by the loss of Willem. His life had been intertwined with Annette's. He had been like a son to us. How was she supposed to go on? Carola was waiting for us at the airport. It was nice to finally meet her. She had been so sweet and supportive all week. She told the driver to take us directly to Ho Chi Minh hospital. Once we were on the road, she turned to us with a serious look, and I knew it had all been too good to be true. "She really isn't in a good way," she said. "You need to prepare yourselves for that." Oh, how that journey seemed to take forever. So much traffic. All those bikes! I wanted to get out and push our car through.

When we finally got there, a team of doctors was waiting for us. They wanted to take us to a room to show us Annette's X-rays first. I couldn't believe it. "I want to see my daughter!" I exclaimed. "Where is she?" My husband gestured that he would stay behind. A timid-looking nurse took Eveline and me to Annette's room. Walking through the corridors, I was horrified by the mess. There were people camping out everywhere, paint was peeling from the walls, bats were flying around a rusty staircase. Cockroaches.

Then I saw her. She looked so tiny! Such a little hollow face. And it seemed like she didn't have any teeth! The thought of false teeth flashed through my mind. Her eyes lit up when she saw me. "Did you come all the way here to see me?" she said. "Pasje is dead." I threw my arms around her. A little heap of bones, flushed with fever. I could feel that the sheets were soaking wet.

"Would you please change these?" I asked the nurse in French. When I turned back the sheet, I saw the terrible wounds. Gaping, black wounds. The bone was showing through. How brave she was! Just moving the sheet made her cringe with pain. My husband joined us. He was very emotional. They had hung up all of Annette's X-rays and shown him her collapsed lung and the multitude of factures. In her jaw, her hips, and her legs. "Her pelvis looked like a broken *kerstkransje*," he said. (A *kerstkransje* is a Christmas cookie shaped like a little wreath.) Broken in pieces. Also, her jaw was split in two: she still had all her teeth!

Personally, I was most worried about the wounds. I knew that the gangrene would kill her if it got into her bloodstream. In fact, any infection would kill her. Had no one seen the pile of dirty potties, covered with flies, in the bathroom? How could a hospital be so filthy? There were rats! We had to get her out of there, out of Vietnam, as soon as possible. We knew that SOS, an emergency medical assistance organization, had a plane at the airport, waiting to fly her to Singapore, where she could get the best medical treatment. But the Vietnamese authorities would not allow it. "She can be treated perfectly here" was their patriotic opinion.

"With that collapsed lung, leaving the country would be more dangerous." Pigheaded patriotism, and that was putting it gently. My daughter Eveline, who had originally insisted that the medical facilities in Vietnam were better than in other third world countries, became more and more convinced that the Vietnamese authorities did not really want Annette to survive this. That they would prefer it if she didn't live to tell her story, because of the growing tourism industry.

Thankfully my husband, who had grown up in the Dutch Indies, was more accustomed to patient negotiation. He and Chris talked for hours with the officials in charge, some army colonels. It was like a slow game of chess. They came up with one elegant argument after another, for instance, "Annette's French is so rusty; she would feel much more comfortable in an English-speaking place, like Singapore." Finally, it was decided that Annette could leave if she would have an operation whereby a tube would be put in her chest to stabilize her collapsed lung.

All subject, though, to the final approval of the vice minister of health, who was flying in from Hanoi.

On the way to the operating room, she could only moan. She woke up when we were already at the airport, on the tarmac. Her ambulance was parked right next to a little plane, two doctors inside, ready to take off. Waiting endlessly. We didn't know why. For the vice minister to arrive, maybe? There was quite a crowd: officials, soldiers, reporters, I don't know. It made me anxious that they would change their minds again. The more publicity, the more they would want to save face.

Annette stayed in the ambulance slipping in and out of consciousness. We were not allowed to go inside it, but we could talk to her through a little window at the back to calm her down. Annette was visibly scared and claustrophobic when she was awake, and we still had to get her into that tiny little plane! The window was too high for me, and I couldn't manage to stay on my toes for long. Eveline took over. "Hang in there, little sister; hang in there just a bit longer." At some point I really had to go to the bathroom. Two soldiers accompanied me all the way back to the main terminal. One on each side of me. They took up positions outside the bathroom as I went in. What did they think I was up to?

Finally the vice minister of health arrived. An older woman. When she was about to sign off on the trip, Annette's lung appeared to have collapsed again. At least that's what they told us. Again Chris showed his negotiating skills, now together with one of the SOS doctors. Right there on the runway, they managed to talk us out of there. I was the only one allowed to accompany Annette. My husband, Eveline, and Jaime would have to take a commercial flight. When I was about to go on board, the vice minister came over to say her final good-bye. "I hope you will come back to Vietnam one day and see it under happier circumstances," she said. Then she hugged me and whispered in my ear: "I am a mother myself. If it would be my daughter, I would want her to leave too."

And then, finally, we were in the air. I saw Eveline on the runway getting smaller and smaller. Then one of the doctors demanded my attention. "Annette's blood pressure is dropping steeply," he said. "You have to talk to her now, keep her awake, otherwise you'll lose her."

I talked and talked to her. I gave it everything I had. "Please, Annette, please don't leave me. Don't leave me now, after all you have been through." I talked and begged throughout the two-hour flight. And she made it. Just about.

"Very good job," the doctor said when we arrived in Singapore, where an ambulance was waiting for us. "Without you she would have died. You have given her life for the second time."

My bruised face, Singapore,
December 3, 1992

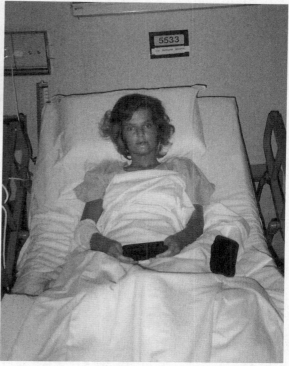

Put back together, Singapore, December 3, 1992

# Survivor of Viet plane crash undergoes surgery here

## Dutch woman went through eight-day ordeal with no food but only rainwater

**By Tan Hsueh Yun**

THE only known survivor of a plane crash in Vietnam, Miss Annette Herfkens, underwent surgery yesterday morning at a private hospital here.

Doctors worked for about two hours to mend her fractured jaw and her collapsed lung, and cleaned a deep wound on her left leg.

The 31-year-old Dutch woman was taken to Mount Elizabeth Hospital early on Tuesday morning after she was flown in from Ho Chi Minh City.

She was dehydrated and suffered multiple injuries, including fractures, infections and some internal bleeding.

She also lost about 10 per cent of her body weight, said Dr Paul Zakowich, who heads a team of four doctors looking after her.

But he added that she has a good chance of recovery and could be completely well in about three months.

Miss Herfkens went through an eight-day ordeal before being rescued from the crash site. She had nothing to eat, but was able to drink rainwater.

The Vietnam Airlines Yakolev-40 plane she was travelling in crashed on Nov 14, minutes before landing at Nha Trang, a coastal resort in southern Vietnam.

The plane was carrying about 29 other passengers and crew, including her boyfriend, Mr William van der Pas, who died. He headed the Vietnam office of the Dutch Internationale Nederlanden Bank.

News agency reports said that villagers found her sitting in the wreckage in a valley of dense jungle, surrounded by the mangled bodies of about 20 other passengers.

They then carried her in a hammock to the town of Khanh Son. From there, she was taken to Nha Trang by ambulance and then flown to

**Miss Herfkens: Dehydrated and has multiple injuries.**

Cho Ray Hospital in Ho Chi Minh City.

A decision was then made to send her to Singapore for further treatment.

AEA International, a Singapore-based group which provides emergency medical services in the Asia-Pacific, received a call from its Vietnam office at noon on Monday.

Dr Lyndon Laminack, who treated Miss Herfkens, said the group was contacted by both Mr van der Pas' employers and Vietnamese authorities.

A Lear Jet with Dr Laminack and a nurse on board were then sent to Ho Chi Minh City, and they arrived there at 10 pm.

Miss Herfkens was taken to the airport at about midnight. There, Dr Laminack stabilised her before she was flown to Singapore accompanied by her mother.

The plane landed at Seletar Airbase and she was taken to Mount Elizabeth Hospital at about 3 am on Tuesday, according to Dr Zakowich.

He said that she will remain in the critical care unit for another two to three days, adding that if her condition remains stable, she will be moved to a medical ward for another 10 to 14 days.

Said Dr Zakowich, a specialist in internal medicine:

"She is now on a lot of strong antibiotics because of the infections.

"But the final plan is to bring her back to the Netherlands for further medical care."

Dr Zakowich said that besides her jaw, her pelvis is also fractured in two places, but he added that these do not need surgery and will heal slowly. She also has fractures in her toes, feet and left leg.

He said: "She's young, and she may be able to walk with supervision in about a month.

"She was confused and delusional when the rescuers found her, but now her mental status is good."

Dr Zakowich said that so far, she has been fed through a gastric tube, but starting today, she will be fed orally with liquids and porridge.

Her parents, sister and brother, who is a radiologist, are also in Singapore, but they declined comment.

Singaporean newspaper, November, 1992

# THE REAL WORLD

I am in Mount Elizabeth Hospital in Singapore. The room feels like a good hotel. Large, nice wood, and my own refrigerator. There are flowers everywhere. My mother, my father, my sister, and Jaime are constantly moving around. And I cry. I cry for Pasje. I cannot stop crying. I sob convulsively. I cry and ask for water. I cry more and ask for more water. They all jump up when I ask.

My father keeps on saying that he loves me. Nice but weird; we don't say that in Holland. I am very happy he is here. He keeps on bumping into my toes, though. I scream with pain. How can toes be so sensitive? My mother. Oh, my mother! Her dear face switches from sheer happiness to worry to pain. She feels what I feel. Pasje . . .

Doctors are coming in and out. A triumphant Indian, who operated on my wounds, a dedicated Jewish American, who worked on my fractures and lungs, and a lovely Chinese woman, Myra. She has fixed my jaw, with screws. She insists that I eat soft food. Lots of soft food. She reminds me of my half-Indonesian aunt who has recently died. Nice, round, and very smart. She keeps on bringing more and more food. She is worried because I keep on losing weight no matter how much I eat. No matter how much cream I drink. Myra has suggested getting a few electronic gadgets in Singapore to distract myself. There are so many medical procedures yet to come. My sister gets me a Game Boy. With Tetris. I was the unbeaten master at that game in the office. I used to play it while I was trading. When I was a mistress of the universe. When I was carefree. Blissfully so.

What a chicken I have turned into. I am frantic when they wheel me through the hall. Frantic if I don't have water with me. Frantic when they leave me alone in a room on a bench to take another X-ray. *How long are they going to leave me here?* I hold on to my little water bottle with panicky obsession.

Of course, I am sociable. I laugh with others, make jokes, read all the faxes and letters out loud, enjoy the plentiful food. And I drink liters of Dutch Lady. But my heart is so heavy. Or is it light? Is there a hole, or a weight? My Pasje! I see his friendly face, his soft, brown eyes, his strong and muscled body. I see him smiling, I hear him laughing, I see him dead, I see him alive, I see him all the time. I cry. I wail. *Don't think of Pasje. Don't think of him dead. Don't think of the future,* I think. But I do. I do think of him. All the time. *Drink water.*

They all move around my bed. My oldest brother has flown in as well. He is the doctor of the family, but both my sister, Eveline, and Jaime feel at their best when they are in control, making decisions. There they go again, discussing the next decision to be made. About me. Now they decide that I need somebody to sleep with me at night. At all times. I think of the jungle. How peaceful my jungle was.

# Perspectives,

**MY SISTER, EVELINE:** Today I got a glimpse of the old Annette. She begged me for a cigarette, and when I resisted, she kept repeating that if I *really* loved her I would not hesitate to give her one.

My heart broke, but how could I, with all those oxygen tanks and other mysterious medical devices around her? And as far as smoking bans are concerned, Singapore is at least a decade ahead of the rest. Hard enough for nicotine addicts like Jaime and me; we can only have a quick furtive draw on the way back to the hotel.

Amazingly enough, during the long hours spent at Annette's bedside, I haven't cared. And that bedside is where I have been all week, to look after her and deal with the press. Since we left Vietnam a week ago, Annette's survival has become world news. We have been anxious to keep the press out. Reporters from the Dutch gossip papers are trying hard to get a shot or a quote from the family. It isn't my first and probably won't be my last encounter with paparazzi. I know how to outsmart them. We have been sneaking in and out of the hospital and the hotel through back entrances and fire escapes.

My parents, Jaime, and I have been taking shifts looking after Annette. At the night as well. In case she wakes up from nightmares. During one of my first shifts, I spent many hours untangling and washing Annette's hair, using the brush Jaime had brought. Her hair was a bird's nest, still harboring twigs from the Vietnamese jungle. I had to be very careful, as every movement hurt her. I always resist understanding medical details, but the number and seriousness of Annette's injuries is overwhelming, and visible. And she is thin—so thin, thinner than ever—and she keeps losing weight. I used to tease her when she was little that she was just a bag of bones covered with thin slices of smoked ham. Now she is a bag of broken bones. When she is asleep with all those humming machines connected to her, Annette's face looks strikingly like my father's mother on her deathbed. My father and I both have noticed.

Annette's courage and psychological strength are amazing. She has escaped amputation of her gangrene-infected hands and feet. She has the maggots to thank for that. Those ghastly worms gobbled up the dead flesh and kept the gangrene from spreading. The downside is that the numerous deep wounds have to be meticulously scraped clean several times a day, a painful and time-consuming ordeal. At Jaime's suggestion, I have bought her a Game Boy with a game called Tetris. It seems to help in making the treatment more bearable. She plays it every time they torture her. With complete focus, totally oblivious to her surroundings.

The other thing that seems to comfort her greatly is having a bottle of water in her hand. Whenever things get too much for her, she takes a sip. It works like a pacifier.

Tonight we will have a little celebration. Annette will be moved from intensive care, and even more festive, we will finally be allowed to bring her the only food she has been craving this week: sushi. Jaime and I have been happy to sample the various options to make sure she gets the very best.

# LONG FLIGHT BACK

After a fortnight in Singapore, I am finally allowed to be transported to a hospital in Holland. Jaime has negotiated with KLM a prime location on the plane, taking up twelve seats. Behind a curtain, so that I cannot be approached by curious passengers and reporters traveling with us. He protects me like a bodyguard.

It is time to go "home." My parents, brother, sister, and Jaime are all getting on each other's nerves. I don't mind. Nothing matters. And everything matters.

This flight is claustrophobia three, four times over. I can't move my legs. I am strapped on a narrow bed with big belts around these heavy blankets. Behind a curtain, on an airplane, for twelve hours! *What is this? An endurance test? When are these ordeals ever going to end? How much more do I have to take?* I feel around to make sure the little water bottle is within reach. It is, but it doesn't help. I want to get out. I need to get out! It is so warm! I start pulling at the blankets from under the straps, but I don't have the strength.

There is Jaime. He undoes the belts. Then he opens the water bottle and gives me a sip. Tenderly, as if I am a baby. I collect myself, if only for him. And to keep up appearances for the kind stewardess, the purser, the pilot, all those people coming to say hello and congratulate me. Inside I am screaming.

*Oh my God,* the flight is getting bumpy. Really bumpy! Bumpier than I have experienced in a long time. Except for my last flight with Pasje.

*Pasje.* I cry.

There is Jaime again. He puts the Game Boy in my hand to distract me, but it is too hard to keep it still. We keep hitting air pockets. They feel like they are supposed to feel on a big plane. The exact opposite of what I told Willem the last time, when we crashed. *Don't think of the crash. Feel the rhythm of the bumps. It is like floating in a boat. The sky is like the ocean. Just listen to the rhythm.*

• • •

In Holland my youngest brother, Bernard, meets us at the airport. I burst into tears when I see him. Of my siblings, he is the closest to me. And to Pasje. Pasje already asked him to be his best man. Bernard knows me better than anyone.

I realize how much I have missed him in the family dynamic in Singapore. With one wink he would have put it all in perspective. Like Pasje. He would have made it all right. *Thank God I still have him!*

I am very pleased when he gets into the ambulance to accompany me to the university hospital in Leiden. Just happy to be near him. But he is so emotional. He seems not to be able to control himself. He just keeps looking at me with tears rolling down his cheeks. And telling me that he loves me! This is my brother! My macho brother, my buddy in mischief! I pat his arm in an effort to comfort him. I want to make him laugh. "Bernie don't worry, the jungle was not bad at all. It was actually beautiful." He stops crying. "Evil weeds don't wither," I add, "Certainly not in the jungle; they flourish there." He laughs.

When I arrive at the hospital, everyone treats me with awe—and gloves, caps, and masks. I get a double room all to myself, to seal me off from the other patients and for my privacy. Everyone keeps talking about avoiding the press.

The next day I am cleared for tropical diseases. The visits begin. Family member after family member, friend after friend. They are very nervous when they come into my room the first time. They obviously have no idea what to expect. It is weird. I feel the same as always, yet they treat me as if I have come from another planet. *Hellooo! It's me you are talking to! Be normal! I am OK!* Well, perhaps I did visit another planet, but that was the good part. Now I am just back to being me. With this big load on my heart. Pasje is dead. That is all that counts.

I do what I always do: focus on who and what is in front of me. Some people cling to me, some are too nervous to talk, others cry. I try to make them feel at ease. By making a joke, a gentle one. Not the cynical ones I make in my head: pretending to have no arm or having some fake convulsions.

I get loads of mail, very kind, some very awkward, even some artwork.

I open the letters and read them out loud to the visitors, who come from morning till evening. My best friends return daily. Bernard serves them beer and tapas from the refrigerator he has brought. It is like a social club. Everyone's presence is priceless.

If only Pasje could be here.

# Perspectives

**MY FRIEND DORINE:** A month had passed since the accident. Annette had risen from the dead and was in a hospital in Leiden. It didn't cross my mind to visit this mythical person; she had more intimate friends. But I thought of her a lot.

I tried to put myself in her shoes, but as usual I failed. Physically she would be able to recover, I had heard, but how was she going to cope mentally? Was it going to be a convent or a psychiatric ward? Those were the only options, surely.

A mutual friend called. She had visited Annette, who had asked if I would like to come and see her sometime. Me? Did she still know who I was? And what could I possibly do for her under circumstances?

I sat next to the telephone, holding a piece of paper with her telephone number. Come on! Four times I picked up the phone; four times I put it down again. How do you make a call like that? The fifth time I carried on, a funny feeling in my throat.

"Hello?" Her voice sounded surprisingly familiar.

"Hello, Herf," I said, softly. The voice suddenly sounded very cheerful. "Hey, buddy! When am I going to see you?"

I went the next day. I lingered a bit outside her door. Then I went in, not knowing what to expect. Annette was lying in her hospital bed, looking pale and weak. Except for her eyes, that is. Like her voice, that look in them hadn't changed. It was sharp, full of interest.

She wanted to know how I was doing. I thought that would be adding to her burdens, but the patient is always right, so I went along. Perhaps she wanted to repress what had happened. Wasn't that what many trauma victims did? If that was the case, she certainly managed it very well. After I told her pretty much everything I had been up to in the past few years, I cautiously asked how she was. I hardly dared mention the word *accident*. But she told me about it without any restraint. Without any fuss, clearly and to the point. No drama. It was familiar and alien at the same time. As if we were just having a drink and a chat.

The next time I visited her she was at her parents' house. They were delighted to see me and so pleased that I had come to visit Annette. That's what they were like, always opening their home to everyone. By then Annette was able to sit up, and she was wheeled into the sitting room. A muscular, stocky man in a white T-shirt and jeans was pushing her wheelchair. He had very long hair, like a girl. Someone from home care, I gathered, a male nurse.

"Meet Jaime," Mrs. Herfkens said. Jaime? Annette's reputable colleague, the bank director? The man who had told Annette's parents after the accident that he was certain their daughter was still alive? Who had gone to search for Annette in Vietnam? He didn't look like a banker, or a smooth, macho Latino. He had long hair!

To hide my confusion, I asked Annette a question. I wanted to ask, "When is your operation?" Instead I asked, "When is your funeral?"

# THE FUNERAL

The day of Pasje's funeral I am taken by ambulance from the hospital to his hometown in the south. My sister travels with me. A two-hour ride. In her upbeat way, she keeps up my courage. Courage I have to summon up from every painful part of my body. My mother did not want to let me go; she thinks it is too soon, too risky, and too cold. She is still afraid of losing me.

I am to be carried in and out of the memorial service on a stretcher. I remember beforehand to put on some makeup. "There will be a lot of press," my sister is saying while twisting my hair into the new hair clip I bought in Tokyo. That hair clip I was never going to wear. It is black. I have to wear black. I am a widow now.

My arrival could not be more dramatic. Flashing lights and a crowd of people greet me when the door of the ambulance opens. Two paramedics maneuver me swiftly into a little medieval church. They carry me through the hall on a stretcher, into a separate room, where I can catch my breath. Somebody explains what is going to happen next. Like a wedding planner. I don't hear. I can't. I have no idea what to expect, but I am too anxious to listen.

When they carry me in, it does feel like a wedding. Slowly, with a steady step. The bride of a corpse. People turn around to look at me. Row by row. I keep my eyes fixed on my groom at the altar. In a coffin.

My bearers continue their solemn step. Ten rows, five rows. One more. What now? I can almost touch the coffin. My bunch of white roses is lying on top of it. "Dag -bye- Pasje," the silk ribbon reads. We turn to the left. They put my stretcher slowly on the floor. As if they are putting me in a grave.

They might as well.

The funeral is almost unbearable. The van der Pas family has taken control and reclaimed Willem. I have no say and have had to insist on every piece of music. Had we been married, they would have had to ask me about every single detail. Now I am treated like a guest. What a difference a little piece of paper can make. They tell my parents that they don't want to bother me.

Oh, and after the ceremony, they hope I won't mind not being in the line of family members accepting condolences. Mrs. van der Pas is anxious that otherwise all attention will go to me, with the survival story and all that. They hope I won't mind being in the far corner, away from the crowd. I don't mind. I don't want any attention. I want Pasje to put his arm around me. He would have laughed his family away. Would have told me all was well.

I have chosen some of his favorite music for the ceremony: U2's "With or Without You." Gluck's "What Is Life?" It cuts my heart. But "Gracias a la Vida," written by the Chilean musician Violeta Parra and performed by Mercedes Sosa in the version I selected, gets to me most. The fragile sound of the guitar intro and the strong voice of Mercedes Sosa.

"Thanks to life, which has given me so much.
It has given me laughter and it has given me tears."

26 dagen geleden was ze samen met hem uitgelaten in het vliegtuig gestapt, dat hen van de Vietnamese hoofdstad Ho Chi Min-Stad zou brengen naar Nha Trang, een badplaats aan de Chinese Zee.

Zij was daarvoor speciaal overgekomen uit Spanje waar ze al enige tijd een staffunctie heeft bij de Madrileense Banco Santander. Ze had hem al een hele poos niet gezien en ze wilde met hem hun toekomst bespreken.

'Annette en Willem kenden elkaar bijna twaalf jaar en ze wilden wat dichter bij elkaar zijn. Er waren voorzichtige plannen voor een huwelijk en de familie hoopte dat ze in dat bewuste weekend aan de Chinese Zee zouden besluiten te gaan trouwen. Zover is het niet gekomen,' aldus de hevig geëmotioneerde Eveline Herfkens die zeven jaar getrouwd is geweest met de Amsterdamse burgemeester Ed van Thijn. Twee jaar na hun scheiding vertrok ze naar Washington waar ze directielid werd van de Wereldbank.

Na haar kwamen zes andere sprekers tijdens de anderhalf durende herdenkingsplechtigheid in de Hervormde Kerk aan de Bredase Duivelsbruglaan, die vooraf ging aan de begrafenis.

Eveline vertelde hoe er kort na het bericht van het vliegtuigongeluk door beide families plannen werden gemaakt over de begrafenis van Annette en Willem. Ze zouden in Den Haag naast elkaar ter aarde worden besteld.

'Alle passagiers waren omgekomen, hadden we uit Vietnam vernomen. Niemand rekende erop dat er overlevenden zouden zijn en we probeerden al te wennen aan het idee

VERVOLG OP PAGINA 8

Spread of Pasje's funeral in *Weekend*, a Dutch magazine, Breda, December 26, 1992; photo by Peter Mulder

# 3

## AFTER

### BACK HOME

My family arranges for me to be home for Christmas. They think it is important. It is. How lucky I am to have parents who can take me in like that, in a hospital bed with a handgrip, in their dining room.

I come with many instructions. The wounds on my arms and legs have to be nursed. I have received two skin grafts. Two parallel strips of skin have been taken from my thigh. They look as if they have been sliced with a cheese slicer, the same type we use to slice the cheese for our daily bread in Holland. Sliced with a little too much enthusiasm and too thick for my thigh ever to heal properly, leaving an obvious souvenir: two perfectly parallel scars. Like two little landing strips.

The yielded skin has been stretched out to cover the giant, gaping wound on my shin, or rather to cover the bone, and to cover two other big wounds on my right arm. One is on my elbow. I can hardly move that arm.

There are four screws in my jaw. I still can't chew properly. I am so thin. I am almost getting bedsores. Like an old lady. My mother knows what to do. She treated her mother's bedsores toward the end of her life. I end up with a silicone pillow to cushion my bony behind.

Visitors come and go, from morning to evening. My friends, my mother's friends, cousins, aunts, and more friends. I forgot how many

I have in Holland. My mother entertains. I am entertaining. In the morning the pain is only throbbing, but as the day and the many visitors go by, it gets worse and worse. In between visitors I cry. By nighttime, when everyone has left, I cry that I cannot take it anymore. In Calvinistic Holland, I am only allowed paracetamol.

My toes are the worst. Two tips are missing, and the nerves have gone haywire. The other tops are still black. A month or so later the black tops will just fall off. Like thimbles.

Jaime has bought me a new Nintendo system. It is even better than the Game Boy I had in the hospital. Others can now join in or watch me play on TV. It mesmerizes my guests, who are not yet electronically savvy. I play all the time. To distract me from my thoughts. To distract me from my pain. To distract me from me. It helps.

It is strange to be back in Holland in such a different role. Or rather, many different roles. It is the first time I have been lost and I am seeing life from the other side. Empty-handed.

I become a listener. Many of my friends seem to want to confide in me. Perhaps because I am an outsider, no longer living in the country. Perhaps because I have become a person who has seen and faced death. Whatever the reason, it is fine; it seems natural. I am somehow in a serene state of mind; I want to help. Though I have become softer overall, my sharp tongue is still intact. I sound out my new reality by joking about my instant membership in several "losers' clubs." I have noticed that certain people feel a special connection with me: people who have lost, one way or another. Some of my mom's friends who have been widowed. The widows' club. A friend who has diabetes. The hole-in-the-leg club.

I do connect to some extent, but I also feel the need to separate myself. I only get one foot wet.

*Hey, that's you! Not me!* I think all the time, partly out of bravado, partly in self-defense. I still find it hard to believe what has happened, and the established club members make my new reality more final by treating me as if I am already a member of their clubs. I am still learning my new lines. I haven't considered yet what it will be like not to be invited to dinner parties because I am not part of a couple. I have not thought about buying special tights to hide my scars, or whether I will wear a bikini on the beach. I am not mentally there yet. But now that I think about it, what a bummer about my legs. They used to be quite an asset.

Of course, I am also a plane crash victim, a survivor. That is a very small club. I get a letter from a Dutch man who survived a crash in 1954. He advises me not to settle with Vietnam Airlines right away. He had many more injuries than initially diagnosed. "The extent of the damage can only be seen over time," he writes. It isn't uplifting, but it prepares me for the consequences of that lonely membership and for what might come with it.

While I am in the hospital, two planes crash into each other on a runway somewhere in Portugal. All the passengers survive. It is constantly on TV, on all channels. It doesn't affect me, but everyone keeps looking at me, waiting for a reaction. Like I am supposed to have one.

My mother marvels at the teams of psychologists, instantly ready to support the crash victims. "You didn't even have one therapist!" she says.

The truth is, I really don't want a therapist. I am annoyed that my family whispers about it behind my back. The nation's trauma expert, a professor in psychiatry, has analyzed me on a whole page of a popular newspaper. He has never met me. Then he writes to my parents offering to treat me for free, as I am such an interesting case. "Thank you, but no thank you," I say.

If anything is driving me crazy, it is all the fussing over me. And of course, the throbbing pain. Constant pain. My body is traumatized, not my mind. And my heart needs mending, not my mind.

# Reflection: Analysis

It wasn't clear to me back then why people thought I needed therapy. Was it about what I felt, or was it about what they felt I should be feeling? Did they think I was uncomfortable talking about the accident? I wasn't. Were they? Anyway, I did talk. About Pasje, nonstop. And I have continued to talk about Pasje, uncomfortable or not. My biggest wound was that I had lost Pasje, that even though we had not officially been married yet, I felt "widowed." That was hard and sad, but there were millions of widows in the world, I was just another one of them.

Looking back I understand now that people thought I needed to talk more about the jungle. About the smell and sight of the dead people. They were worried I was suppressing a trauma. But I wasn't. I had no issues there. If anything, my jungle experience helped me through the pain. They didn't know, and I hadn't yet defined how that worked.

Therapists may shed light on things that are too painful to remember, or that a person is unable to look at, at the time they happen. But I have never forgotten the jungle. I remember every detail. I am aware of it, and I can recall it whenever I want. I have not pushed away what happened to me. I integrated it. I talked to everyone about it for a long time afterward. Then I no longer did. And then I decided to write about it.

I know that therapy can give a safe environment to process painful memories. For me, though, the jungle was that safe environment. The safest of all. So much so that I often go back to it in my mind when I want to feel safe. In those eight days I felt protected, unafraid. I stayed in the present. I did not get into a panic. First it was mind over matter, then it became heart over mind. I surrendered emotionally and physically. To the moment. To nature. To God, really.

Nobody asked, and I didn't tell. I hadn't defined yet that I had had some kind of unity experience. It turned out to be a gift. A gift beyond my psyche. I had looked the beyond in the face.

And why did I not think about the maggots? About the smell? Because I made them secondary to the beauty, the peace, and the safety of the jungle. Both in the jungle and afterward, I chose not so much to suppress the bad things as to shift my focus. I chose what to see. I chose what and what *not* to dwell on. That is different from suppressing memories and forgetting something happened. I had the option to move my eyes away from the maggots to the beauty, and I did.

# CONNECTIONS

A fortnight before Christmas, lying in my hospital bed, in the comfort of my parents' living room, I feel compelled to help the other bereaved. My heart is broken, and I think and act from the depth of that wound. I want to be of service, and thus I make a big effort to get hold of the relatives of the other European victims of the crash: a Swedish man, a British man, and a French woman. I want to let them know I did not feel anything while we were crashing.

With some effort I manage to get their phone numbers from the embassies. I have to convince the embassy staff that I really am that woman who was on that plane with their citizens. That I have good intentions. That I just want to tell the families their loved ones did not spend their last hours or even moments in agony.

The family of the French woman refuses any contact, but I do get the phone numbers of the British and the Swedish families. When I call the father of Hamish, the British victim, I get his sister on the phone. She says her father cannot get to the phone, but she asks me to tell her as many details as I can remember. I do. She thanks me politely and says she will pass it all on to her father.

When I call the Swedish widow, she bursts into tears. She is very grateful for my call. She has been imagining over and over what her husband must have gone through. It has kept her awake every night since the accident. They had been married thirty-eight years. "We were really happy, and I have so many friends who are not. *They* would be glad for their husbands to die. It is so unfair," she cries. This was going to be her husband's last business trip. They had bought an apartment in Portugal and were eagerly looking forward to his retirement. I feel for her. She feels for me.

I have become part of my parents' daily routine. With my bed in the dining room, I am literally in the middle, between the two of them. I can see my father doing his paperwork in the adjoining living room. When I turn my head, I can see my mother in the kitchen, cleaning after the nonstop visitors. They go back and forth to each other's domain to talk about things.

One day my father is paying the bills and telling my mother he still owes Willem's parents half the cost of the notice they put in the newspapers about our disappearance. Mr. van der Pas actually called about that.

"Oh, now that I think of it, they wanted me to ask you if you know whether Willem bought that piece of land in Chile as he was planning to," my father adds.

I am suddenly furious. I rant and rave about the Dutch, how their cash flow will always come first. In any circumstance, however dire. "Why are they even thinking about money?"

I dealt in the jungle, under great pressure, with shock and denial (the first two phases of grief, I later learn). Now I have to deal with guilt, anger, and depression. I have to deal with them in between the visits. The whys: *Why me? Why not Pasje? Why, why, why?*

When my mother puts the coffee cups, the teacups, and the beer mugs and wineglasses in the dishwasher, the physical distance between the dining room and kitchen facilitates my cries. I shout my heart out.

My anger is very much compounded by how Mr. and Mrs. van der Pas behave. How they have so obviously separated themselves from me. And from my parents. Even though my parents have loved Pasje as a son, the van der Pases's grief is now different; it is theirs. My parents understand this. I don't. Don't we share grief?

Then one day, Pasje's parents finally come to visit me. When they enter the room, Pasje's mother is one step ahead of his father. He follows her dutifully. Willem used to say he did not want to become like his father. That he had made that decision when he was sixteen, when his first love left him to go to Paris. "I knew then that I had it in me to be like him, but I decided not to become a pushover." Well, he didn't. But he did keep that same warmth as his father. With his mother's good looks, though.

They sit down next to me. She is cold. He is shy. I look at her eyes. Willem's eyes, but not quite! I decide to look at his father's eyes instead while I talk.

I go back to the role I used to have when I stayed at their house. When I was eighteen, nineteen, twenty. Before Pasje's mother turned on me for reasons that were never clear. I loved their house. Everything about it. The interior, the food, the garden, and all his family. I always felt at home.

Like I did then, I tell Pasje's parents stories. I tell them I spoke to the families of the other crash victims: the sister of the Englishman and the Swedish widow. "Can you believe it?" I say. "It was his last business trip! They were going to retire and move to Portugal. Poor woman."

Willem's parents look more relaxed now. "The British woman was less eloquent," I continue, "not as forthcoming. Perhaps you'd like to have their telephone numbers? You may want to organize some kind of class action." I intend this as a nice gesture, because I am not a beneficiary. They have made it crystal clear to my parents that they are Willem's legal heirs. I am not! We did not get married, after all. I hand them all the phone numbers. It looks like they are defrosting.

I tell them about Noemi. She called last night and asked whether we would like a school to be named after Pasje.

"The Willem van der Pas School," I sound out. Now they look thrilled. On the way out, Mr. van der Pas tells my mother that, in a way, he is happy he can share grief with his wife. He has never been able to share the grief from her hard childhood. Now he can, and for that he is grateful. That is seeing the glass half full! If he indeed is a pushover, he is a saintly one. His weakness is his strength.

ING 🦁 BANK

## Willem van der Pas School

The Van der Pas family (in the middle), together with German Tagle, general manager of ING Bank Chile, and his wife, at the inauguration of the school

The memory of our colleague Willem van der Pas, who died in a plane crash in Vietnam, lives on in Chile where a school bearing his name was opened in May.

The 'Willem van der Pas School', a small boarding school located 120 kilometres north of Santiago de Chile, serves 19 students. It symbolizes Willem van der Pas' attachment to a country which he grew to know intimately while working for ING Bank in South America.

This rural school was funded by the Van der Pas family and by members of the Dutch community in Chile. Mr. and Mrs. Van der Pas, together with representatives of ING Bank Chile, government authorities and friends, attended the inauguration of the school.

The Willem van der Pas School with Mr. and Mrs. van der Pas, Santiago, Chile, 1993

# GETTING BACK ON MY FEET

On New Year's Eve, I take my first steps. My whole family is present. My father walks next to me with a look in his eyes he must have had thirty years ago when I first walked on that same carpet. In that same living room, covering the same distance. I am relieved when I make it to the couch. Next to the Christmas tree. The Christmas tree is all silver with tinsel around the white bulbs. As always, there are real candles on it as well. My siblings and I used to sit around the tree and watch them. Each of us would pick one candle and wait to see whose would last the longest. At the end, each candle would flicker as if fighting for its life. My father would compare it to a struggling soul. Pasje would smile wryly. He, and some others, thought my father's jokes were a bit perverse. My Pasje, who did not get to struggle.

I receive a letter from the international director of Vietnam Airlines, mailed from Hanoi, December 28, 1992: "On the occasion of New Year 1993, I would like to extend to you our warmest wishes. I hope that your health will be recovered soon. Merry Christmas and Best Wishes for a happy 1993 to you and your family."

Not a word about Pasje.

A week later I am notified there is a package for me at the post office. It's a box sent by Vietnam Airlines. It contains our belongings, found in the jungle. Surrounded by my family, I open the box. My hands are trembling when I open the first package inside. Pasje's 1940 Rolex! It is rusty and has stopped at twelve p.m.

My belongings are in a separate container: three packets of Philip Morris Super Lights cigarettes, a Bic lighter, and a camera.

It is an emotional moment. My brother ends up making light of it by saying he will have to stop smoking now: "I didn't quite believe you when you said that you did have cigarettes when you decided to stop smoking. But if you managed to do it there, I should be able to do it here!"

As it turns out later, the camera still works. And there is film inside. I have it developed: the pictures slightly yellow but clear. Shots of

Numachi and me in Tokyo, and the last picture of Pasje, taken by me on the balcony of his hotel room, November 13, 1992.

Numachi comes to visit me. He brings two bottles of sake all the way from Tokyo. They are made with splinters of real gold. He shakes one bottle like a snow globe to show me the golden flakes spinning. It touches me profoundly. Numachi was the last person to see my old self. He had also been with me in the jungle in the form of the dead Vietnamese man. In spirit. Now he is in the house that I grew up in. My worlds are colliding.

The whole month of January I spend getting back on my feet, literally and figuratively. After more than a month in a hospital-like setting, the outside world seems a dire place. My world has become so small. My first haircut feels like a huge undertaking. Riding in a car is scary, even as a passenger. And everyone knows my face from the papers, where I am being described as a "hero." In reality I feel like a captured and nurtured animal being let back into the wild. The first time I enter a restaurant, the place falls silent. I finally become self-conscious.

Numachi visits, The Hague, January 3, 1992

There are still screws in my jaw that will need to be removed, as well as the many stiches on the skin grafts on my arms, legs, and feet. They will need plastic surgery. My hips are a bit twisted. One of my kidneys has dried up and died. My right foot lacks two toe tops, which creates diabetic-like nerve pain. But I can stand up and walk. And smile—though more witchlike and slightly deformed with my forward chin.

On February 1 I fly back to Madrid. With Jaime. My first flight as a normal passenger. It is awful, even with Jaime tuning in to my every need. But I have no choice. I have to resume my life and go back to work, as a frequent-flying banker.

I start in the office a week later. Nervous colleagues welcome me. My boss is warm and welcoming, but she seems to avoid eye contact. Many others do the same. One of the maintenance officers has made a special stool for me, to put my legs on, as I need to keep them elevated to prevent swelling. It is covered with red carpet.

I return to my old reality with a new skin: a thin one. So far, my friends and family in the Netherlands have provided a warm blanket. They all knew and loved Pasje. In Madrid, nobody knew him. Not even Jaime. This is both better and worse, in addition to the fact that Pasje and I did not share our daily life here. It makes it easier to shift my focus. I have more than enough distractions: the all-consuming job, the nightlife, Jaime's company. All things that Pasje has not been part of and that I can take part in, albeit with a heavy heart.

It is when I am alone in my apartment that his absence hits me hardest. When I feel the finality of the verdict. The verdict of never and always: my Pasje—my compass, my alter ego—is gone. I can't call him, hear his voice. Can't get his view, his perspective. Ever again. *Our* perspective, gone. We are gone.

As great as they are, my friends cannot make up for my lost future. And I can't blame them for having their own futures. But I do. Their lives have not stopped. They go on living. Their waning attention, compared to the overdose I received after the accident, hurts. They are busy getting married. Busy having children. It is difficult not to be jealous. I am angry. Angry at death, angry at life, at all my unmet expectations.

There are more than enough things I can focus my anger on. There is Pasje's family, who I feel have abandoned me and repossessed him. There is his employer, by whom I also feel neglected. And there is the Vietnamese government. Just before Christmas, only one month after the crash, it passed a law specifically aimed at the crash victims and their relatives, limiting the airline's liability to compensate foreigners.

I don't believe the people in Madrid really notice. On the outside I am the same as ever, cheerful and making jokes. Inside the same bitter thoughts run through my head, day after day:

*A whole new law! Just for us. What a nice Christmas present! Couldn't they have used their energy to launch a proper inquiry into what happened? Why we crashed, why it took eight days to find us? Twenty thousand US dollars. Is that what Pasje's life is worth? Is that what my future, my health, my kidney is worth? And ING Bank. Now I know why they call it the grocers' bank. Why don't they take care of me? They always treated us as a married couple, in good Dutch spirit. But now? A bunch of flowers, that's all. No legal assistance, no financial assistance, as if I was just a fling! Bloody cheapskates. In good Dutch spirit indeed! If only we had gotten married. If only we had that piece of paper! Then his parents couldn't have gotten away with all they did either! They would have no choice but to include me. And as a relative, at least I would have the right to organize a class action against Vietnam Airlines, killing several birds with one piece of paper.*

And thoughts against Pasje's parents, who seem to believe more and more that they are entitled to his belongings:

*"It's the law," they say. Simple as that. The belongings of a grown man. Thirty-six years old! His things from our thirteen years as a couple are now at his parents' house. Pictures, letters, the many things we bought together, collected bit by bit for our future home. Never mind the money I gave him to invest in the piece of land in Chile: for our retirement. And on top of that, they monopolize our friends! My friends. Mr. and Mrs. van der Pas have started a trust benefiting*

*the school Noemi named after Pasje. They involved everyone but me. Thank God for Miebeth. At least she lets me pick up my personal belongings. She has orders to write down, meticulously, what I take. Two silver salt and pepper shakers Pasje and I bought in Chile. The many letters and notes I wrote to Pasje. He saved them all, tucked them so neatly into a tin box.*

I am bitter. Very bitter. If only I were an official widow. Dressed in black, even. People would have to take notice of my loss. I wouldn't feel so alone.

I resolve my anger with both ING Bank and Vietnam Airlines by writing them what I think I deserve. Although both efforts are to no avail, it gives me relief: I have done what I can.

By accepting the verdict of *never,* I have planted the seed of *always.*

# Perspectives

**MIEBETH:** It was two months later, at the end of January, that we heard of a possible body exchange. That the bodies of the three European men who had died in the crash might have ended up in the wrong coffins. Jack, the father of Hamish, the British victim, had suspected foul play by the Vietnamese after the crash. He had ordered another autopsy and had found out that this was not his son's body. Hamish was not blond like the Swede. He had dark hair, like Willem.

The British authorities had approached the city of Breda. They wanted to exhume the body we had buried. In March we heard that it was indeed Hamish's body, that we had not buried Willem in Breda but the British crash victim.

It turned out that Willem had been cremated in Sweden. The Swede was still in a morgue in the UK. My parents went to Stockholm to pick up the ashes.

We all felt we should have some kind of simple ceremony, but my mother started to plan a complete second funeral. She was determined to have it her way, all the way this time.

I understood my mother's grief, but she and I reacted in the exact opposite manner when it came to Annette. Where my mother chose to exclude, I had simply shifted all the love I felt for Willem to Annette.

# A SECOND FUNERAL

In March my mother tells me that Pasje's body has been inadvertently exchanged. It is difficult to believe that Pasje's friends had carried an Englishman to his grave. That he has been cremated in Sweden. Apparently, Pasje's parents traveled to Sweden to pick up his ashes and hid his urn in their carry-on to avoid formalities. Apparently, there would be a "second funeral" in Breda. I am invited for the ceremony but not for the tea afterward in their home. My parents, however, are able to arrange for me to be alone with his ashes on the day of the funeral, before everyone arrives.

At the cemetery, I walk past all the graves. It is a beautiful cemetery. Rustic, quiet. Surrounded on all sides by Dutch landscape: meadows of bright green grass with sturdy trees; dense, dark green bushes encroaching around the sides of the tombstones, pulling them into nature. I hadn't noticed the view the first time. I remember pictures of the cemetery I saw in magazines but none in my mind. Just the white roses on the coffin. My roses. I am anxious. How can I not remember my Pasje's grave? I look around. How did we get here? How did our story turn from a fairy tale into a horror movie into a soap opera?

Last time I remember being in these woods, Pasje and I were still on track. He had been bragging about his beloved Breda. As always, he was trying to convince me to settle there one day. I was extremely reluctant. Having grown up both in a bigger city and by the sea, I found it a strange notion to think of settling away from either. We had gone for a walk, against my lazy will. It was more than worth the effort. We had walked and talked for hours, with his arm around my shoulders—his favorite way.

The trees are even more beautiful to me now, with my new affinity for leaves, acquired in the jungle. I breathe them in, for energy. Then I see the tombstone marking his grave. It is not rectangular like the rest. It is round, with a hole with a piece of copper. It stands out among the neat rows of stones, literally. It is not like him. Not modest, not subtle. I have heard a lot about this stone, brought here from the family's country home in Normandy. His mom had planned to use it for her own grave. Fate let Pasje have it. But now with Willem in an urn there is unexpected room in the grave. She is planning to use it for herself as well. Mother and son reunited. Forever. She has claimed his possessions, his history, and now his body. It hurts.

In a sudden impulse, I grab the wooden urn from the grave. It is a simple box made of lightwood in Sweden. It looks like it could have been made for IKEA. With the urn in my hands, I move away from the grave, beyond a group of bushes. I sit on the ground, under the trees, overlooking a meadow with grazing cows. It is beautiful. It looks like a painting by an Old Master, but not as cloudy. It is a bright, sunny day. I hug the box. I rock it back and forth. It really feels good. I had pretended not to care. "They are only his remains; it isn't him," I had said. But this is the body of my love, after all, and it comforts me to hold it, even in this box. It gives me peace.

Miebeth is calling me. She has come looking for me ahead of the rest, but she can't see me through the bushes. She turns around and starts to walk back. She thinks I have taken off with the ashes! I quickly come out from under the trees carrying the wooden box. She smiles, relieved, and hugs me. Together we put the box back in its resting place. We wait for the other thirty people to gather around the stone. I stand a bit off to the side.

Willem's father starts by welcoming everybody. He looks at me meaningfully and repeats with emphasis, "Everybody."

The ceremony proceeds. Willem's father asks his mother to put his "favorite" things in the grave. They are all presents she has given to him.

His bathrobe with "Breda" and "Santiago" embroidered on it, the attaché case she bought him for his first job, and some kind of toy.

I can't take it anymore. I run off. Over the graves. Away from the scene. I sit down on a bench and look frantically for the little gin bottle filled with water that my father has given me. He chose the bottle intentionally, for its small size. I put it to my mouth. High up, like a Coca-Cola commercial.

"Herfkens, put that gin away!" It is my friend Jet, who has come to my rescue. I laugh through my tears.

"It's water!" I get up and stick my arm through hers. Together we return to the grave and rejoin the others.

It is the last time I see Pasje's mother. I leave straight after the funeral with my parents and my oldest brother for his house in Dordrecht. Everyone else goes to the tea at the home of Pasje's parents.

In The Hague that evening, my mother answers a phone call from my brother that Mrs. van der Pas was trying to get hold of me to offer Willem's ashes. She has heard from Miebeth "that I care so much." So she was prepared to dig them up? But when she later calls my parents, she says that, actually, I can only borrow them. My mother does not know what to say. She answers that this would not be practical, as I am going to London and Paris before returning to Madrid. Mrs. van der Pas suggests that I could take the urn as a carry-on: "We had no problem at all getting through customs!" I ask my brother to decline the offer on my behalf. "Let Pasje be in peace. I wouldn't want him to be dug up a second time. Besides," I joke, rather bitterly, "I do not aspire to become a modern-day Joanna the Mad, traveling with the body of my beloved through Europe, checking in his remains on airplanes instead of a golden carriage."

## Reflection: When Somebody Dies

When people die, everyone wants a piece of them. Like children wanting to sit next to the birthday boy or girl. But what matters is what the dead person has given to you in absolute terms, not in relative importance to someone else. I am still running on what Pasje gave to me.

At a funeral you often learn a lot about the departed from the stories of others. All the signs are there that this person had a whole life beyond you.

In the isolation of your grief, you can choose to ignore that. A wife can let herself listen to previously unknown details of her husband's office life and his surprising sportsmanship, but tell herself that in the end he always returned to her. That she was the most important part of his life. I reckon this is not the same for a mother who has survived an adult son, which must be the loss of all losses.

It was only natural that, at the time Pasje died, Mrs. van der Pas was no longer the center of his universe. To her, the eulogies must have felt both like compliments for a job well done and knives in her heart, confirming the separation. Understandably, she blamed me. If only for surviving.

At the first funeral there was no way of getting around me. The press had portrayed me as a national hero. It did not help matters that I was dramatically wheeled into the church on a portable bed and was later carried behind the coffin on the way to the cemetery, looking like a corpse myself. At least the law was on Mrs. van der Pas's side and assigned all Pasje's belongings to her.

By the time the second funeral was held, history had been rewritten. Pasje's mother had decided to skip her son's adult years, which she had played little part in, and had rewound the tape to the innocent childhood.

That is how she could claim eternal ownership of her child.

After a long struggle with life, Mrs. van der Pas died of grief fifteen years after Pasje's death. When I visited the grave she and Pasje now shared, I was afraid my fragile forgiveness would be compromised by seeing the concrete evidence of their reunion. But instead, I saw the beauty. The stone that I hated so much when it bore only his name had become beautiful with time.

# TRADING PLACES

I am lucky to have the job I have. I get to continue trading as before within three months after the accident. I am also lucky I share that job with Jaime.

My jaw, my feet, and my heart hurt, but trading is the best distraction. Every other Friday, Jaime flies from Madrid to New York to see his sons. It is part of his job package: two business-class tickets per month. He will leave me to "woman" the fort. Though we are in charge of only a small trading unit, we have huge cash lines.

Because of the extended lunch and late dinnertime, Spanish offices stay open until at least seven in the evening. On our floor there are usually people around until nine, but not on Fridays. On Friday nights you could shoot a cannon on our floor. However, someone from our trading unit has to be there until 11 p.m., when the New York market closes.

Our office is not very elegant—yet. A giant space with randomly placed desks and fluorescent lighting. No trading system with touch screens yet, just old-fashioned phones with a couple lines served, unreliably, by Spain's Telefónica. Though I'm generally coolheaded when trading, phones that stop working can totally tick me off.

One Friday afternoon the lines were down for three hours when we were short on Mexico. That is not a strategic position but an arbitrage one. I swapped out of some Mexican bank loans in the morning intending to buy them back later when New York opened. When the phone lines went down, I panicked. I ordered a trader on our floor, who was now reluctantly reporting to me, to get them at any price. He was only too happy to oblige and pay a premium to his very good friend at J.P. Morgan. That was the last time I let my emotions influence a trading decision. Even when the big boys from New York kept on trying to get me to do otherwise:

"Hi, young lady, what are you doing?"

"Nothing much, just hanging in there."

"Are you there all by yourself?"

"Yes." *Patronizing prick.* "I am. Why the honor of speaking to you?"

"I just thought: *Let's check what big and upcoming Santander is doing.*"

"Right." *He knows Jaime is not here.*

"Are you familiar with dealing prices?"

"Of course I am." You have to define the amount at stake and agree to deal, once you do you cannot tighten the spread.

"You want to start with a few million?"

"I can do more."

"Five?"

"Ten, if you want," I say, showing off.

"OK, what country?"

"You name it," I answer, showing off even more. "In Eastern Europe or Latin America," I add. "Or do you want to do Africa?" Now I am bluffing.

"Mexico," he says. Of course. Mexico is Morgan's number one country. That means I will have to be that much sharper. "You choose the assets," he continues. I quickly check my position sheet. We have a decent trunk of Mexican par bonds, and I wouldn't mind having more. The average price is well below the market, and with an additional ten million we'd still be under. I like Mexico pars anyway. I think I'd rather buy, so I have to price it that way. But I am going to let him think I want to sell.

"You start," he says.

"Forty-five, forty-five and a half," I say. That means I buy at forty-five cents on the dollar and sell at forty-five and a half cents.

"Forty-five, forty-five and three-eights," he answers. That means he wants to sell. Good.

"Forty-five, forty-five and three-sixteenths," I answer, pretending I want to sell as well.

"One-sixteenth, three-sixteenths," he says. Is he bluffing? I think so.

"One-sixteenth, one-eighth," I answer.

"Ten million yours," he answers. Bingo. I have bought them at the price I want. He doesn't realize it yet.

"Wanna do more?" I ask, happy with my acquisition. No answer. "Or, if you want, I can play again, with bigger amounts?" He obviously wants to get off the phone.

*Got you, big shot!*

# COMPLEMENTARY COHEADS

Our bosses in Spain value and respect us. They aren't very corporate, more like traders. That's how they manage the bank. They sell and take losses when common sense requires them to do so. They always keep a good amount of cash so they can purchase cheap assets in bad times. They manage the money as if it is their own, and in a way it is. They are major shareholders in the bank that their fathers and grandfathers built from scratch.

We like being part of this dynamic, growing entity, however feudal it can be. Sometimes our chairman summons us in on Sunday to get our views on the world economy. It could be worse: some of our colleagues are made to jog with the boss, play a round of golf, or come on board his jet to brief him on the way to Brazil.

Our direct boss has become head of Santander Investment, the investment bank, and she is taking us with her. Technically it is a promotion. We get a seat on the board. But we have our reservations about the move. We like being part of the "real bank." Commercial banking is based on the good old practice of putting money to work. Investment banking is all about making a fee and moving on. Snotty MBAs who come up with sexy constructions, make a profit, and don't look back. December is their horizon: bonus time.

We like the straightforwardness of our business. We trade for the bank's own account, as if it is our own. I love my job. It is all I have left.

How do Jaime and I manage to be so profitable year after year? Even survive in a market as volatile as ours? Brazil is like a yo-yo, the Soviet Union falls apart, Venezuela has a coup d'état. How do we do it?

We both love our business. We have that in common. On first impression, Jaime and I also seem similar. Charming and full of it. Together we will fill up a room. But we could not be more different. We complement each other, in fact.

I like the big picture, Jaime the details. Jaime manages the numbers,

I manage the people. I read and read, Jaime watches the news. I travel, Jaime stays put.

As our market matures, we get screens monitoring the latest whim in every country. Jaime is glued to them, only moving his eyes to make his minuscule notes. While I continue to have conversations on the phone, all Jaime needs is to trade. To be in it, to win it. I need to communicate. Dialogue. To get a sense of the market's mood. To clear my head and hear my own thoughts.

For the longer-term outlook, I travel. To feel how a country is doing. I talk to taxi drivers, see whether the shops are busy, and listen to the local bankers.

I also look at graphs and printouts. I draw lines between the curves and come up with a level where I think it makes sense for a price to go. And so often it goes there.

Sometimes I sleep on it, sometimes the number just pops up in my head. I can only describe it as an educated guess from my clever unconscious. I don't get the number through conscious thinking, but it isn't gambling either. It never works for me in a casino.

As Jaime listens to my intuition, I follow his due diligence. Jaime makes sure all our transactions are properly processed. All the way through. We never fail to get an A for accounting.

But what we are best at is decoding. Reading each other. Taking the other's personality into account. Separating the ego from the instinct, the noise from the music.

# Perspectives

**BASTIAAN, JUNIOR TRADER:** I joined Annette and Jaime's desk in the fall of 1995. I had just finished my MBA in Amsterdam and didn't feel like lining up with my fellow students for that one trainee spot at the usual Dutch companies—ABN, ING, Heineken, Shell, Unilever. I wanted to postpone an office life and left for Madrid. To learn Spanish, play a bit of hockey. And maybe, if I really needed it, I would land a job.

Money goes quickly in a city where you live at night. Mine lasted three months. A Dutch relative put me in touch with Jaime and Annette, who happened to be in search of a young desk assistant. They interviewed me for about thirty minutes, and then took me to dinner. I remember suggesting Vietnamese, which wasn't very clever. We had Japanese instead, Jaime's favorite. For hours they introduced me to the "wonderful world" of emerging-market debt trading. My head was spinning from yields to maturity, the Russian Vneshtorgbank, debt-to-equity swaps, sake, and Kirin. But most important, we hit it off.

It was a good thing I had not been warned about them beforehand. I had no idea what to expect from a first job, but it wasn't this! They worked hard; were very dedicated and profitable; and excelled at Nintendo games, Super Mario Brothers and Tetris being their specialties. But we were also very secluded in our little trading-room shrine. It was us against the world. Probably due to the outbursts Jaime was famous for directing at anyone who was not on his level of intelligence, the only persons who dared enter the room were Ana Botín and her husband.

One day—a Wednesday I believe—Jaime and I had been discussing buying Mexican debt all morning. We had covered all angles: GDP growth, US economic numbers due the next day, crude oil, peso devaluation, even the personal life of President Vicente Fox. In the end, we were convinced we should go long. The only thing left to do was to see if Annette would agree. Then we could start building a position with some $20 to $30 million worth of debt.

Annette, as usual, came in a bit late—let's say just before lunchtime.

We ambushed her immediately, giving her all possible reasons for buying Mexican debt and telling her why it would go up. She didn't take the time to remove her coat off or put down her shopping bags, and instead went straight to her screens. She watched them for about five minutes, drinking in all the prices, which were blinking like a Christmas tree. Then she looked at our graphs, drew a line, and said: "No, we better go short on Mexico. It doesn't feel right."

Jaime and I looked at each other in disbelief. Had we done all those fundamentals for nothing? But Jaime knew never to trade against Annette's instincts. When she wasn't in the office, we often used our nickname for her: *la bruja*, the witch.

Jaime did sell short, and we made almost a million US dollars in one week. *La pinche bruja!* (That damn witch!)

# WOUNDS AND WEDDINGS

The first year after the accident, I combine almost every trip to Holland with some kind of doctor's visit. Every month a dental surgeon checks the screws in my jaws until they are finally removed in the summer of 1993, slowly and painfully. But then a dentist has to construct a special tooth to fit into the fracture. Afterward my jaw is left protruding a bit, and my face is slightly asymmetrical.

The eight days on rainwater had taken a toll on one of my kidneys: Repeated sonograms show it shriveling up. Eventually it will disappear altogether. The other kidney ends up looking enlarged.

A plastic surgeon cleans up the scars. For those procedures I am under general anesthesia. Lucky for me, his colleagues in Madrid can change the dressing afterward, but I still have to come back for regular checkups. The results are OK, but the scars stay, visible on my arms and legs. I don't mind that much.

My toes remain painful. With the tips missing, I feel a phantom pain where they are supposed to be. Nerves take a long time to heal. The scars on my ankle do not tolerate stylish shoes very well, or travel and standing around for long periods. Nerves play up; that is what they do.

When I am not at the doctor's, I have weddings to attend. All my friends seem to want to tie the knot. For most of them, I fly over from Madrid, put on my party dress and a big smile, and choose a gift from the couple's wedding registry.

Because my wedding is no longer happening, I decide to take material matters into my own hands. I hear Harrods has a big annual sale of china and silverware and decide to purchase my own wedding registry. I do the research on silver and china. I make list after list and interview my friends. What items do they really use, and how often? I even speak to a salesperson in Stoke-on-Trent, the English town where Wedgwood is made. He says that as a Dutch person, I would probably want Edme Queensware, although living in Spain, I might prefer

Amherst. However, I might also like the plain white bone china, which the Italians tend to buy.

I go the Italian way. The white makes the food stand out, and I love food. On a business trip to London, I buy the entire Wedgwood china set at Harrods and an Old English silver set in a wooden "military case." Both at half price. I arrange for it all to be sent to Madrid. Then I walk over to Harvey Nichols and buy some fancy charger plates, which I carry on the plane.

Now I am all set.

# Reflection: Fear of Flying

People always asked how I kept on flying after the accident. How I dared enter a plane at all.

Truth is, I didn't. But what was my alternative? Stay in Holland? Give up on my life and my apartment in Spain? Give up on my career? On what was left of my life?

Flying was an important part of my job. A means to experience what I had always enjoyed most: other cultures and viewpoints. Traveling put things in perspective for me; it gave me a different perception of myself. Luckily, the same job that compelled me to travel also allowed me to travel in a way that made it just about bearable. Our travel agent always booked me a seat in the very first row. On European flights, that meant flying business class. On intercontinental flights, it was first class.

And Jaime was there. On the very first flight from Singapore, the first flight to Madrid, and the first flight back to Amsterdam. He accompanied me on those flights with such compassion that it eased my pain and fear. Just seeing the outline of a plane would make me nervous. Jaime would describe the type and make of the plane and normalize the situation. I was fortunate to have Jaime around.

Even today I need legroom on a plane. I have long legs and still have difficulty when I feel the seat in front of me against my knees. I immediately associate it with that seat on top of me, weighed down by that dead body.

My first flight alone was from Amsterdam to Hamburg, to the 1993 Inter-American Development Bank meeting. Something had gone wrong with my reservation. The seats in the first row had been assigned to the directors of ING Bank, of all people. I was sitting behind Pasje's bosses!

I was too proud to ask them to swap with me. I chose to eat myself up instead. Not only was I uncomfortable with my knees against the seat in front of me, but I was also consumed by anger and envy. They were all alive and kicking, and Pasje wasn't. Pasje, who had so much more to give to this world than all of them together, I thought. They were relaxed and cracking jokes among themselves, oblivious to my grief-fueled thoughts.

After that "solo" flight, things got better. Once we are gliding through the air, I actually like flying: reading *The Economist* and having a real bird's-eye view. The few times that a flight has been bumpy or we have had to circle for hours, a friendly fellow passenger has talked me through it—like the time we couldn't land in New York and we circled for more than an hour after an eight-hour flight from Amsterdam. An elderly board member of ABN AMRO offered to hold my hand. He held it the entire time until we ended up landing in Boston. I learned that people are always willing to help. I just have to ask.

# ONLY A SEED

It is Christmastime again. A year has passed since the crash. Jaime knows I have no idea what to do with myself. I do not want to be anywhere. For thirteen years, I spent every Christmas vacation with Pasje in whatever place we happened to be. Last year I was in a hospital bed at my parents' house, and the night passed in a blur. So it really feels like this is the first time without Pasje. Jaime understands. "Come with me and the boys to Aruba," he offers. I accept. The Caribbean climate, looking after his boys, and the fact that they all are Jewish makes it easier to keep my emotions in check: I can pretend it isn't Christmas at all.

After Christmas I go on to Curaçao by myself. I stay with a school friend who has lost her first husband, our childhood friend. It is good to be with someone who has gone through the same experience. Then a friendly ING banker invites me to a New Year's Eve party at his house. He was Pasje's boss in Amsterdam. We all used to go out together in those days. Now he is managing ING Curaçao. I know the party is going to be difficult, that the whole atmosphere is going to take me right back to the past. But I feel I shouldn't avoid the confrontation. Face reality. So I force myself to go. It turns out to be an informal get-together with many of my ex-colleagues.

When the clock is about to strike twelve, the pain hits me. So hard that my stomach contracts. I feel like I am drowning, like a giant wave is sweeping me off my feet and I am choking. Drowning in pain and choking on fear. Pain for Pasje, fear for all the Christmas holidays and New Year's Eves to come. That throbbing pain, the feeling of amputation I have been living with, is taking me over completely. With such a sharp edge, it is as if Pasje is dying in front of me again, here and now. I go outside into the garden and sit down on the edge of the pool. I put my feet in the water to cool down the painful scars. The scars on my feet and the scars on my heart. I start sobbing.

"If you have loved once, you'll love again," I hear. It is a pleasant voice, with a German accent. My host's elderly mother sits down next to me. I look up. Her eyes are full of compassion. She knows. She has been there; I can see it. I put my head on her shoulder and cry.

# BIG SHOES

When my good old friend decides it is time to get married, I am his obvious choice. We used to go out in college and we had been really good friends ever since. We both happen to be single, and we can still give each other a thrill.

It had been two and a half years since the accident, and I had not consciously thought about filling Pasje's shoes. Yet, as girls do, I discussed it with my good old girlfriend. She said, "Yes, he would be the only one who could."

And I started thinking: "Hey! Why not Jaime? What's wrong with Jaime?"

# HOTLINE

Once Jaime started working in Madrid, he didn't enjoy business travel anymore. He'd done his fair share of it. I had liked his stories of trips to Scandinavia and Switzerland. How a senior Swiss banker had taken his arm when crossing the street and invited him to his house to meet his family. How he had shown Jaime the big vaults with all the gold, right under the head office in Zurich.

He only wanted to travel to the developed world anyway, and definitely not to meetings, so I would go. By myself. To all the countries we traded, to the conferences, the forums, and the big bankers' meetings. Jaime let his world shrink and mine expand.

The IMF/World Bank and regional development bank meetings are held alternately in Washington, London, and elsewhere. Thousands of senior bankers and government officials come together to give or ask for loans. A lot of the wheeling and dealing is done in the hotel lobbies and at the parties.

While other bankers travel in groups and coordinate their meetings, I am always operating on my own. It is part of the divide-and-conquer policy of our bosses: the different groups within the bank compete with each other and do not share information, let alone their contacts.

I fly first class, take taxis to the hotels, have a few meetings, and dress for the parties where the bankers share wine, delicacies, and information. The parties are often held in galleries and museums. What is there not to like: walking around holding a glass of champagne, seeing the country's renowned art, chatting with friends from the market, meeting the key officials of the countries, and picking up information to trade on in the process.

It is an indulgently privileged way to see the world: Eastern Europe, Latin America, Russia, the Far East. The poorer the country, the more lavish the parties. I feel a pang of guilt seeing the ice statues in Bangkok, the mountain of caviar in St. Petersburg, steaks in Buenos Aires, goose liver in Budapest. Especially when we bump into demonstrators. In

Prague they throw stones at our buses. But I felt a bit exonerated since we were offering solutions for these countries' debt burdens by selling the debt back to their governments at a steep discount and making the banks take a loss . . .

Jaime is always with me—virtually, so to speak. I call him all the time. Before the event, sometimes during the event, and definitely after. I tell him about the Jewish cemeteries in Prague, swimming in the Dead Sea, the paintings in the Hermitage, or the Peruvians doing buybacks. But I also call him to whine that I left my favorite scarf on the sightseeing bus during the ladies' program—what was I doing there anyway? Or because I cannot sleep in the hotel I was assigned to—in then-communist Moscow—because of the noisy industrial refrigerator.

Jaime can see the enormous changes in Russia through my eyes. On every visit to Moscow I report on them, from the first McDonald's to brand-new shopping malls, wondering out loud how much longer five-year-olds will sit through operas and chess matches or taxi drivers will quote literature. I walk across the Large Moskvoretsky Bridge from the newly built Kempinski hotel, listening to Jaime's thoughts about the markets. At the Red Square I describe Lenin's body to him.

I successfully corner some new Russian bankers and central bank officials and tell Jaime the results right on the spot. He talks me into the night on the train from St. Petersburg to Moscow, the one on which passengers are often drugged and robbed of all their belongings overnight. The alternative is a Russian plane—something I am reluctant to try again. When I wake up the next morning with my clothes still on, I call Jaime immediately. He is my first thought in the morning and my last at night. We share everything with each other.

Our line is hot, indeed.

# PART II

## THE RETURN

### 1993–2006

"A human being is a part of the whole, called by us 'universe,' yet we experience ourselves, our thoughts and feelings, as something separate from the rest, a kind of optical delusion of our consciousness. This delusion is a kind of prison for us, restricting us to our personal desires, and to affection for a few persons nearest to us. Our task must be to free ourselves from this prison by widening our circle of understanding and compassion, to embrace all living creatures in the whole of nature and its beauty. Nobody is able to achieve this completely, but the striving for such achievement is in itself a part of the liberation and a foundation for inner security."

—*Albert Einstein, letter of 1950, as quoted in the* The New York Times

# 4

## MOVING ON

"Ana, it has been three years now since my boyfriend died, and the inevitable has happened." She is sitting behind her desk, working her way through a pile of memos. Our boss is now in an ivory tower. I have to make an appointment to see her and need to punch several codes to get into her office.

"What?" She sits up, alarmed.

"I want to marry Jaime." She looks shocked, if not horrified. "But we want to keep on working together," I add quickly.

She remains quiet

"It is your fault, really," I joke. "I did not get to meet anyone else. I am always with him, working."

Finally she smiles and asks, "Have you been planning a big wedding to which you want to invite the whole bank?"

"No," I answer, "not at all."

"Then it is OK," she says "Don't make too much noise about it. It's fine. Congratulations." In the old days, when she was still working on our floor, she would have kissed me. Now she remains behind her desk.

I am thrilled, but I linger.

"Is there anything else?" she asks.

"Yes, we would really like to move our trading desk to New York. I am getting older, and we want children. It would all be so much easier if we could work normal hours."

So, we move to New York City from Madrid in the summer of 1995. Jaime wants to live on the conventional East Side. I prefer the more relaxed West Side. I bluff that I will only move to the East Side if he cuts his hair. People in the market once collected and offered $70,000 to get rid of his mane, and he has notoriously refused. He calls my bluff and we settle in an East Side co-op. The hair grows back, slowly but surely.

## Reflection

"Love is the name for our pursuit of wholeness, for
our desire to be complete."
— *Plato*

Several people asked me how it was that Jaime and I got together after
the accident: "How did you know he was the right one to fill Pasje's
shoes? Did it feel like betrayal? Did you feel guilty?"

The truth is, I dared him. I dared him with all my heart, body, and
spirit.

A spirit I had met in the jungle. A spirit that had taught me to get
over myself and to go beyond myself. A spirit that only shows itself in
surrender.

The ultimate bliss is in the surrendering itself. Any self-awareness
or self-consciousness gets in the way. As Einstein describes it in a letter
to Queen Elizabeth of Belgium: "When one feels free from one's own
identification with human limitations and inadequacies, when one
gazes in amazement at the profoundly moving beauty of the eternal,
the unfathomable: life and death flow into one, and there is neither
evolution nor destiny; only being."

So that is how it was to love Jaime after the accident. It was beautiful.
Like *la petite mort* as the French call it. The little death, just like in the
jungle, where the big death took my hand.

# FORWARD CONTRACT
## NEW YORK, 1996

I have to focus on the "terms" of my agreement with Ana Botín. Specifically, how to keep my pregnancy under the radar at the office. Getting pregnant, however, is different than a typical assignment. No forward delivery on this or that date. My years of professional training are rendered useless. It is also a different type of surrender of control. A painful surrender, as it turns out: I have three miscarriages.

Ana asked us to keep it all a secret, so I feel compelled to plan how to do so. My first step is the clothing. I buy the same suit in different sizes, so as I grow in size, my suit will fit me the same. But I miscarry. Three times. The season changes: A suit I bought for a summer pregnancy will not work for winter, and vice versa. My planning gets all messed up.

I must have bought at least twenty pregnancy tests. "Relax," I am told. "That is the only way." *Relax? Really?* I am obsessed! Trying to become and stay pregnant is all-consuming. First having to wait for the date until I can do the test. Then waiting, praying, with anticipation, to make it to three months, the "safe" date. After eight weeks, I start— hardly daring—to have hopes. Every time I go to the bathroom I expect to see blood again.

What I like about being pregnant is the effortless bonding with other women. A real, equal connection. Nobody is rating. Once born, children are rated on various scales of success—intelligence, athleticism, sociability . . . But when you're pregnant, you are united in uncertainty. You share expectations; you don't rank them. There is purity in the pregnancy connection that is not quite there when you compare the final product.

I enjoy that connection. Women from both the West End and East End of London, Spanish women, Dutch women, multiracial American women, and women who would normally stereotype me and stay distant now look at my bump and ask me when I am due and share their own experiences.

The third time I lose my baby, I am at work. I have just passed the thirteen-week mark, and I am so happy that we have made it—third time's the charm! I am about to call everyone with the good news, when I start bleeding. In the office.

Jaime takes me to the hospital, where I have a procedure to remove what was going to be our child. But my body keeps on producing hormones and emotions as if it is still there. I am heartbroken. Jaime desperately wants to comfort me. Helplessly, he says that he will buy me "anything, whatever I want." I look at the many strollers in our street and start sobbing, "A baby. I just want a baby."

The loss feels enormous, and the prospect of going through the same anxiety again is daunting. But then I remember the jungle, and I just stay

With Jaime off to the Stuyvesant Ball,
New York, 1996

Nine months pregnant and celebrating my 36th birthday with my brother,
New York, April 1997

still—stay still with the loss. Lean into it even, and feel the pain. I do not move on immediately. I let the loss absorb me first, completely.

After that, I can stand up and go on living.

When we finally tell our subordinates that not only are we a—happy—couple, but also that I am seven months pregnant, their jaws almost split. The trick with the suits has worked.

# GARDEN OF EDEN

Creation derives from opposites. Having children must be the highest form of duality—if only for the most excruciating pain combined with the greatest joy. The ultimate creation.

When I finally manage to stay pregnant, I assume my jungle pains have seasoned me. That giving birth should be easy. I wouldn't really need to do the breathing or the pain control. Even my gynecologist says it would be "peanuts" for me, so during our Lamaze classes I focus much more on my classmates than on my breathing. Luckily, Jaime pays attention, and when the moment comes, he holds my hand with his typical tenderness and care.

But he cannot take care of this for me. It isn't like doing a deal ticket or my tax return. I have to do this myself. Or rather, I just have to let go . . . and surrender. In the jungle I disconnected from my body, whereas in childbirth the mind-body connection is essential. In the jungle I had a collapsed lung, forcing me to really breathe. Now, I just can't do it! After eleven hours of suffering and holding in my breath, and my baby, I am told to have either an epidural or a cesarean. I choose the first.

Josephine is born an hour later. Seeing Jaime talking to his girl through my tears of joy while they stitched me up says all there was to say about the duality of life.

My mother gets a granddaughter after all: Josephine Leonie Lupa. We nickname her Joosje.

# TWO BLOND BABIES

Joosje makes me a mother on Mother's Day. As it happens, it is also the last day before the maternity ward of New York Hospital closes, and I am the last mother to give birth there. A nurse asks me whether I want to be interviewed for a New York TV station, while she intends to move us to the new Greenberg Pavilion; I politely refuse, because it is not the time to out Joosje yet, and definitely not on TV. In fact, I'd rather go home, and we decide to sneak out. It is an exhilarating experience to go into the hospital with the two of us and come out with three. If only we were not suddenly approached by a camera crew. A man I recognize as the Republican senator from New York, Al D'amato, comes forward to congratulate us. I reluctantly shake his hand and smile wryly for the camera, hoping that my Wall Street brothers are watching another TV channel.

We set up my office in the living room from which I trade happily while dancing with joyful Joosje in my arms.

Jaime interprets Ana's wishes to keep our domestic arrangements quiet in the strictest possible way. He is absolutely adamant that *nobody* in the bank or in the market should find out.

The second pregnancy is much easier to hide than the first. A year has passed, and our colleagues have gotten used to seeing me infrequently in the office. They assume I am traveling. Our subordinates, on the other hand, get used to reporting to me at home. Once in a while, they come to my apartment to fix my computer. They merrily play with Joosje on our terrace. I think they are proud to share this secret with the great Ana Botín, the charismatic co-owner of the bank.

Because I work from home, I have the double life of the working mother in a very literal way. When I am hanging out with moms from Joosje's preschool, who do not have or want to work at all, nobody sees me as a working mother. Although I often excuse myself to talk to Jaime on my cell phone, they view it as hubby stuff rather than market stuff. When sitting on the bench at a playground, I listen in wonder to their timeless conversations. When a toddler interrupts, they just forget the previous subject altogether and move on to the next one. It doesn't matter, because they are in the moment with their children. I don't feel that yet. I feel like an imposter. As I also do with the working moms when they complain about the lack of focus of the nonworking mothers. *Why are they creating camps?* I wonder. Perhaps it is done out of insecurity. Motherhood is prone to constant judgment. And so are the children, as a result. Collective judging functions to bind one group, for they are right, leaving the others out in the wrong.

Considering we are living in the lion's den—the Upper East Side, the neighborhood where most investment bankers live—we have surprisingly few sticky situations. Until my neighbor takes me to a playgroup, by invitation. Girls only. I am a novice at motherhood, but these mothers own that role fully and efficiently, with a distinct Upper East Side twist.

I am in a large apartment with a playroom, maid's room, and eat-in kitchen. Framed artwork in the kids' corner, the frames matching little benches. There are schedules everywhere, and multiple printed invitations on the fridge. A special Lego table with a hole in the middle and a bag underneath to catch the bricks. The kids' bedrooms are in different colors but match with extreme consistency. The curtains, the bathrobes, the multitude of cushions, everything is coordinated.

The nanny is minding our daughters in the playroom; the mothers are in the dining room, having bagels and coffee. They talk about their husbands, their likes and dislikes at dinner parties. They talk about their most-wanted private school. I watch and listen in awe.

Suddenly, I hear the hostess say, "My husband has moved to ING and is much happier now; he is an emerging markets economist." *ING? Emerging markets?* I gasp for air. I grab my friend's arm and guide her into another room. "I have to go. He must be working right next to my old pals; I am finished if they find out." The market is a place full of gossip. My friend is cool. She hands me Joosje's coat, when she notices a pile of passports on the desk near the window. She quickly skips through them and shows me a picture of a man in a suit. "Do you know him?" she asks. I don't know. I can't focus; I am too nervous to look. I just have to get out of there.

I sneak out and let my friend do the good-byes for me. And I resign from the playgroup.

When Joosje is two months old, we bump into a trader from Salomon Brothers near the hospital. Jaime tells him he is babysitting his niece, and not knowing what to do with her, he called me to help him out. The trader tests: "And does Annette know what to do?"

"I am a natural," I answer, with my best poker face.

A year later, pushing Joosje in her stroller, we almost bump into a colleague from Santander at Blockbuster, but Jaime turns around just in time. As he does in the park, when he spots his ex-boss from Citibank.

We only get busted by the market after Maxi is born, when a fax is sent from a New York office to a London office. Someone has just seen Jaime Lupa pushing a double stroller with two blond babies, both with Annette's face.

Two blond babies, New York, 2001

# THE ORANGE MAN

Jaime and I often find that we are invited to dinner parties just to tell my story. Jaime will oblige beautifully, with pathos and drama, always exceeding our hosts' expectations. By contrast, I always play it down. I just shrug and say, "It wasn't that bad," or "No, it hasn't really changed me." I know that I fall short of everyone's expectations.

Inevitably and thankfully, the conversation then turns to the mystery of the orange man. The man who I believed had been watching me in the jungle.

"He must have been a monk," the other guests suggest. "They do wear orange in that part of the world."

"But it was bright plastic orange," I counter. "Official orange. He might have been a government official, waiting for all of us to die. To avoid paying damages, perhaps. They obviously go to great lengths to avoid that."

Of course, they ask why I didn't get any money. I explain the law passed by the Vietnamese government soon after the crash, limiting liability to twenty thousand US dollars, way below international standards. "Twenty thousand dollars? That's all you got?" our hosts exclaim, horrified.

I tell them that I have refused to accept it. "Thank you, but no thank you. I would have had to sign off on all further claims. And who knows what will happen in the future. They might start caring about tourists, and me! I could still become disabled in some way, mentally or physically. I am not waiving!"

"That could establish motive," my hosts suggest. "Sending the orange man to watch you die." That has crossed my mind.

Someone asks, "But didn't they send a helicopter to rescue you?"

I shrug again. "That's what I heard, but I never saw a helicopter. You'd think I would have noticed. All I did all day was look at the sky."

"And the orange man, what did he do? Did he say anything? Did you do anything to get his attention?"

"I screamed, I waved, I cursed in every language, but he just stood there, like a staring statue. He did not lift a finger."

In the end, everyone agrees that I must have been hallucinating.

# YOGA, 2001

When I finally turn forty, I am more than ready for my next decade. So much happened in my thirties: Pasje, London, Madrid, New York, the crash, Jaime, Joosje, Maxi. The only drawback is that I promised myself that at this estimable age I would finally begin exercising. I've never really worked out before. I've never believed I needed to. Not until I turned forty.

I decide on yoga, which seems the path of least resistance. I target a friend to come along.

We join a yoga place with an established yogi somewhere in Midtown. It turns out yoga was the new "in" thing to do. It seems to have its own breed of women: long hair, skinny, with straight backs and serene smiles. They are dressed in tank tops and leotards. They sure hug a lot.

"That sweater is *soooo looovely*," says one to another. *It should be; it's Prada.*

At the center of these long-legged nymphs sits a short-legged, pot-bellied yogi, well into his fifties, with long, gray hair. Even less-dirty minds would not be oblivious to all the sexual joy that charges the air. Hugh Heffner comes to mind.

One of the most beautiful nymphs, Rachel, becomes our semiprivate yoga teacher. We meet in a little room with a view of the diligently stretching, cool Midtown crowd.

I listen to Rachel's instructions with uncharacteristic focus. It's always been a challenge for me to listen and act out instructions in sync. It makes me want to joke around. Not anymore. Now I oblige. I am forty.

Rachel makes us balance on one foot. I am supposed to cradle the other foot while focusing on a single spot on the floor. I look at my scars and at my missing toes while rocking my foot like a baby. The remaining toes are in obvious need of a pedicure. I stumble and step back.

"Focus!" Rachel says.

I have to breathe deeply, in and out, like some pervert making an obscene phone call. In and out, in and out. One leg toward the back, both arms to the front. My seemingly fit body feels awfully limited. I can't even straighten my legs.

"It has to come from your core strength," Rachel says. *From where?* "Body and mind in balance. You connect your mind to your body through your breath," she says. *Mind over matter!* I held my breath and pushed myself up to plank position.

"Don't judge," Rachel says. "Don't compare."

Now that she says it, I notice that my friend is doing a much better job. She is more focused and stronger than I am.

*Don't think of her. Focus!*

I look at my friend focusing. She doesn't bother judging her surroundings. Not now, anyway. *The rest of the day she judges loud toddlers, non-potty-trained toddlers, fat toddlers, skinny toddlers, working mothers, and nonworking mothers with nannies. She even judges childless women for loving their cats as if they were children.*

How can you rate someone else's love?

*Let it go! Stop judging her. Focus on your breathing.*

I look at the clock. Fifteen more minutes. Rachel makes us do a headstand. That is easy for me. As inflexible as I appear now, I have been good at gymnastics since I was little, and I loved standing on my head. I might lack core strength, but I am still light and supple. Up went my legs, against the wall. My friend is still struggling. *Hey, look at me!* I breathe in, I breathe out, sounding like a grungy dog.

"No ego!" Rachel says. "Just let go."

And finally, I do. During the meditation at the end of the yoga session. Out of nowhere, after a class of battling my overly active mind, there it is: my jungle. My jungle in all its glory and beauty, with its lush green and energizing leaves. My mind goes blank. In a golden silence and a silent gold.

The teacher later describes it as Samadhi, the superconscious state of union with the divine. When the fluctuations of the mind stop completely. When the little self connects to the higher self, to the center, to the universe.

I can tell from her face that she finds it hard to believe that I would make it there at all, let alone that fast. A materialistic, opinionated, bacon-devouring, outgoing, left-brained investment banker.

It is beginner's luck. Like my first golf lesson, when I hit the ball really far and straight, with that perfect *ping*.

It takes me years of practice to get back up there. Many yoga classes and teachers later, I learn to connect to my body through my breathing. To breathe into my painful shoulder and leg. I even learn to use the breathing as reins for my brain, to get that same neutral mind I had in the jungle. The mind that lets me be a witness to my surroundings and to myself. In the jungle, my labored, one-lung breathing steadily reminded me that every high and low arises from and returns to a neutral place. That there is a stillness in the pause between breaths that is always there and available. To everyone, at any time.

# SENTENCED, 2001

Jaime and I are sitting on a couch. A two-seater, which makes us sit closer together. It occurs to me that we are supposed to be holding hands. Like the couples on TV, waiting to see what prize they will be awarded or making a plea for their sick or missing child. Of course, we don't, but something tells me it might not be a bad idea. The whole scene feels like a play: the elegant office with striped wallpaper and heavy curtains; the ottoman with the damask fabric and gold trim; and the matching Victorian couch, with us sitting on it. Enter the Upper East Side therapist, a Hermes scarf wrapped around her shoulders, her reddish hair up in a bun.

She is here for couples like us, couples willing to pay hundreds of dollars an hour for speech therapy for their two-year-olds. She had evaluated Maxi the week before. I was on that couch alone then. With curled toes and white knuckles. Maxi was so obviously not complying with the therapist's instructions. Like he didn't comply at his posh music class at Diller Quaile, where I often got dirty looks from the other mothers for letting my son disrupt their perfect world. After class they whispered. They avoided eye contact as we strapped our children in their strollers. They made an obvious effort not to have to walk down Madison Avenue with me. They turned silent when I caught up with them because of a red light. It was OK. He was my second child. I had been there and I had done that. Literally. I had walked down that avenue with the other mothers, listening to the cocky—or rather, "henny"—conversations about that one odd child. If only by walking with them, I had gone along with avoiding the "unfortunate" mother. Now I knew how she must have felt.

The speech therapist insists Jaime and I come together this time. So here we are, not hand in hand, on the couch. She looks at us with trained compassion, which we are still unaware we deserved.

"I am very worried about your son," she says. Something in my ears start ringing. "I have tested him for more than just speech."

*Oh, God.* "I have reasons to believe that he has PDD." Jaime looks blank. I know what she is talking about. Only a fortnight earlier I had woken Jaime up, crying that Maxi could be autistic. It was four in the morning. I had spent two hours surfing the Internet with my heart racing. Mothers know best, they say. Fuck it. I wish I didn't. PDD stands for pervasive development disorder. This diagnosis had been invented for those who do not fulfill all criteria for autism. No two-year-old does, so this diagnosis leaves some room for hope. Autism does not. It is a prognosis of never and always. I knew that. "You are lucky that we caught this early," she says. "With intensive therapy he might still live a full life." Now we are both nodding, as if we are listening to the details of a sentence. "You have to get on it now! I'll send my report to the best agency for early intervention."

Walking to the appointment, we felt upbeat. A winning couple striding down Park Avenue. Well dressed and self-possessed, we had passed our daughter's preschool in a church on Park and 85th. She was safe and sound inside. It was a good feeling, especially as we discussed a guy who had just paid a million bucks to get his child accepted. We congratulated ourselves. As foreigners we had beaten the odds without even realizing it. We had no trouble being accepted, whether it was for the co-op, the preschool, or the preppy music classes, and these things were apparently the neighborhood's highest purpose. After this preschool, it would be kindergarten, and from there into the best college, and so on.

We had not even changed in the process: Jaime's hair was still longish and I still blurted out whatever came to my Dutch mind. We lived off Fifth Avenue. We made good money. We had a busy social life. Invitations to Upper East Side events decorated our refrigerator and we wrote thank-you notes on personalized stationery. We had two adorable toddlers. Our future was bright.

As our sentence is being pronounced, I struggle to hear above the roar of emotions flooding my ears. I watch myself taking down phone numbers given by the therapist and picking up my bag to leave the office. What now? I am trying to adjust to our future. All I could come up with is the vanishing image of the four of us in two golf carts. I try to picture Raymond from *Rain Man*. Blank. I feel an ice-cold hand around my heart.

We have just lost Maxi's future.

# DOOMED, 2001

We are invited to a dinner party at our friend's house. I am early, so I wander into Barnes & Noble. I walk over to the Special Needs section. Reluctantly. I still feel that with every book I read Maxi's diagnosis becomes more irreversible.

There are only a few books on autism. I pick one out, open it at random, and glance at the page. "Autistic children break up families," I read. "The sleepless nights, the constant unpredictability: eighty-five percent of the parents end up divorced." I close the book.

I walk over to my friend's house in a daze, in a world of my own. A new, scary world. My friend opens the door with her apron on. She is still cooking. I tell her what I had read. She hands me a glass of Sancerre.

I burst out crying.

# ADJUSTMENTS, 2001

After Maxi's preliminary diagnosis, I first have to mourn his future as I picture it. Define what is lost and stay still with it, the things he and I would never be able to do.

I see happy families everywhere. "Normal" families. Fathers and sons playing baseball. Brothers and sisters playing tag. Mothers taking pictures. Each child looks straight at the lens and smiles. At least now I knew why lately Maxi does not. Autism. Full-fledged. That final diagnosis comes eventually. Years later, after we'd spend thousands of dollars and hours on special therapies and tests. There is a whole market out there for tired and desperate parents like Jaime and me.

We submit to countless evaluations and questionnaires. I discover a whole new use of time. Already at that very first speech therapy session, it strikes me that I am sitting in the waiting room for a whole hour doing nothing, just waiting, with other parents. Just seeing their resigned faces shocks me. It is only the beginning.

In the years to come I will bike, bus, and taxi Maxi all over Manhattan to occupational therapy gyms and socialization and listening classes. I get to know new neighborhoods and I learn the relativity of time. I slowly broaden my horizons by opening up to this new world—a loving world.

The city offers an early intervention program to New Yorkers with disabled children. An army of young men and women comes to our house to give Maxi speech, physical, and occupational therapy and applied behavior analysis, known as ABA. The latter is one of the few proven interventions for autism. It is rough. I often hear Maxi cry with frustration in the other room. Maxi's first fifteen therapy sessions are spent on pointing and following something when it falls on the floor. He is prompted to do so. Autistic children don't learn anything by themselves. They have to be taught the most basic skills. Over and over again. It's the only way. Maxi has to be taught how to point, how to copy, how to look, how to make word shapes with his mouth, how to play with toys, how to draw. Nothing is automatic. He has to be taught how to live.

Time after time, the therapist drops a toy from high chair only to have Maxi respond by staring into space. She will then take his face in her hand, turn it to look at the toy, and hold his finger to point at it. She speaks very loudly to get his attention. Not my style at all. But the only way to make progress is to find a way to penetrate Maxi's world.

When Maxi executes the prompt, he immediately gets a piece of a cookie. If he doesn't, he will not get anything. It makes him cry, but it finally works. He becomes eager to comply. He begins to love being given small and achievable tasks. To begin with, touching his nose or sitting down. Then, as he better understands what is expected of him, more complicated commands. He likes the praise (and the chips and cookies) that come with his accomplishments. He actually becomes eager to please!

Our luck doesn't stop there. Not only does Maxi learn the skills relatively quickly, he retains them. Many autistic children can mysteriously lose an acquired skill just like that after all those hours spent on learning it. And contrary to common belief, autistic children are not necessarily brilliant. Eighty percent have lower than average IQ, and most have no special talent. Only special interests.

Keeping track of all the therapists is a full-time job. They are constantly telling me what we should and shouldn't do. I end up having to resign from the bank to accommodate them. Each therapist comes with her own manual. Each has a master's degree in my son's condition.

At one point I find myself in an intervention meeting with all of them for not sending Maxi to a special-needs school. That is a big step. At the time, he is still going to the same preschool as Joosje. It has been our luck that siblings don't get screened as much as the first child. He is given a full-time "shadow," a person who is prompting him to be good. He is not aggressive, so why take him out of the regular preschool? Max is happy and I feel that good role models are essential for him. *Mother knows best.* But the older Maxi gets, the more obvious a misfit he becomes. Everyone feels uncomfortable: his teacher, the other parents, and his shadow. Uncomfortable is not why they pay the school or what the school gets paid for. I have no choice but to take him out.

Finding a special-needs preschool is a daunting task. Practically a nightmare. Wherever Maxi gets an interview we are welcomed warmly but are soon bonjoured coldly. All the schools I hope for reject him. We are lucky that Maxi falls into the twenty percent of autistic children who have an average or higher IQ, but most children in that category have Asperger's syndrome and are, unlike Maxi, highly verbal. That means he is either too high functioning or too low functioning to get into many special-needs schools. Despite all the tea I drink with board members and the many pleading letters I write, there are always better fits on their lists.

Maxi finally gets into a preschool in a guarded building for the handicapped. That is a real adjustment. We help blind and severely mentally disabled kids find the elevator on the way up. My first reaction is to separate ourselves. To define that at least we are better off. I cannot yet see beyond disability. I still act out of pity, not out of compassion. Pity assumes superiority and feels condescending on the receiving end. It creates a separation. Compassion connects. It is a hard lesson, but I am starting to get it.

# TOUGH LOVE

As he gets older, Maxi becomes more difficult. For months he just refuses to turn left. We have to take a taxi around the block in order to pick up Joosje from a playdate next door! That is, if I can get him out of the house at all, and not find him naked again after having dressed him four times.

For years he wakes up in the middle of the night and turns on all the lights and all the TVs at the highest volume. "Daytime," he says. After that period he still wakes up at five a.m. every day. If I take my eye off him even for a moment, the craziest things can happen. He breaks eggs in a shoe or flushes my watch down the toilet. Yet slowly I come to appreciate the world at that early hour, before everyone else wakes up. Those hours belong to him and me.

Going out with Maxi can be precarious. There are countless embarrassing moments: In restaurants, when Maxi grabs french fries from someone else's plate. At playgrounds, when he takes a toy from another child's hand or knocks over a toddler. At the ice-skating rink, when he eats the ice. I often get scolded for being a poor mother.

Family picture, New York, 1999

Maxi, New York, 2000

Hiking, New York, 2000

I try to find a way between adapting the world to his needs—indeed, very special—and adapting him to the world's expectations. I try not to give in to his need for structure and repetition. I tell him to overcome his fears and shower him with praise and kisses when he does. I do not give him medicine, but tough love. And as time passes, he learns. To listen. To turn left. To skate. To bike. To wait for his turn. To not grab food or eat snow. . . . To adapt.

## SEPTEMBER 12
## NEW YORK, 2001

*"And I don't know a soul who's not been battered."*
—*Simon & Garfunkel, "American Tune"*

That is the song I listen to over and over again the day after September 11, 2001. To comprehend what has happened. To give in to the bewilderment and enormous pain I share with my beloved New York.

I send it to my friends around the world. It best reflects what I am feeling. What *we* are feeling. For the first time in my life, I have become part of a collective trauma. I do not matter. I do not want to matter. I just want to help. Really help. Like a true American. I always have been impressed by how quickly Americans organize themselves in times of need. I want to give my coat to the expressionless strangers walking uptown like robots. A migration of people covered in gray dust. Or is it ash? I want to translate at the emergency centers. I want to tell people to keep on flying, as I have done. I suddenly feel what community spirit means. This is our community. This is our city burning. The gray smoke has slowly overtaken the blue sky. It comes with that smell, the smell of death.

To me, Union Square has always represented the essence of New York, with its variety of people sharing hardship. In our urge to be downtown, Jaime and I walk past the square. There are pictures of missing people everywhere. The restaurants are packed. Everyone wants to be out, to connect. There is a giant banner: "New Yorkers are the Toughest People on Earth." Normally, that would irritate me, how Americans use words like *earth* and *world*, even *universe*, for their own emotions and dreams. Now I agree. It is September 12, and everyone is a New Yorker today.

The day before, I was tidying a closet in Maxi's room with Nana, his nanny. Maxi and his ABA therapist were also in the room, sitting opposite each other. Maxi had his little hands in his lap as the therapist had told him to do. She was teaching him to say, "Stop." She was pushing a wet cloth into his face, again and again, and he just kept ducking away.

Jaime was in our bedroom getting ready to leave for work. He was late.
Our colleagues were already at the office. I was going to be even later, as
I had a meeting at Joosje's preschool.

"You better come and watch this," Jaime screamed from the bedroom.
I walked over and glanced at the TV. I saw a plane hitting the World
Trade Center. Still thinking about the closet, I shrugged it off. *Why does
he always show me planes and plane crashes? As if I have a special affection for
them! And why do they let those little planes fly up and down there anyway?*

I went straight back to the closet. Maxi was crying by then, and I got
more annoyed as my poor little son was being purposely irritated.

"Stop," he finally cried.

"You really have to watch this," Jaime yelled, and there, on my bedroom
TV, we saw one of the towers collapsing like a rectangular mushroom. Or
was it melting? We called in Nana and the therapist. We were all standing
there in silence with our mouths open, looking at each other in disbelief,
when we suddenly realized that Joosje was seeing it too. "I have to go to the
office now," Jaime said, maneuvering her out of the room toward the hall.

"Papa, Papa!" she cried hysterically. "Don't go; please don't go! You'll
burn out there. You'll never come back!"

Jaime left. I comforted Joosje and stayed with the kids, but all I really
wanted to do was go outside. Eventually I left, too.

"To get water," I said.

The scene on Madison Avenue reminded me of silent film foot-
age when the Second World War was declared in Europe. People were
plainly stunned. Cars were stopped still in the middle of the road with
their doors open and the radio on. There were enormous lines at the supermarket. Mobile phones didn't function, but everyone held on to them
for dear life. Everybody was talking to everybody. Pain connects.

# ALMOST A HOMECOMING

That autumn after September 11, we are busy applying to schools for Joosje. It is the strangest thing having to sell my four-year-old as deserving entrance into one of the elite private schools. She first has to do an IQ test. Then every school wants to interview her and then Jaime and me separately. Each school has a presentation night. Ten schools, thirty visits. After all those hours spent writing, interviewing, talking, and thinking—if not obsessing—about it, we are convinced that such a school is exactly what Joosje needs. What we need. What everybody in our neighborhood needs.

It is a strange game on a rather uneven playing field. All cards are in the hands of admissions officers, who trade information. Crucial is the first-choice letter, in which you show your cards in a buyer's market. Jaime and I are traders by profession, and Joosje is a smart kid, so we thought we should keep our options open. I include one Catholic school among our choices because I know a few families there. More as a safety net, I think, not really thinking Jaime will consider it since he is Jewish. We celebrate both Jewish and Christian holidays, but we are not religious otherwise. I went to church as a kid, but my country had rapidly become secularized during my childhood. My generation became cynical, believing religion to be the source of all conflict.

The admissions officer of the Catholic school turns out to be a bit of an overage hippie. Just like Jaime. They immediately hit it off. "Better Christian values than no values," Jaime jokes during our interview.

"Why don't you give it a try?" she asks him. "Why don't you come to the weekly mass, and see if you can live with it?"

I am neutral at that point. If anything, I find the school a bit fussy and too girlish. I truly dislike the uniform with its red-and-white-checked apron resembling a tablecloth. My kid was named one of the coolest dressed at her preschool, and now she would have to dress like a German waitress?

We go to mass around Christmastime. The elegant building, already

With Jaime at the Central Park tennis courts, New York, 2000

stunning, is spectacularly and tastefully decorated with wreaths and bows, matching the ones in the hair of the girls.

We sit in the back of the wooden chapel—Jaime comfortably uncomfortable, I uncomfortably comfortable. Then the girls come in. Without their aprons. They look like little angels and sing like them too. The priest seems as broad-minded as could be, almost New Agey. Gently preaching a message of love. A message we so need that winter after September 11. Jaime smiles. I cry. We want this for our child. We both had this as children. How could I have forgotten? How could we not raise her with the idea of something bigger than ourselves?

The first-choice letter went out the next day to the Convent of the Sacred Heart.

# WELCOME TO HOLLAND, 2002

We now belong to the special-needs world. With its own junk mail. We get lots of letters showing pictures of children with Down syndrome, in wheelchairs, or with other disabilities. At first I would not open them. Then one day there is a booklet in my mailbox with a colorful picture of tulips on the cover and the words "Welcome to Holland." I immediately start reading the accompanying article in the elevator to my apartment.

It turns out Emily Perl Kingsley used Holland as a metaphor for the experience of raising a child with a disability. To imagine how raising a child with a disability feels, the author compared having a baby with planning a dream trip to Italy: You imagine the trip in your head a thousand times. You read books. You are full of plans, full of anticipation. But when the plane lands, it becomes clear you have not landed in Italy, but in Holland. The important thing is you have to remember Holland is not a terrible place; it is just different. Of course you'll have to adjust: learn a new language, read new guidebooks, make new plans. But you will discover some very nice things about Holland, and you will meet new people too. The only problem is that everybody around you only knows Italy. They all tell you how wonderful it is, and for the rest of your life, they will remind you of the fact that Italy was where you were supposed to go in the first place. They cannot appreciate Holland. Nor do they take your appreciation for Holland seriously. The pain of that will never go away. It is even more difficult than the loss of your dream, which in itself is a very, very significant loss. But if you allow yourself to spend your life mourning Italy, you will miss out on the very special and loving world that is Holland.

As it turns out, after all the traveling I had done in my life, I am stuck in Holland.

# Reflection: Hope

I read every book on autism I can find. In any language. To understand my son. To get reacquainted with him. His behavior is so out of whack that I need a blueprint to understand him. I have to break into his world so I can find a place for him in mine.

My favorite books are those written by autistics. They give me a glimpse into Maxi's mind, or what it will become. At first I measure everything he does against "normal," constantly making comparisons, always trying to minimize his condition, marginalize it. *Maxi doesn't have this*, or *Maxi doesn't do that*. "At least . . ." Always "at least." Often my heart is racing while I read these books, because I am nervous to find out about the next hurdle. But I read my way into acceptance. I learn to appreciate how Maxi's mind works, how he sees the world. By fighting it and focusing on "recovering" him, I am missing what *is* there, in the here and now, right in front of my eyes. I just have to take my losses. Take a loss on my expectations.

It takes a lot of effort to learn how to look through his behavior, to stop thinking, *Oh, autistic* with his every move. But at some point I do. Once I learn to take him for who he is, I discover what is there. A beautiful boy with an unique perspective on our world. And a true source of unconditional love. From there, the only way is up. He turns out to be my teacher.

I don't feel there is a "real" person inside Maxi screaming to get out. Maxi is real. He is someone—not a caged someone. He is a person who is worthy in every sense. He sees the world differently. And I like how he sees it. He wakes up smiling, goes to sleep smiling, and enjoys the sequence of moments in between.

Have I given up hope? No, I have taken a loss on the expectations I had for his future. Hope is not an expectation. Hope is not wishing life to conform to what you think it should be. It is staying in what is real.

Hope helped me cope during those very hard early years, when I had to accept that for Maxi there was no "recovery." Not with pills, not with antitoxin treatments, not with listening courses or diets. Maxi endured them all. Sometimes at a great price, and often at the expense of my daughter and my marriage.

I have stopped believing I have control. That is the reality. My hope is rooted in reality. The here and now. I see many possibilities for Maxi, but not in the way I did before. I am looking beyond football teams, prom, or college. I want him to be open to life in all its manifestations. Open to what is real, not to what I want him to be. By really embracing that, I have emerged not only accepting him but also celebrating him.

For me, life is coping with what is. This is what we are given. Maxi could have had a stroke, an accident, or meningitis, after all. Shit happens. Why me? Why us? Why not? I have taken a loss on my expectations, but I have never taken a loss on Maxi. Or on my hope. I do as much as I can, and I will do more when needed. I am living a very hopeful life.

# TIME FOR SINGING

Every Thursday morning I go to mass at Joosje's school. Surprisingly, it becomes the highlight of my week. I drop her off at 8:15, have a coffee with the other parents, and walk back with them, in great spirit, to this beautiful mansion adjacent to Central Park. Our seven- and eight-year-olds will be waiting, already seated in the chapel. Bouncing with anticipation to sit next to us.

Early on in the year, "spirited" Joosje was put on a little separate bench in the front at the window. It became our bench. It overlooked the Cooper-Hewitt museum. Very aesthetic. To the left we could see our apartment building sticking out. Not as aesthetic. It is the only postwar high-rise in our prewar neighborhood.

The sun rays come through the window, lighting up the diverse hair colors of the girls in front of us, their braids and tails done almost to perfection. Joosje is nestled under my arm, with messy hair, playing with my bracelet. We all sing with all our hearts.

It is as good as it gets. Perhaps because every adult is holding his or her own precious child. Perhaps because the mass is overtly inclusive of other religions; the songs seem carefully phrased to that end. Perhaps because the sermon is plain and simple, about love and friendship. Real and relevant to children. Real and relevant to us. This mass, these songs, these voices help me get through some rocky and rough years.

It is a bit of a miracle. Here are all these mothers and daughters in all sizes and shapes, nationalities even, struggling with life and the pressure to fit in. There might be rivalry and triviality, but all that disappears when we start to sing. A simple song. Every time I was overcome with a feeling of brotherhood and sisterhood, solidarity, love even. I am no longer seeing that controlling mother on a nearby bench, but a human being surrendered to the beauty of the moment. We are no longer ourselves, just parts of a whole to which we all belonged.

Why did it have to be an exceptional moment? Why could such moments not be the rule of everyday life?

"We would love to have stars without the darkness," the priest says. "But life is not like that. There is always a presence of sweet and sour, joy and mourning, health and sickness, light and darkness. We need the darkness to appreciate the light. We have to embrace the dark with the light, the bad with the good."

How appropriate. If the moment were not exceptional, it wouldn't be life. Would I feel the appreciation if I had not known its flip side? Would I feel this gratitude if I had not known loss? Would I cherish this moment of belonging if I had not known loneliness?

"But our wisdom does not end there," he continues. "We have the ability to control our focus. We can choose what to look at. If we want to find fault with our family members, our friends, our classmates, our coworkers, we will. But if we look for their good points, we are sure to find them too. We can decide to look at the stars or at the darkness that surrounds them. Life is made or broken by what we consistently choose to look at. We don't pretend the darkness does not exist, but we can choose to concentrate on the stars."

*Oh, jungle!*

I look at Joosje. She is not really listening. Of course not, she'll have to find out for herself. Fill in all those abstractions. As much as I would like to shield her from darkness, I can't and shouldn't.

She'll have to learn on her own, and I know she can. She realizes she'll never have the relationship with Maxi her friends have with their siblings. She sees and accepts that Maxi is different and at the same time she appreciates the "normal" moments as a gift and loves anything he gives her.

After mass everybody goes their separate ways. We all revert back to our roles. Because that is what they are: just roles.

At first it was hard for me to accept Maxi's special-needs world and the time I had to spend there. I felt too cool to be there. I separated myself. I thought I needed to adjust my eyes to what I perceived as a dark place. What really happened was my eyes slowly opened.

Planted in a more "perfect," if not plastic, world, I learned that "perfect" shields us from a different world. A vulnerable world, an imperfect but oh-so-loving world.

I begin to look at things through different lenses: two worlds, two lenses. For a while Joosje and Maxi have after-school classes in the same building at the same time. I skip from bench to bench: from Joosje's dance class to Maxi's special-needs soccer. I go from chatting about the girls' achievements and outfits to talking about how to prevent self-mutilation and bed-wetting.

In the fall, my children always play soccer on adjoining fields in Central Park. I cannot escape the pitying looks from some parents on Joosje's team. So obviously congratulating themselves for not being on the sideline of the other field, where the goalie is in a wheelchair and the other kids, looking like drugged zombies, are running hand in hand with a volunteer.

I know what there is to find at that other field. I know I just need to force myself to get up from that comfortable blanket, to remove myself from the easy talk about the teachers and goings-on at Joosje's private school. I know that I have to walk over to the next field where I don't need to make an effort to relate to the other parents; we are already connected. I know I will find a mother with tears in her eyes because of an achievement she always deemed impossible. I know everyone there will truly share that joy, without rivalry.

So why do I still resist? Because it is easier on that blanket. It is easier to do the superficial thing than the rewarding one. Always. The easy thing, not the right thing. Like going for a run or meditating. You know the benefits, but you still have a hard time doing it. Once you do it though, you feel disproportionately gratified.

It is the same for me during the two years my father is dying. The house in Holland where we stay for the summer is one block away from my parents' house. My neighbors and friends are relaxed and fun-loving people. It is so easy and comfortable to join them for drinks in their gardens. They have easy conversations—comfortable and safe. Walking over to my parents' and entering my father's room means entering a world of very different conversations. About the uncomfortable stuff. About life, death, and the hereafter. "Heavy," my friends would say. When I sit in those sunny gardens, I know I just have to put my wineglass down and get out of that comfortable chair to go to my father's dark bedroom. To the smell of illness. Each time I enter his room, my father's face brightens, shedding a different light on comfort.

"So sorry I'm late," I say, running into the large, empty yoga room where my teacher is waiting for me. "There were just no taxis!"

"Don't worry," she answers, with her lovely smile. "Just made it here myself."

"I can't believe what I am busying myself with," I continue, taking my sweater off and throwing it on top of my big shopping bag. "Party favors," I say, nodding at the bag. "For my daughter's thirty best friends, who are coming to her birthday party next week." I sigh. "And I am having fifteen friends at my house this afternoon for lunch. For *my* birthday. Upper East Side women with Upper East Side standards. What am I thinking?"

I roll out my yoga mat and sit down. I zoom in on my new teacher: a six-foot-tall goddess with long, blonde, curly hair. A top model turned yoga teacher for all the right reasons. Or the wrong ones, some might say: She had struggled with everything that goes with the high life. Either way, she had come out with radiance and wisdom.

"Put your legs up against the wall and calm down," she says. I follow her instructions, still thinking about the gazpacho I am planning to make, wondering whether I bought too much food. "Turn inward. Use your breath." I try. "Put your hand on your belly and breathe into it." I do. "Empty your lungs completely and contract your stomach muscles. Hold it there. Pause. Then fill it all the way up with air, pause, and empty it again. Listen to the pause between your breaths."

I fill my belly all the way up with air and hold it. Exhaling, emptying my lungs completely. I push out all the air and stay still. It is as if the inside of my stomach touches my spine. I hold it there. My head becomes light. There it is. The pause, the silence, the center, the gold. The jungle.

# SPECIAL ED, 2004

Maxi's fifth birthday is a milestone. For taking that last loss. Giving up that last bit of a dream.

Five is the age where early intervention ends and special education begins. Where the records start, countless records. It is now official. Very official. We enter a new world of abbreviations, organizations, and institutions. Of rules and classifications. Another jungle.

It is time to go to kindergarten. So, we have gone from school to school, from the Bronx to Brooklyn, only to be rejected time and again. When we're about to give up, I hear of a special ed school on Roosevelt Island. The Child School. Miraculously, Maxi gets in, but he refuses to go on the school bus in the morning, fighting his way out like a stubborn little bull. He does not mind taking that same bus back home, however. Like an eager little horse on his way to his stable.

We take Maxi to his new school every day on the tram. The tram is the cable car spanning the East River to Roosevelt Island. He dutifully goes down to the tram station with one of us. By the time the tram reaches its highest point next to the Queensboro Bridge, he is wildly flapping with happiness, with his nose against the window, taking in Manhattan's skyline. On the island we have to wait for another bus, and it can be freezing out there, but I cherish these trips. There is something very special in taking your child to school. Any child. Is it because there is a set beginning and end that makes it so enjoyable?

Maxi is the only one of his kind in this school. But at least he has the chance to be intellectually challenged. I strongly believe that he needs to use his intelligence to overcome his disability. He just loves to use that well-functioning side of his brain.

And I am right. He learns to read so fast! From then on, we use written messages to communicate, to tell him what to do and what is coming.

He goes on to first and second grade. With one-to-one assistance.

He does his homework and he learns to comply with verbal instructions. With assistance. He still speaks only in syllables. "With assistance." It is incredible what those involved with special-needs children help accomplish. Teachers, therapists, school district officers—for a less than adequate salary they sacrifice their professional lives to help our kids forward.

# Reflection: What Hurt

What hurt were the attempts to get Maxi to fit in. The interviews at schools that could so easily get a "better" fit—a different student to admit. The failure of admissions officers to make eye contact when they told us so. Hearing no time after time.

What hurt were the endless medical examinations to eliminate any physical reasons for Maxi's "condition." The MRI scan during which he had to be held down, and which ended in an overdose of anesthetics because he was fighting so hard. Like a little lion. I had to wait five hours for him to wake up, anxiously sitting next to him, afraid he never would.

What hurt were the blood tests—I have lost count—during which I had to restrain him, crying, on my lap. They always turned out negative, or positive, however one wants to see it.

What hurt were the dental visits. Brushing his teeth was never an option. To have his cavities filled, we ended up in yet another operating room. His eyes were questioning me, not understanding.

What hurt was lying awake all night, beside him, waiting for the next day's colonoscopy. "To exclude parasites and other possible medical reasons" for the soft stool I stepped in every day. The result would be negative, of course, but who was I to contradict the specialist? I would listen to Maxi's breathing. I would look at his sweet sleeping face, knowing what was awaiting him the next morning. He didn't have a clue.

In the morning, he would be babbling happily to me in the taxi. Grabbing my hand while we walked into the building. Rubbing his cheeks against my arm, planting a couple kisses on my elbow. Just happy. Until he realized where he was. Then he would panic and put up a fight.

It broke my heart every time. It broke my heart wide open. Was that the price I had to pay for a love I could never have imagined?

# Perspectives

**JOOSJE, SEVEN YEARS OLD:** I am Josephine Lupa, and this is my story about my brother, Max, who has autism. He is five years old. He can't talk, but he is a lot of fun. He is nice but sometimes is a bit annoying. But he can't help it, so it's OK with me.

Sometimes he repeats what we say, like if you say to him, "Do you want more pizza?" he might say, "Do you want more pizza?" instead of yes or no. But sometimes he will say yes or no.

Just because he has autism doesn't mean he is bad. Maybe God just said, "I think Max should have autism." So I shouldn't get too mad at Max, even if he rewinds a show that I like. Again and again. Max is very cute, and there are so many good things in Max I can't say them all. Anyway, Max goes to a very good school.

*I loooooove Max.*

A few things to remember about kids with autism.

- Kids with autism aren't bad people. *So don't act like they are bad!*
- Kids with autism don't like to be bullied.
- Be nice to kids with autism!

**DAVID, A PARENT:** The first time I ever saw Maxi was at his home. My daughter was having a playdate with his older sister. I guess I'd heard a little about him. I knew he was autistic, but I suppose I expected someone quite different. He's such a beautiful little boy. Clear, sparkling eyes, an endearing smile, his mother's radiant blond hair. You almost want to say, "Oh, but he looks so normal!"

It was only when I saw Joosje interact with him, or rather try to, that I saw someone else. He was there, but not there. The sparkling eyes focused on no one in particular; his attention and movements were totally random, without any purpose. He flailed his hands as if flustered, but it was apparently just his way. After a few minutes he left. It took another ten or twenty minutes to convince my daughter to get her things

Joosje and Maxi, New York, 2003

together and come home. As we left Joosje's room, someone noticed—uh-oh—Maxi had pooped on the floor. Nothing large or messy, rather like little rabbit pellets. I felt so badly for Annette. Someone went to fetch paper towels. And yet, well, that was Maxi. He's autistic.

I can't remember when in the chronology I was visiting my daughter's art class. The girls were working on projects—a still life of flowers, I think—so there was a lot of chattering in the room. I didn't hear the exact comment, but someone must have said something about Maxi. Joosje, without rancor or tears, looked up briefly at the other girl and said, "Now you know what's wrong with Maxi." It struck me that he was, or rather his autism was, just a fact in this family. She was not apologetic, self-pitying, or—at least outwardly—angry about it. Nor did she try to hide him. I wondered then how I'd cope with an autistic child, and at the same time, I was struck by how they did. Something quite impressive was going on in that household, difficult as it might be.

I'd see him sometimes coming with his mother and sister to school in the morning. The head of security, who welcomes the girls every day by the entrance, hollered out, "Hey, Maxi, what's going on, buddy, huh? Gimme five!" I think Maxi did actually make a somewhat uncoordinated gesture to slap hands. But I liked the exchange. I thought, *He treats him just like any other kid, even though, you know, he's autistic.*

I remember one day, leaving school, I saw Annette crying, being comforted by another mother, Susan, a good friend of ours. She put her arm around Annette and kept saying, "I know how hard it is, I know, I know." I just naturally assumed . . . well, Maxi, you know, he's autistic.

Then one day in early summer, I was walking to the school to pick up my daughter. About half a block ahead, I saw Annette walking with Maxi. It was late afternoon, and they had the sidewalk to themselves. They couldn't see me, and I realized I didn't want to disturb them. They were swinging their arms and she was singing a children's song, something with a lilting melody like "Peas Porridge Hot." I was blown away. Her voice was so playful and tender, and as she sang, she'd lean into him, almost caressing him with her smile. I realized it was the first time I'd ever seen the two of them alone, when they could just be themselves. It was the first time I understood how Annette copes with Maxi. He's her little boy.

# PARTICLES PARIS, 2005

My father dies when I am in Paris. That is where I have my last conversation with him.

Joosje is at the playground next to the Louvre. We have just admired the *Mona Lisa*, with two thousand other tourists: It is free entrance Sunday. I feel so claustrophobic I leave Joosje with our friends. I call my father, thinking he would understand, as I got my claustrophobia from him. My mother picks up the phone. From the tone of her voice I immediately know what is happening. She warns me that he is very weak. That she had been sitting up all night holding his hand. That after almost sixty years together, he had given her the most beautiful declarations of love. She says she could not be more grateful for having had this night with him.

I whisper, in that childish voice my siblings like to make fun of, "Dag Pappie, how do you feel?" He answers with a voice so weak that he seems much farther away than the five-hour train ride from Paris to The Hague.

"Dag Popje," which means *hello, little doll*, "I don't feel so well."

"Oh, Pappie, you can let go now, you have been so strong. You can be strong again and let go," I say, with a lump in my throat. "That's how I love you, Pappie. How we all love you."

He answers ever so faintly, "Ja, I have to go now. Bye, Popje."

I rejoin the group. The people, Paris, the playground—it all seems surreal. I feel physically removed from them, as if I am walking on floaters. I change our train reservations to go back to Holland that same day; we will be leaving after lunch. In my friend's eyes I see an understanding that both surprised and comforted me. She tells me she had lost her father.

We set out for a quick lunch near our hotel on the Champs-Élysées. We eat our steak frites in silence. I get the phone call as we leave the café. My eldest brother, always the messenger, conveys in an almost formal way: "Our father died at twelve thirty p.m. He has left us peacefully."

As I walk back to our sad little group, something has changed. I feel my father so close, it is as if he is in the air particles.

"Feel, Joosje," I say. "When you rub your thumb over your index finger, you can feel Opa, really. As if he is everywhere." She does so and smiles. A relieved smile. Relieved for me, I think. Relieved I took it that way. She did not expect this sheer happiness on my face. Sheer happiness is what I feel. For my father, who is finally released from himself. I am almost dancing back to the hotel. My father had been dying for more than two years. He is free!

I spend most of the train ride on the phone with my youngest brother. So different from the eldest one. He is overcome by emotions. He just can't cope. This is his first death. He cannot take himself out of it. I feel serenity and acceptance. Is that what I learned in the jungle? Or from grieving for Pasje?

While Jaime and Maxi are on their way from New York City, Joosje and I finally arrive at my parents' house. My brothers, sister, and sister-in-law are all sitting around our table, having dinner. As we have done so many times. I embrace my mother, who has just lost a part of herself. Then I go straight into my father's bedroom, where he has spent the past two years. The room I have left so many times thinking it was the last time I would see him and devastated I was leaving for another continent. I called him every day from New York.

He is lying on his side, facing the window. I walk around the bed to get a look at his face. A beautiful, serene face. It isn't just his skin that looked so much younger. He has the expression of a child. I burst into tears and walk into my mother's arms in the kitchen. "He is so beautiful, he is so beautiful," I cry.

"Isn't he just?" my mom whispers. She is proud, fragile, heartbroken, strong.

My heart breaks for her; she has lost more than half herself.

We eat and drink as we always do. Loud, with lots of jokes. My father is more present than ever. After a while I have to get up, to go back into his room, to see his face again. I sit on the windowsill next to him. I pick up a pile of books. On top was *The Seat of the Soul*, by Gary Zukav, which we had both read and reread many times.

If the perfect alignment of personality and soul have a face, it is my father's.

## Reflection: My Father's Prophecies

My father was a one-man think tank. He practically invented "operational research" at Royal Dutch Shell. They put him in an office just to think. To calculate the probabilities of finding oil in this or that place.

In fact, probability was something he applied to just about everything. It is great to be raised by a father who calculates the chance that there will be a pervert around the corner when he sends you to a shop. Or estimates the best place to wait for you when you're going down a French river on a raft. It leaves no room for irrational fears.

He also used probability to tackle existential questions. He believed that the chance that our world had been created by physical accident was smaller than the chance of a monkey producing Shakespeare when put in front of a computer. And although traditional physics could not explain the universe as we know it, quantum mechanics, the new physics, did leave room for the existence of God.

My father believed that God had been co-directing ever since the Big Bang. That doubts about God's existence stemmed from the images of God that people had come up with. "As soon as you form an image of God, the whole concept becomes more improbable," he used to say. He tried his whole life to visualize God but never succeeded. There was one thing he was convinced of, though. The chance that God did not exist was too minuscule for it to be true.

His next question was what the intentions of that God were. He felt that you could only probe those intentions by finding out how life had developed so far. My father saw the answer in a purpose for which God needs people.

So this is where he would ask the age-old question. The one Job asked in the Bible. If God is good and almighty, why does he allow there to be so much misery? The religion in which my father was brought up would say, "Only God himself knows, and we shouldn't seek to understand it." My father could not accept that. The only convincing answer for him was that God had not been able yet to manage all of the chaos. God is mighty, but not almighty. He is still in the process of inventing himself. He is under way, to create himself and to get somewhere. To achieve his purpose, God needs people. They must somehow grow toward an ethical and good society.

And my father thought that we were doing that. Millimeter by millimeter we are learning to control the chaos. For centuries we have been heading in the right direction. My father believed that we are on our way to a world community, all people sharing a culture and morals. The computer already connects everyone in the world. One day, the human consciousness will resemble one big mind. A coming together of the thoughts and consciences of all people, whereby we learn to go beyond our ego. The driving force of that ego will continue to exist, but it will function better socially and religiously, resulting in a better society. I share my father's optimism.

# THE BUMBLEBEE

When my father was still alive we talked about my friend who was regularly surrounded by white butterflies after her mom died. Her mom had promised she was going to send messages that way. We asked my father to do the same, but we all agreed a butterfly wasn't appropriate for my Buddha-like father. Maybe a big fly or a bee of some sort?

Two months before he died, my father asked my mother to buy a piece of jewelry for herself. As a gift from him. My mother delegated the task to me. She wanted a brooch. I bought her two little golden bees, one covered with white diamonds, one with black onyx. Both my parents loved them.

When my father finally passed away that warm summer's day and his body had been taken away, a bumblebee appeared in my parents' bedroom. It stayed there all morning.

Later that week, we are dressing for the funeral. As I am putting the little bee brooches on my mother's black suit, a giant bumblebee flies in. "Hi Pappie," I say, "How good to see you." The bee buzzes around us for quite a while. When it settles in the corner of the open window, I almost panic, and yell, "Please move! You'll be crushed when the wind closes the window. Please *move!*" But the bumblebee stays put. I literally have to shoo him to safety.

The next day we hold the funeral service for my father. Eight-year-old Joosje reads 1 Corinthians, Chapter 13, about love. She does it beautifully. Afterward we have a celebration on a terrace outside. When my friends come over to praise her, Joosje tells them the story of the bee. And at that same moment there he is again, circling around her little blond head, a very big, very fat bumblebee!

# BEYOND, OVER, AND ABOVE

One Saturday I take Maxi to his special-needs indoor soccer. Usually he goes to the Friday afternoon class, where I wait outside the glass walls with the other mothers. Sometimes I am in the mood for other special-needs moms, sometimes I am not. When I am not, I ponder how we all seem to share the same child, and I feel connected.

That Saturday it is a different ball game: There are fathers. I cannot help comparing them to the fathers of the soccer league for which my Joosje plays. My tears return.

Mikey, who is the only other autistic child in Maxi's class, must be nine or ten years old. A bit chubby, beautiful face, and very autistic. He repeatedly "inappropriately" caresses the teachers. He takes off his shoes several times and sits—or, rather, lies down—on the floor. Maxi is, naturally, all over the place, but he complies better by comparison. With special-needs children, however, that is not so relevant. There are none of those little triumphs parents feel when their "typical" child does an activity better than the child's peers. A special-needs child's parent learns to get beyond, over, and above comparing.

Mikey's father seems to be reluctant to look at the soccer game. He paces up and down the hall where his younger, "typical" son is running back and forth with a little fire truck. He distractedly tells the boy to be quiet. He seems to take this son's imaginative play and motor skills for granted: two children, two standards. A few times he has a short conversation with another man who, teary eyed, stays away altogether from the soundproof windows of his child's classroom.

When Mikey's father finally sits to watch the soccer game—next to me—his son kind of scores a goal. The three teachers gave him a loud high five, but his father does not respond. This seems to me to create some tension on our bench. But when the door to the room opens and our two boys come out, it is as if the hall fills with warm air. Gone is the tension. Mikey's father closes his son in his arms with pure, unconditional love. Beyond, over, and above comparing.

# STARRY NIGHT

When Maxi is six, I take him to see his favorite Van Gogh painting. He has seen it on the TV show *Little Einsteins*, with Beethoven's *Für Elise* in the background. Another favorite. He plays the beginning of that piece on every piano he encounters.

The MoMA is as crowded as I have ever seen it. Maxi behaves surprisingly well, waiting in line after line. But when we finally enter the exhibition, he pushes his way forward, getting more than the average number of dirty looks in the process. I can barely keep up with him, but I catch up when he pauses for a second in front of a painting that is very similar. In fact I thought it is *The Starry Night*, though different than I remember. "No!" Maxi screams, and elbows himself to the next room. It is *Starry Night Over the Rhone*.

Maxi works himself to the front of the biggest crowd in the room. I run around the wall the painting is exhibited on, coming out on the right-hand side of the painting. There is Maxi, reading out loud: "Star-ry night, oil on can-vas, Eighteen eighty-two, Ly-on . . ." Then he steps back to be in front of the center of the painting and looks, his eyes wide open, silent, in complete awe. Mesmerized. So is the crowd behind him. Some by the painting, viewing it over Maxi's shoulder, but many by Maxi, seemingly under a magic spell. What does he see? Does he see what we don't see?

Then the spell is broken by an irritated elderly couple; I recognize the lady from earlier dirty looks. The old man tells me boldly to take my son away from there. I try, but Maxi pulls himself loose and establishes himself firmly back in the same spot. He sings *Für Elise*. He holds his head sideways and squints. Then he makes gestures in the air, following the curves of the painting with his finger. The man starts to shout as if Maxi is touching the painting. He isn't, by ten inches. I quickly pull him away from the approaching guard, behind the wall of the painting, the last in the exhibition, and hold him tightly. Tears fill my eyes.

"These people have small minds, Maxi," I say.

The man appears next to us and hears me. He tells me again it is up to me to control my son.

"He has autism," I answer.

"So?" he asks, angrily. "What about all the other people? For you, he is the most important in the world, isn't he? But what about all the other people?"

He has a point, but I whisper in Maxi's ear, "And he has a small heart." My tears come down now.

Three other people come up to me.

"My grandson is autistic, my niece, my nephew. . . . You are doing a great job." But it does not take the edge off. Does anyone know what it takes for Maxi to even enter a museum? How many times I have waited outside with him while my friends went in with their children? How many times have Maxi and I had to walk up and down the block, often in the freezing cold, waiting for the others to come back out?

Fortunately, my friend, with whom we came to the exhibition, finds us. She tells me all the lovely comments she has overheard about Maxi in the back of the crowd. Then she muses, "Isn't it ironic? Isn't this just the type of man who would have been the first to harshly judge Van Gogh in his times? Dismiss both him and his work as crazy? Have him locked him up without a paintbrush? Who do you think connects to the artist here?"

# Reflection: Maxi's World

Maxi does not talk. He does not like to talk. Yet our silent communication seems much greater and more essential. We feel the language rather than speak it. From soul to soul? Maxi confirms my suspicion about words—the limitation of words to communicate what is invisible.

Whoever is with Maxi syncs with him. Jaime, on the way to the park, or bathing and feeding him. Me, falling asleep next to him, or ice-skating with him. Nana, our nanny, moving in unison with him on their way to his therapies. His "shadows," the special caretakers, walking hand in hand with him at school. When I ice-skate with Maxi, it is like the sum of all romantic love. As portrayed in a movie, on a cloud. Everything else is a blur and unimportant. There is just Maxi, his smile, the music, and my heart bursting. Time stands still.

With the men I've loved, I always ended up thinking about something else: the next thing to do or to buy. I definitely saw the moment as an obstacle to the future. When in sync with Maxi, I have no desire for anything other than being with him and savoring his smile. It must be the definition of Zen. Moreover, with Maxi I can act as crazy as I want, as much as I want. He will not define me, let alone judge me. He will just grab my face and pull it toward his. Give me a quick kiss. A pure, matter-of-fact kiss, without conditions.

# Reflection: Flip Sides

There is a flip side to any situation. When you look back on unfortunate things that have happened, you can always find something good in the misfortune.

For me, everything got much easier when I started to see the advantage of disadvantage, and vice versa. To own my luck, both good and bad.

Now I can't help noticing how the more fortunate take ownership of their blessings.

"Everyone makes his own bed, so they should lie in it," they say, taking credit for their soft sheets and good health, their happy marriages or successful children. When they define, discuss, and judge the less fortunate, they seem to find a reason to hold them responsible for their fate.

This blame must surely be rooted in fear: "If it's not his or her own fault, it could happen to me." Finding fault gives the illusion of control. "If the mother of that drug addict is to blame, it won't happen to my son." Or "He got cancer out of stress, a bad diet, a karmic debt."

But pain gives depth, and even dysfunction brings its own brand of love, with an intensity that functional families can't always understand. That is the flip side to good fortune: you can miss out on the possible benefit of experiencing hardship. But by achieving compassion, the fortunate don't have to experience misfortune to acquire depth; they import it for free, without the misery. And the less fortunate don't get an extra kick in the gut by being blamed, frowned at, looked down upon, and excluded.

If the fortunate would see the limitations of their luck, perhaps they would not judge or pity. They would be less fearful and thus more open and more compassionate. True compassion strips away superior-inferior feelings. You see through the other person's eyes without thinking of yourself as being on a different level. All you have to do is focus on the other person, put yourself in his or her shoes and forget about yourself for a few minutes. Completely. Don't think. Compassion comes from the heart.

Just flip sides, and everyone is up.

# HURDLES AND PERCEPTION

"Joosje, move away from that picture. A little bit farther. Otherwise you won't be able to see what it's about. You will only see the details but not the whole painting."

We are at a museum. "That's how Papa sees the world," I mumble, thinking that she can't hear me. When I see she has, I quickly add, "Of course, I would stand too far away and not see any details."

Now I have her thinking. With a wrinkle in her brow, she repeats, "So Papa stands too close and only sees the details. You stand too far and only see the picture. So where should I stand to make sure I am in the right place?" The wrinkle deepens. Then her little face relaxes, and she says, "You see? There is none. That's why you and Papa need each other!"

Jaime and I both like beating the odds. In business and in life. Again and again. But the odds always win in the end—or what appears to be the end. We had too many factors against us. We should have known. Different cultures, different religions, different personalities—all those hurdles that parents warn their children will matter over time when the romance wears off. That is why all Romeos die. Love is not enough. Could it have been any more romantic? How Jaime came looking for me, brought me back to life, to give life? Hadn't we deserved to live happily ever after? Together?

But life kept on happening.

In the end, marriage is a marriage of egos. And culture, religion, and personality matter. For egos.

What's love got to do with it? Nothing. And everything. For Jaime, Maxi's love became all-encompassing and sufficient. He does not need more. As it turns out, Jaime prefers Holland to Italy.

# COUNTING

Every year, on the 14th of November, I commemorate.

First, Pasje, of course. "Today he would have been thirty-eight, thirty-nine, forty-two, fifty." And so on.

Then for the next eight days, I also count. How much I eat and drink. From seven a.m. on the first day, the second, the third, to five p.m. on the eighth day, when I was rescued. It is a lot. Two slices of brown bread with cheese and tea with milk every morning. Coffee with milk and another slice at eleven a.m. Lunch. Tea with cookies, a drink with salami and olives, dinner with wine, tea with chocolate. And water. Many glasses of water.

No hang-ups. Just counting.

# 5

## PREPARATION

### MEANING? WHAT MEANING?
### NEW YORK, 2005

Every Thursday morning I have coffee with the other parents before attending mass at Joosje's school on East Ninety-first Street. One morning someone somehow mentions my story. Many of the parents don't know about the crash; it just hasn't come up. I don't mind talking about it, but I do mind the overwhelming attention that comes with it, especially in a group. Like now.

"You have to make a movie!" "You have to write a book!" "You have to tell your story."

"I will, I will," I say, as I always do in an attempt to close the subject. "One day. First I have to go back to Vietnam, and writing a book is such a big mountain to climb."

"Then I know the perfect guy for you," one mother says. "He is a published writer looking for a new subject. He would be perfect, and you will really like him!"

I do like him—at first. He gets me thinking, writing even. To him. E-mail after e-mail. But he does not seem to get me. Nor do I get him. He comes to our apartment to get a sense of his potential subject. He tells me that he is overwhelmed by the strong European coffee and the flood of daylight coming through our big windows. He doesn't ask me any questions, so I volunteer what has been going on in my life. I tell him that after I stopped working to take care of Maxi, Jaime lost his job. "Jaime and I are not in the best place now that we are both at home," I confess. "But please don't write about Jaime or our relationship. As interesting as it might be for the reader." *Or the writer*, I think, as I look at his disappointed face. "For our family's sake," I add, "for their protection." I try to make light of it: "Our kitchen is a bit small for the both of us. It gets too hot!"

The writer looks puzzled. And incredulous. "So you have an autistic son, no job, a failing marriage, yet you look as if you have no care in the world. How can you be so *happy*?"

"How can I not be happy?" I answer, gesturing at my surroundings—the family pictures on the piano with the Central Park reservoir and skyline visible from my window.

He looks at me in awe. I look back at him with irritation. "You sound like a romantic," he says. "I am a realist. I don't fixate on how things should be. I take things the way they are," I say. *Happiness is not having what you want but wanting what you have*, I think. The writer still tries to figure me out—and my story. He says he needs to "translate." Not translate from Dutch to English but "distill what it means and define its merits."

I don't quite get that. Why not just tell the story? Let the reader interpret. Doesn't my story itself serve as a concrete example of life holding meaning even under the most miserable conditions? *You don't get meaning; you give life meaning.*

Another point of friction is that I want him to write about Maxi. For me the crash turned out to be a stone thrown in the water. It definitely showed me depth, but the ripples have subsided and I have been able to go back to the surface. Maxi has a chronic condition; its ripples will never subside. It forces me to dive deep every so often.

"Nobody likes chronic," the writer says. "People like accidents, a mourning process, and recovery. People want a solution."

*The solution is right in front of them*, I think. There is beauty in every situation. Once you see the beauty, happiness will follow.

• • •

Soon after the writer's visit, I find out I need surgery. I have to stay in bed for two weeks. To accommodate the writer, I decide to turn lemons into lemonade by finally writing everything down. How it was, not what it meant. I never could find the words to express what I had learned. Now the words find me.

I sit at a trendy downtown restaurant, flanked by a high-flying, A-type book editor, a reserved book agent, and the writer. The writer has turned my pages into a book proposal: *Accidental Life*. His proposal includes a trip with me to Vietnam, to climb my mountain. The editor and the agent are meeting me to assess whether the book may be a worthwhile investment.

The writer insisted there is no need to prep me for this meeting.

"Simply be yourself," he said. I should have known better.

I've just returned from a summer in the Netherlands, where we buried my father. I am still a bit emotional and very much in Dutch mode: sarcastic and straightforward. What's more, I have come here directly from Roosevelt Island, where I dropped off Maxi for his first day of school. It was a long struggle to get him inside on this hot September morning. Quite a different universe from the cool one I sit in now.

My hostess, the editor, is confidently dressed in black, her dark hair elaborately blown out. She knows the writer well, having edited one of his earlier books.

"She is one of the best," he has told me. She behaves like she is. They chat about the Condé Nast Building, the Soho House, and the grooming needs of the writer's wife, a senior editor at a prestigious fashion magazine. They talk about my looks and compare them with the agent's. "Scandinavian," they call it.

Suddenly, the editor turns to me: "So tell me, Annette, what did you learn out there in the jungle? What is it that you know that I don't know?" I glance at the writer. I knew I should have come prepared! I can't oblige her with an on-the-spot, profound summation of my experience in the jungle. I begin blurting out secondhand one-liners: That I had a mystical experience, that it had something to do with trust and surrender instead of fear and control. She looks disappointed.

I tell her that I really don't know what to believe in, but that I have a strong feeling about going to Vietnam. That I always follow my intuition. That I believe in an extra dimension, and that I have entered it.

I can tell from the way they are looking at me that this is not at all what they want to hear. They want tragedy and recovery. No beyond.

Besides, if my story can be reduced to one line, what is the point of writing it? The cliché says fact is stranger than fiction, and I believe that's true. So why do people who willingly take a journey with a fiction writer expect real-life storytellers to condense their story to one line? "What did you learn? How have you changed? What is the essence?"

Then the writer joins in the grilling. And I thought he was on my side! He looks at me meaningfully and asks, "Where does this passion to return to Vietnam come from? Why do you *need* to go back to the place of your misfortune?"

*Misfortune.* I let the word sink in. Again, my reasons are so different from what they seem to expect. I am not going back for closure, but for a different kind of coming-to-terms. An opening. For the realization of what love is. To see that place of beauty with today's eyes, after all I have lived through and learned. About loss and love. Loss by loss. Layer by layer.

"Why now?" the writer urges.

*Because it is time.* After the accident, I spent most of my energy on becoming and appearing "the same." The same as my old self, as well as the same as my peers. Perhaps I did this to comfort others, perhaps to comfort myself. I wanted to be as "normal" as possible. So I kept the jungle to myself and worked hard to blend in and make the world forget the survivor part of my identity. I just brushed it off. Not only did I try to hide my physical and emotional pain, I also hid my spiritual gain. I had seen the secret, but I kept it a secret.

Until my father became ill. Until he was dying. For more than two years, he and I read our way through all kinds of spiritual books. He had always been interested in quantum physics and its link to spirituality. When I joined him in that quest, I realized that I had actually experienced what those books try to describe. That perhaps I should try to translate in my head what my heart already understood from my jungle experience. In German they call it an *aha erlebnis*—an aha experience. I realized that the jungle had given me a treasure—a story to tell. That perhaps it was just a matter of finding the right words.

"It was like an orgasm," I blurt out. "You can compare my experience in the jungle to an orgasm." Seeing their flabbergasted reactions, I add quickly, "In my head, I mean. I had this near-death experience."

Never mind. Their real question was, Why should anyone give you fifteen minutes on a talk show? Definitely not to make the host blush.

The next day the writer calls to tell me that the project has been canceled. The editor feels that I am not yet quite able to articulate what it all means. She might have a point.

# Reflection: Going Back

I always knew I was going to go back. Back to Vietnam. Back to the jungle. Back to my mountain. Fearful or not, it was only a matter of when.

I also knew I had to tell my story. About surviving and surrendering. Surrendering to the ultimate—the ultimate beauty, the ultimate end, and the ultimate beginning.

But for me to tell my story to the world, everything has to be objectively true. As a rational Dutch citizen, I have to check it out first. See it with my own eyes to understand what I have gone through. See that place in Vietnam where I experienced the worst and the most beautiful at the same time, ending life as I knew it.

It is difficult to go back into that little body when you have seen and been the universe. That tiny little body with that small and limited mind that cannot possibly behold all knowledge. A now-broken, wounded body with a hole in my heart for being on my own. Never mind how little my old self was: I needed to find it to go on with my old life. To go back to the survival of the fittest, albeit a whole less fit.

In the thirteen years that have passed, sometimes it seems a dream drowned by the drumbeat of daily life. Sometimes it seems like the ultimate vehicle for understanding. Understanding how to deal with Maxi. With life. To observe, not judge. To focus on what is in front of me and accept what is real. To overcome my little self. And to connect.

Now I need to connect to my story. Own it. Go back.

I am terrified. Ironically, while the jungle taught me not to fear death, the accident made me fear life. I'm afraid to travel, afraid to be hospitalized, afraid for people even. Fear closes off the mind. I want to go back to confront and connect with the object of my fear, to see my fears in perspective, and most of all, to let go of fear itself. I've raised my children to face their fears and insecurities—and to connect. Now I have to practice what I preach to them.

It will be more than just a mental challenge. The accident has some physical repercussions as well. The nerves in my right foot have never recovered, and my hips are tilted, leaving my right leg more than an inch shorter than the left one. I am used to the continuous pain this causes, but climbing a mountain will be a challenge. If I can manage that, crash injuries aside, it will be a sure kick in the face to my middle age.

On the upside, I have learned to meditate at will and I have let love become my drive. And curiosity. All these years I have held on to those lingering questions: Who was the orange man? Did he exist? Who were my rescuers? Why did it take eight days to find us? And where are they now?

Now let's see whether I can face the answers. And that little plane.

# JACK
## NEW YORK, 2005

The first thing I do is contact Jack. He is the father of the British victim we accidently buried in the Netherlands. He has been on a mission for years to find out what happened. Why the plane crashed, why it took so long to find us, and what the Vietnamese authorities tried to cover up. The postmortem of his son's body, after it was returned to the UK, suggested his son had had a prolonged period of survival. Several days. That he did not necessarily die of his injuries, but rather from severe dehydration. In Jack's mind, his son could and should have been saved. Jack's member of parliament submitted questions to the Vietnamese authorities. After much delay, they finally invited Jack to visit Vietnam and check things out for himself. It is in Jack's footsteps that I hope to find my way back to the wreckage.

From: Jack Emerson
To: Annette Herfkens
Date: 1/11/2005

Dear Annette,

Thank you for contacting me again; I needed a kick-start to continue the quest. I enclose a copy of what I sent to a friend after my visit, which gives an idea of the site, the walk in, and the accommodation that we were given at To Hap, the administration center for the commune and only two miles from the road's end, passing the hospital on the way. I shall also attempt to send a picture of the prayer flag (more like a tapestry) and myself at the site. I have more photos that I could send if you would like them. Does the ground look familiar? The trees may have grown since. To the left was a tower over which the aircraft had come bringing the trees with it, leaving

a gap that may have been where you are reported to have seen
a man at some time. To the right was a sort of overhung cave
(where the woodcutters appear to work now) with a steep rock
slab beyond. Please let me know your reactions to the enclosed,
and ask any questions you wish.

Delighted to resume communications,
Regards,
Jack

    I was delighted too, but did not recognize any of his pictures, and
much of the following correspondence was Greek to me, for all the
technical terms. To some, Jack might seem obsessed, even creating
a website for his mission, but I enjoy his tough sense of humor as he
cynically cheers me on.*

---

*http://www.vietnamairaccidentinquiry.org.uk/

"If you go to Vietnam you have to involve Chris," Jaime says. "He saved your life then; I am sure he wouldn't mind helping you now. He has the contacts."

I guess he is right. I am already exchanging e-mails with the Dutch ambassador to Vietnam. The embassy reopened shortly after the plane crash. The ambassador has promised his support and has told me he will keep all correspondence in a secret file called "Pilgrimage."

Chris is Jaime's hero. Jaime speaks with reverence about Chris when recalling his input at the time of the accident. Still, I have never contacted him. Mrs. van der Pas has. She has monopolized that relationship the same way she has everything else that was Pasje's. I have not minded in Chris's case; I don't know him. Nor do I have any emotional ties to Vietnam. Which just makes it stranger to seek contact with Chris now. What should I say? "Hi there, I have been told that you saved my life. Sorry that you have not heard from me for thirteen years, but I am planning to come to Vietnam now, so would you be so kind as to help me again, please?"

"Chris will not mind," Jaime says, almost solemnly. "Just e-mail him."

Chris doesn't mind. He e-mails me back right away, sounding extremely nice and wise indeed. And to the point: "I will do all for you short of climbing that mountain," he writes. "I smoke."

Again he is a savior. He coordinates the contacts with the Dutch embassy and Vietnam Airlines. He puts my mind at ease; he seems to find the right tone and words in every e-mail. He obviously cares. He even worries about the accompanying writer's motive. Then I write to him that the players have changed. And changed again. Another writer has backed out, as well as a journalist/filmmaker. They were both enthusiastic until they read Jack's description of the climb and its hardships. Chris is apparently so worried I will suggest yet another journalist who "might take advantage of my story," he tells me he plans "to climb that bloody mountain after all."

# FEARING FEAR
## NEW YORK, 2006

The ball is rolling. My trip to Vietnam is set. Chris, Vietnam Airlines (from Singapore only), the Dutch ambassador—they are all counting on my return.

I have booked my flight for March. I really wanted to go last November, on the thirteenth anniversary, but the plan and the players kept on changing. Perhaps it is for the best. November is the monsoon month. I should know. The flights could be canceled; the mountain might be too wet too climb. Better not push my luck again.

I have to prepare myself, both physically and mentally. To manage that horrible climb. Jack says I really need to "build up endurance." Yoga once, maybe twice a week will not cut it in the jungle. The crash site happens to be at the top of the mountain. "Six hours straight up, in the sweltering heat," he writes.

I start by running around the reservoir in Central Park with a friend. She makes sure I finish at least one lap without stopping. I walk up the stairs to my apartment on the twenty-first floor every day. At first I am breathing heavily and my heart is pounding by the eighth floor, but eventually I am walking up to the fortieth, and then back down. Then Jack scares me more. "You should run up, walk down, run up again—and put some stones on your back."

And then there is the mental part. "Mind over matter," Jack says. I keep on telling myself I don't need to make it to the top. Reaching the foot of the mountain—"my mountain"—is already an accomplishment. Just getting there, claustrophobic as I am. I am facing a twenty-hour flight to Singapore. Then a Vietnam Airlines flight to Ho Chi Minh City. Then a domestic flight to Nha Trang. In the same-size plane I crashed in. It won't be Russian-made this time, but still. Then a van—another confined space—to the guesthouse. "It has running water and electricity, some of the time," Jack wrote. I need to stay the night there in order to leave at five the next morning for the jungle. "Our van broke down and we had to wait hours for a new one to come," Jack says.

I am dying a thousand deaths. I am afraid to be afraid, to finally get that posttraumatic stress syndrome everyone always warns me about. Even seasoned mountaineers suffer from it when they go back to the location of an accident.

I try hypnosis. Magdalena Agabs. I got her number on the train to Roosevelt Island, while taking Maxi to school. A crowded train that goes under the water. A double confinement. I asked the lady next to me if I could borrow her *Metro* newspaper, to distract my phobic thoughts. She gave it to me and told me how Magdalena had hypnotized her son's fears away. When I got up, she handed me the phone number. "We met for a reason," she said. So I had to follow up.

Magdalena is an exotic type—as exotic as her name. She tells me to relax. I have to stare into her dark, velvety eyes. I think of *The Jungle Book*, the scene where Mowgli looks into the snake's eyes and they turn into a kaleidoscope. It makes me laugh. Again and again. It doesn't work. Every time I am at the point of slipping away, I cross my arms and get myself back.

"You have too strong a mind," she says. "For you the only way is to hypnotize yourself. Focus on two things at the same time with the exact same focus."

It works. With a bit of yoga breathing and a touch of New Age thinking. I take the subway to Brooklyn at rush hour. Under the water. To practice. The subway is packed. I struggle even to find a car I can fit into. It is quite a test for a claustrophobe to stay nonjudgmental when sharing a tight place with many people. "You love them, you love them, you love them," I tell myself, and suddenly I do.

So am I prepared? I better be.

# AMULETS
## NEW YORK, 2006

"The angels will carry you up that mountain; God will protect you. The energy of the trees will lift your spirit," my various supporters say to boost my morale.

They tell me to buy special mountain shoes, Teva sandals, lightweight ski poles, a UV-protection blouse, and treated socks to ward off mosquitoes.

I carry an energy pendant; a picture of Saint Francis, friend of nature and animals; a silver pillbox from my friends; and a good-luck letter from nine-year-old Joosje.

# THE OLD JAIME
## NEW YORK, AMSTERDAM, 2006

To say that Jaime and I are estranged is perhaps too much, but over the past few years, he has definitely withdrawn, if not isolated himself. From our friends, from life, from me. From everyone but Maxi and Joosje.

I did not fully understand the extent of his withdrawal until recently, when I start planning my trip. He slowly but surely gets drawn back in and returns to me, and I realize how much we have grown apart.

After I leave for Vietnam, I call from the car to say good-bye one more time and hear it in his voice. The warmth, the interest—devotion almost. Just the way he used to be.

When I call from Newark Airport, he is the same. And again after I arrive in Holland. I get his call in a shoe store in The Hague. I am buying yet another pair of hiking shoes. "Sandals that just fit around the scars," I tell him. I am nervous my damaged feet will not carry me up that mountain.

"You can do it; I know you can," he tells me over and over.

Finally, I am talking to him from Amsterdam Airport, just before boarding that endless flight to Singapore.

"It is ten hours!" I complain. "What if I get claustrophobic?"

"You won't. You'll be in the front. Just enjoy, talk to your neighbor. Think of the old days. You have been there and done that, and much worse. " His warm voice is there again. He has come back to me. *Think of the old days.*

# HEALED
## SINGAPORE, 2006

The twenty-hour flight from Amsterdam to Singapore turns out to be quite pleasant. The lady next to me senses I am nervous, despite my perfect seat in the first row. By the time we are in the air, we are chatting. She is Australian, on a world trip. I tell her what I am up to. She gives me a crucifix. A little wooden one, with silver corners and a minuscule Jesus figure.

"I don't know why I collect them," she says. "I'm not even a Christian. One day you'll give it back to me." It is beautiful. I add it to my collection of charms given by my friends. I relax.

I am looking forward to seeing Myra. She is the orthodontist who fixed my jaw after the accident. She also fixed my resolve, by feeding me Japanese and Indian takeout and suggesting to my family to get me my first Game Boy. Now she will fix my nerves. She is waiting for me at the world's most efficient airport. What a warm and open person she is, and how right she had been to suggest a stopover, to acclimatize both mentally and physically before climbing my mountain. Better to ease into it slowly, with her motherly guidance. We have been exchanging letters since I recovered, and hers are always warm and wise.

Myra takes me straight to a supermarket and asks me to pick out what I want to eat. I marvel at the international choice. When we get to her house in a quiet Singapore neighborhood, she gives me a beautiful room and her house key.

"You can keep it," she says. "You never know if you'll be back one day." The guest room opens up to an orchid garden, tended by her husband, a psychology professor. They make a wonderful couple. He is a native Singaporean, born to idealistic British parents who set out from England to help build the perfect state. She is a Chinese immigrant. Her mother walked with her young family all the way from China to freedom in Singapore.

Myra has a busy orthodontic practice at the hospital and flies all over the world to repair cleft lips. She also bakes elaborate wedding cakes for anyone who wants one. She is even more generous to me. When I admire her ring, she tells me she had the band made in Thailand especially for the stone. She shows me how the light forms an asterisk-like shape on the surface of the blue stone. She takes it off and says, "You have it; it matches your eyes." Of course I protest, but she insists. It fits perfectly. Another amulet.

We discuss how many religions coexist in peace in Singapore. Rather than being politically correct, people allow gentle jokes about each other's choice of worship. Myra and her husband are rational and erudite intellectuals who say they don't buy spirituality or religion of any sort. But they are both so dedicated to others, to this world, and to paying such close attention to every aspect of their daily lives. I can only define it as the perfect example of how spirituality is rooted in reality.

The next day Myra takes me to work at Mount Elizabeth, the hospital where I was reassembled thirteen years earlier. She asks me if I recognize it. I do, a bit.

"I recognize the feeling," I say.

"Now, that I don't get," she answers. "How do you recognize a feeling?" I just do.

The doctors and nurses are great. They actually remember me. They have many versions of how fragile, ghostly, sick, anemic, dehydrated, and close to death I was the last time they saw me.

The next day I meet up with Numachi, my Japanese colleague who described my last days in Tokyo so meticulously thirteen years ago. Who brought me sake with real gold flakes while I was recovering in Holland. We have stayed in touch over the years by sending each other lengthy Christmas wishes. From time to time, I have picked up the phone to ask him how he is doing. He will always remind me of that Vietnamese man in the jungle, the one who lent me his trousers. I remember how I called him Numachi in my mind, how the similarity was comforting.

Numachi has his own company now, partly in Japan, partly in Singapore. I insist on playing golf with him, picking up where we left off last time. He takes me to a golf course near the Malaysian border. When our taxi gets stuck in a huge traffic jam, I get an anxiety attack, fueled by fears about my impending climb. Numachi smiles at me cheerfully and says, "Well, you can't do anything about it. You can't get out!" It takes me back to the crowded subway in Tokyo all those years ago. He said something similar on that occasion. Then I was amused by his lack of empathy. But then I was younger and braver.

I think of Joosje. Once, when she was doing her homework, she quoted, "Courage is not the absence of fear, but the knowledge that something is more important than fear." I tell myself to get over it. I turn inward. By using both my breathing and my new self-hypnotizing techniques, I succeed.

From Singapore to Ho Chi Minh City I will fly Vietnam Airlines. A free flight. On the airline's invitation. I have to collect the ticket at the Vietnam Airlines office in Singapore, somewhere on the eleventh floor. I take the elevator with apprehension. Seeing the logo gives me the creeps. It is like facing an old enemy.

The girl behind the counter smiles when I introduce myself. I ask her politely whether I can sit in the very first row of the plane.

"I was in an airplane crash, you know. I was the only survivor and I woke up with a dead person in a chair on top of me. I have long legs and get anxious when I feel the chair in front of me, against my knees." The girl smiles, sympathetically.

But when I'm boarding I am really nervous. Even more so when I find out that I won't be sitting in the front row after all. Sure, it's the first row in economy, but my knees are squashed against the business seat in front of me. Even though the whole business section is empty. I feel uncomfortably closed in. My mind starts racing: *They don't care!* When they close the curtain separating the two sections, my heart starts pounding in my throat. I have to get up. I approach the stewardess.

"Excuse me, but I am extremely claustrophobic. Is there any chance you would upgrade me to the first row of the plane?"

"No, madam, I am not authorized to do that."

"I was in a plane crash with your airline. It is because of Vietnam Airlines that I need to sit there in the first place!" I say more urgently. Her doll's face shows no emotion. She won't budge. I panic even more. It really seems she couldn't care less, like the men in the ambulance and in the hospital in '92. That same indifference and distance. It all comes flooding back. *What am I doing here? What was I thinking?*

I go back to my seat and have no other choice than to breathe and to befriend the Singapore businessman next to me. We talk throughout the flight. He wishes me luck.

I also breathe my way through the bus ride to the terminal. The bus is packed with people, many Vietnamese. They might as well have sat on my chest; that's how it feels.

The other business class bus is empty. *What would it have cost them to treat me as if they cared?*

# 6

## BACK IN VIETNAM

### FINALLY, CHRIS
### VIETNAM, 2006

By the time I meet him at the airport in Ho Chi Minh City, Chris has taken on legendary status in my mind because of all the heroic stories Jaime has told me about his interventions after the crash. And in his e-mails after I contacted him, he has always said the right thing. Dutch common sense meeting Eastern wisdom—something like that.

It is awkward seeing him in person. He is definitely older than I had imagined, and looks like an average European—though, I reckon, so do I—a bit of a bulky body, profusely sweating in the blazing heat. I let my disillusion evaporate by concentrating on his nice voice, and I relax. Once we are in the car, Chris fills in the thirteen-year gap since we last "met." First, his business made him quite wealthy. Then he married a Vietnamese pop star who turned out to be a taker. Gone were the marriage and the wealth. He had to start from scratch again. The good news is he has remarried. His new wife is Cambodian, and they have two little children.

"I am ruined but happy," Chris laughs.

He takes me to the restaurant at the roof of the Rex Hotel. That rooftop, with its French Colonial atmosphere, tropical plants, and the constant buzz of the city as background music. The same rooftop where Pasje took me on my first night in Saigon. The same rooftop where Chris told Jaime I was alive.

When we sit down and order our drinks, Chris looks straight at me and asks, "So, what do you want to know?"

I am startled by his sudden directness. After a few moments, I answer: First of all, I want to thank him for everything he did after the accident. For all of us. And I have to apologize for my long silence. I tell him Pasje's parents and I have separated, so to speak, and they got to "keep him," as he was Pasje's good friend in Vietnam, the last one to know him.

Chris looks thoughtful, then says, "I guessed as much. But the truth is that I hardly knew him. We only went out a couple of times. I just helped him along, the same way I always do with new expatriates." Chris must see the shock on my face. He adds, "But I have to say that I liked him so much that I thought we might become real friends. He was grounded and genuine."

I am still taken aback. Isn't that alleged friendship the whole reason for me being here with him?

"If it isn't out of friendship for Pasje, why would you go up that damn mountain with me?"

"Because you made a deep impression on me, that's why."

To keep my composure, I open my camera bag, put the camcorder on the table, and say, "Well, if you don't mind, could you start telling me why?"

# *Perspectives*

**CHRIS, VIETNAM, 2006:** My stock was up in 1992. My business and everything else was flourishing, and I was living in a big house near the center of Ho Chi Minh City. It was so big that I had rented out a room to Carola, Pasje's deputy. That's how I knew her. When the plane crashed, I first followed the events but stayed in the background. I gave Carola some tips on how to deal with the communist bureaucracy. Poor girl. She was dealing with all this on her own, with only a few guys from Willem's bank in Hong Kong to support her.

I knew Willem a little bit. We had been out a couple of times, and there had been something there. I could see he was making an effort to get to know the country and the people. He was different from the other expats. He wasn't trying to score cheap points by criticizing our host country. A week before the crash we went out for a drink and Willem mentioned the upcoming holiday in Nha Trang with his girlfriend. It was obvious from the way he talked about her that she was very important to him. That she was someone quite special, and that he had planned many surprises for her visit to Vietnam. It was an enjoyable evening. We felt a kinship because of a shared curiosity and thirst for adventure. It was clear that we would seek each other's company more often, but we never got the chance.

After the crash, families and embassy staff were getting extremely frustrated with the perceived lack of commitment and efficiency of the Vietnamese authorities in handling the rescue operations. It was 1992, and Vietnam was still new to being a member of the global community. The American embargo was still in place and was lifted just a year later. Dealing with an incident involving foreigners was clearly a challenge.

Communicating with foreigners was not their strong suit either. Who was responsible and who would coordinate the rescue efforts? It is quite possible that these questions were asked for the very first time. The frustrations were justified, but that did not translate into results. The only way to get somewhere was to be cooperative and not confrontational.

By the time Carola asked me to help her, I was already on alert. The Dutch ambassador in Bangkok had called and asked me to get involved. There were so many rumors flying around; he wanted me to use my contacts to cut to the chase. I did and managed to forge a good relationship with a deputy director at Vietnam Airlines who was in charge of coordinating the matter in Ho Chi Minh City.

On Saturday morning, I was called to come to the VN Airlines office to listen in on a rescue mission, a joint effort by the military, VN Airlines, and other officials. Apparently, the wreck had finally been located and they knew where to go. But fate struck again: not much later we were informed that the rescue helicopter had crashed and everybody on board had been killed. Until today very little is known about this accident, but I am sure that it heightened the tensions in what was rapidly becoming a major affair.

The next day a rumor was spreading that there might have been one, possibly more survivors! It was not clear who had survived and how. Expectations and pressure were mounting. Had the rescue team been too late? Had there been survivors who had died while waiting to be rescued? For us, the only question that mattered was whether Willem and Annette were alive, but we got no answer. By now I was getting more involved, and we adhered strictly to our policy that we were not seeking blame, only clarity. Sometime later, we learned that a rescue party was on its way, on foot, to the crash site. It must have been Carola who first heard that Annette was alive. When I heard it too, I could not believe it. I had been in similar jungles and would not expect a Western girl to last for more than a day!

The news that Annette was found reached Bangkok. The ambassador's instructions were clear: "Make sure she gets out of there as soon as possible." That was my priority.

Carola decided to go to Nha Trang to take care of her upon her arrival. Once again, we had agreed that we would focus on getting the job done and not confront anyone with contentious questions. After Carola had left, my primary task was to deal with the families. The first delegation—Annette's colleague Jaime and Willem's brother and sister—was about to arrive, unaware that Annette was alive. Her parents and sister had heard the news and would also fly to Ho Chi Minh City "to pick up Annette." I knew a bit about her sister's bulldozer reputation from the newspapers and the grapevine. I had also learned that her colleague was someone to be reckoned with. My first concern was to keep communications with the authorities clear and open. I knew that good relations would be crucial in getting Annette out. I didn't need any loudmouths, but I have to say that I liked the mercurial Jaime right away.

I remember telling Jaime, Miebeth, and Jasper the sad news that Willem hadn't survived the crash, and the great news that Annette was alive. Jaime jumped up and cried, "I knew it. I knew it!" It was a long night. I learned that it was impossible to reconcile joy and devastation.

I met Annette on the tarmac in Ho Chi Minh City. I rode with her in the ambulance to the hospital. She was on a stretcher on the floor of this rickety old Russian thing with a wailing siren and hard springs. Although clearly very uncomfortable on that bumpy ride, she was incredibly lucid. Her eyes were shining brightly, and right away she started talking to me. About Pasje. And the horrible smell. And that she had heard other passengers moan. I then decided not to leave her side. The last thing anyone needed to hear at this time was that she was saying out loud that people had been alive after the crash. After eight days and frustrations galore, it wasn't far-fetched to think that such provocative details might be counterproductive in our mission to get her out of there.

When we got to the hospital, I stayed glued to her side. When they parked her in the hallway, when they took her for X-rays, when they took her to her room. Once her parents had arrived and everything she said switched to Dutch, I decided that she was "safe." From then on, I just focused on the negotiations to get her out of the country. All the various interests involved did not make it easier for me. I tried to keep her parents and Eveline in line with how I wanted to approach the authorities. After a week of experiencing total defeat and sadness, their emotions were raw.

The smallest of things could have caused them to explode, and although relieved and ecstatic, they were also understandably frustrated. But given how fragile the situation was, I didn't need anyone stepping on those sensitive Vietnamese toes.

Another challenge was the presence of curious onlookers and, of course, journalists. While waiting for test results to come in, Annette was resting in a room on the tenth floor. I had left her by herself, just to stretch my legs for five minutes. When I returned there were two people in her room. They had a lens sticking in her face and were trying to ask her questions. I managed to throw them out. They were oblivious to their insensitivity and intrusion and were incensed by my intervention.

The most important person to deal with was Mrs. Chien, the vice minister of health at the time. She was the one who had to give final permission for Annette's departure and sign the release documents. She was a tough woman who didn't smile much, but she was realistic and straight. She had been a medic for the Vietcong in the Củ Chi tunnels during the Vietnam War. She was proud of everything the Vietcong had achieved. She was all too aware of the international press. Annette was a high-profile case, and the effects of her decision could reach beyond Vietnam's borders. That is probably why she changed her mind a couple of times about clauses in the handover protocol. The situation remained tense until the last moment on the tarmac. Something caused a delay. I personally believed that it had to do with the company that was flying Annette out. I just hoped that those doctors were giving her a sedative. I was surprised to see how small the plane was.

Once the aircraft took off, my mission was accomplished. I could go back to normal. But I never forgot those defiant eyes that would not surrender, no matter what.

# PERCEPTION AND PERSPECTIVES
## VIETNAM, 2006

My ears are ringing. Chris has revealed so many facts I did not know. I can't believe there actually was a helicopter, and that it had crashed on its way to pick me up, not while searching for the plane! Eight people died rescuing me!

In general, Chris has a different take on the things that happened, yet another version of the truth.

After our lunch, Chris drops me at the Continental. It is really local, like the state-owned hotels in Russia I used to stay in. None of the obligatory goodies they offer in international hotel chains but with its own national pride. It pleases me; I like being immersed in a different culture. I walk around the block to orient myself. The crazy traffic is overwhelming. Crossing the street is like playing double Dutch: dangerously difficult to decide when to get in. I buy a locally printed book at a street booth. Chris told me they copy anything and everything.

*When Heaven and Earth Changed Places*, it is called. By Le Ly Hayslip, a Vietnamese woman who grew up during the Vietnam War, or, as they call it here, the American War. It seems appropriate to tackle this book now, so I order room service. I start reading right away and get completely immersed in the memoir. *This strong woman has seen it all! With all the atrocities the French, the South Vietnamese government, the Vietcong, and the Americans have inflicted on this country, how can I blame the Vietnamese for not caring about one foreigner?* My sudden understanding does not calm my paranoid thoughts, though. *Should I blame their government for sending that orange man to watch me die—if that's what happened—to protect the desperately needed tourist industry? One life sacrificed for the good of many? Who am I?*

# REGRESSION, 2006

Early the next morning, Chris picks me up to show me around town. On a motorbike. I hold on for dear life. The traffic is manic: Motorbikes are shooting around left and right, cutting each other off, running red lights while honking incessantly, driving just inches from one another into oncoming traffic. Some carry whole families, dead hogs, chickens. Everyone is wearing a triangular handkerchief over their face. *The Wild East!*

I have asked to go to Pasje's office, a thirty-minute ride. We stop in front of a colonial villa. I am happy to finally see it, knowing how much effort it took Pasje to get this office up and running.

Willem had to start a foreign branch from scratch and play the cards he was dealt. There were hardly any other foreign bank offices at the time. I am impressed!

When we have lunch at a local eatery, we get to know each other better. Chris has a great sense of humor, probably inherited from his Welsh mother. That, combined with his Dutch father's common sense and his knowledge of Eastern culture, makes him a very likable person.

I just wonder whether I am regressing a bit to my old persona. When he takes me to his office and temporarily installs me behind a desk, I somehow feel like a trainee again. Chris's trainee. Or like his younger sister? When under pressure, it takes much more effort to apply my acquired wisdom. It feels safe to return to control scenarios from both my childhood and my personality. I'd better get over myself, build up my confidence so I can tackle that mountain!

Back at the hotel, my anxiety about the rest of the trip and the upcoming flights has not eased at all. I decide to take the bull by the horns by writing an e-mail to the Dutch ambassador in Hanoi. I tell him so far I have not been treated all that hospitably by Vietnam Airlines, that I would very much appreciate it if he could try to arrange for me to at least be given special seating on airplanes. I copy Chris on the e-mail.

Five minutes later the phone rings. It is Chris. He seems a different person. With an ice-cold tone in his voice, he tells me I might want to have a good look in the mirror, that I should ask myself what I have come here for, that he wonders whether he truly wants to be involved.

I freak out. *What have I done? Why is he so angry? Why has he suddenly turned on me?*

Now I start to doubt him: *Whose side is he on? Who is he, anyway? Is he working for the government, as Jack suggested before I came?*

Jack also warned me more than once to be careful when talking on the phone or sending e-mails, as "they watch everything." *What do I know? Is anything ever what it seems?*

And the Vietnamese government: How interested are they truly in my well-being? I remember vividly how little empathy the military man had for me when I was found in pieces. How much tolerance will they have for the hysterics of a spoiled foreigner now?

Then there are the theories about the orange man: that he was ordered to find the wreckage and watch everyone die before coming to the rescue, that he was ordered to wait until no one was left alive to tell the story. That I am lucky he did not kill me. Suddenly I fear that he might actually exist. That I might bump into him while visiting his village! *Maybe he will want to finish the job now.*

My mind runs off, seeing conspiracies everywhere.

# FEELING LONELY
## VIETNAM, 2006

After a sleepless night, I decide to roam the streets of Ho Chi Minh City by myself. I call Chris and say I need to take a break for a day. I need some time on my own to digest all the impressions.

His voice is warm again. He apologizes for yesterday's outburst and assures me that everything is under control. He has spoken to the ambassador: Vietnamese Airlines has agreed to treat me like a VIP. They also have apologized for not realizing I have issues with flying, certainly at the back of an airplane. Chris sounds genuinely concerned, involved, worried. He offers to pick me up, but I tell him I really wouldn't be good company right now. I am tired and grumpy from a night full of soap operas in my head.

I aimlessly walk around in the city. I like to absorb, to experience a place, which is really only possible when you are alone. I try to imagine Pasje here in his last days. I thought New Yorkers were tough, but the Vietnamese must have invented the word. When you look at the people, you feel a true toughness underneath.

And the sex. The sex is in the air. You can sense it everywhere. It is not bad, but it is not good either. Loveless, just to titillate the senses. Still, it doesn't feel like it is a loveless city; it just functions on tough love. Like New York. And there seems to be a huge discrepancy between the coldness of the military and the warmth of the other people.

I think of Chris, who has lost his money and had so many challenges in his life here, yet still chooses a tough Vietnamese life over a comfortable Dutch one. Comfort and love don't always walk on parallel lines. They sometimes step in each other's way.

I picture Chris when I left him at his bus stop yesterday, waiting in the sweltering heat to commute to his small apartment in the suburbs, his face glowing with the anticipation of seeing his family. By the time he boarded the overcrowded bus, his shirt was soaked. When he waved at me through the back window, squashed between the other commuters, I remember thinking, *Now that is love.*

How can I not trust him?

I resolve to shake off my blues. I turn toward the various market stalls on the way to the Saigon River.

*When the going gets tough, the tough go shopping*, I think. I get a fake Patek Philippe man's watch. A very good fake, Pasje would have agreed.

I also pick up the nightgowns for my mom that I ordered less than twenty-four hours ago at a little atelier next to the hotel. Three copies of a gown she purchased in Singapore thirteen years ago, when I was in the hospital. It has turned out to be her all-time favorite, worn to threads. The girls in the shop are extremely friendly, despite their fifteen-hour working days. I have told them the reason I am in Vietnam, and when I enter the shop, one of them immediately runs upstairs to get the goods. Apart from the nightgowns, they hand me a dress they have designed especially for me. It is a gift and token of good luck.

# EXPECTATIONS
## VIETNAM, 2006

Later that afternoon, I call Chris. Hoping to clear the air between us completely, I ask him whether we could visit a Buddhist temple together. I fancy Buddhism. I have finally picked up the book that I smuggled out of my hotel in Tokyo. I like Buddha's lack of dogma and his emphasis on compassion, going beyond personality, both divine and human. It makes sense to me.

Chris says he will be happy to take me to a temple his wife often visits. It is Cambodian, just like her. He says he will bring his family.

His wife, Akim, is stunningly beautiful, with an aura of je *ne sais quoi*. Chris explains she has grown up in Angkor Wat, on the ruins of the most impressive Hindu and Buddhist temples in the world. She was born during the Pol Pot regime. Her grandfather, the grand abbot of the Angkor complex, saw to it that she was raised by Buddhist monks. They seem to have done more than just keep her safe: she exudes grace and wisdom.

We take a taxi to an ordinary-looking street packed with traffic. It is late afternoon and people are on their way home from work. We turn into a tiny alley you wouldn't normally notice. At the end is a large, well-tended garden with tiny cottages and a colorful temple. A true oasis—green with plants and trees and a manicured lawn. Young bald men dressed in orange robes are quietly shuffling around; others are sitting on benches, reading. Chris's children run in as if they are visiting their grandparents. They confidently break the silence with the typical enthusiasm of three- and five-year-olds. Like their mother, they obviously feel at home.

I am introduced to a young monk with the sweetest face. Beautiful, with small, standard features and soft eyes. He also has an air of authority, maturity even. In broken English, he suggests we have a service first, and then he will show me around. That sounds great. I am impressed. My expectations are high. We sit down on a carpet in a little room with candles and a small shrine. He starts to chant. I am thrilled. *This is just what one would expect. The real deal!* He goes on and on in his monotone voice. My thoughts are drifting off. To the jungle, to the mountain to be climbed. My eyes follow the children, who are jumping around in a remarkably unrestrained way. I think of Christian churches, where children have to sit quietly with their hands in their laps.

When he stops chanting, the monk looks at me and asks something in Khmer. "He wants to know if you have any questions," Chris translates.

Questions? Many! About what? About life? Death?

"Why don't you ask him how our climb will be," Chris translates for him. I don't quite get it. Is this man a fortune-teller now? With surprise, I look at the dice he throws on the carpet. He calls out the numbers and starts explaining. Chris translates with an equal amount of respect and cynicism in his voice. "He warns us against bad weather. We will have problems at first, but we'll definitely make it up the mountain."

*Oh, good*, I think, still startled. When we go back outside, I am relieved. "So what do you feel?" Chris asks, with a twinkle in his eye.

"Confused," I say, pondering.

"Imagine the reverse. You grow up here in Asia, and one day you get hold of the Bible and get really impressed with its message. Years later, you go to Europe to attend a Catholic mass. You see the ornaments and the saints; you join in the rituals of confession and communion. Afterward, you try to find all that in the Bible, but you can't." Chris smiles, shrugs his shoulders, and says, "Well, like everywhere else, people need something to get them through their hard lives. Here it is numbers. That's why gambling is so big in Asia."

We are about to leave when Chris beckons me to follow him. We walk around the cottages where the monks live. At the back we have a view of the balconies, filled with clotheslines. Orange garments are hanging neatly side by side.

"Look!" Chris says, pointing.

I don't understand. I look at the cute cottages instead, but he insists: "Look at those! Don't they look familiar?" His face is full of expectation.

"Why?" I ask, blankly.

"Look again!" he exclaims. "The orange man! Wasn't that his outfit?" I look up at the monks' robes. I see almost every possible shade of orange. "No," I answer. "I hate to disappoint you, but it was *plasticky* orange!"

How often do I have to tell people!

# A FALSE START
## VIETNAM, 2006

It is Tuesday morning, and we are finally leaving for Nha Trang. On the same flight as the one I took thirteen years ago.

I am almost happy to go into my crucible. After more than a year of planning and plotting, I am prepared, if not eager, to take that plane and meet the challenge of my mountain.

I wake up before five a.m. with much anticipation. I organize the many chargers and batteries for my cameras. I separate my suitcases just as I did thirteen years ago: one for storage, one for Nha Trang. This time I also have an extremely well-equipped backpack for the jungle.

Chris picks me up, reliably on time again. I am really happy to see him in the hall of the Continental Hotel when I walk downstairs. I have just checked out and called for a taxi when Chris receives a call on his mobile: our flight has been canceled due to an impending storm! Chris is visibly upset and amazed.

"That never happens at this time of year; it is not supposed to!"

I know that. That's why we planned this climb for March. The initial trip scheduled for the November anniversary of the crash was too risky, because of the rainy season and typhoon risk. In March the skies are supposed to be clear and sunny.

I try to shrug it off with, "Shit happens." This trip has already been plagued by so many changes of plan, I have become resigned to "just my kind of odds." I suggest we go for coffee across the street. I am still trying to shift my focus to the surprisingly tasty cappuccinos when Chris gets another call: Come immediately to the airport. The flight has been reinstated. It will leave on time, after all!

Back to the Continental to get my luggage and off we go to the airport. I tell Chris how it was still dark the morning I left with Pasje for Nha Trang, that I remember the many bicycles and the "pajamas," now replaced by motorbikes and Western outfits.

The ring of Chris's mobile interrupts me: all flights canceled again for the entire day. He tells the taxi driver to turn around and head back to the Continental Hotel. It is fully booked. So are many other hotels, due to the airport closure. Thankfully, the manager of the Hyatt is a Dutchman. So that's where I end up, completely exhausted, in busy Ho Chi Minh City, and yet again not at the beaches of the South China Sea. Crucible postponed, and who knows what else. More than ever, I am convinced I am never going to make it up that mountain.

The new plan is to leave the next day on the same flight, skip the beach, go straight into the jungle and to the guesthouse, and set off the following day before dawn to climb the mountain. But only if it will not turn out to be too wet, slippery, and dangerous on the mountainside after all the rain.

Great! More variables and uncertainty. I realize with some incredulity that the monk's prediction has been accurate so far. Let's just hope he continues to be right and we make it up the mountain. More than anything, I hope I finally get to see that sea. Where Pasje and I were heading to begin with.

I send an e-mail to Jack to keep him posted and almost immediately get one in return.

To:      Annette Herfkens
From:   Jack Emmerson

Dear Annette,

Look on the bright side. If only someone had made the decision to delay the flight all those years ago, you would not be having all this hassle now. See if my Prayer Flag is still hanging in tatters there. And no more talk of doubt. You told me that you had a wonderful physique. Glad that the arrangements are now in order. If it is Mrs. Anh again, give her my regards. No, better not; deny any knowledge of me. If the river is swollen from the recent rain, insist they carry a light rope for your safe crossing.

Regards, and to Chris (I hope he has a sense of humor),
Jack

I hope I can keep my sense of humor.

# ANTICLIMAX
## VIETNAM, 2006

The Hyatt is a far more comfortable hotel than the government-owned Continental. As I take a bite of the usual bacon and eggs at breakfast, I look at the girl sitting next to me. She is dressed in a business suit and reading the *Financial Times*. Just like I used to do. The newspaper shields you from men. The hotel separates you from the country's culture. The suit separates you from yourself and ups the self-esteem when you are negotiating in a foreign environment. Good for business, but bad for blending in.

Again Chris picks me up early. We make it to the airport this time. A smiling Vietnam Airlines employee welcomes us and guides us through security. Chris is very supportive and sensitive, tuning in to my much-stretched nerves. It is all so eerie. The airport has changed a lot, but the atmosphere is the same as I remember. I recognize the spot where I watched the Vietnamese man eat his soup the last time I was here, while I was waiting for Pasje. I think of Pasje and all the things I have lived since he checked in here. For the last time. All the things he didn't get to experience.

We are taken into a lounge. I am treated like a VIP, thanks to the intervention of the Dutch ambassador. When we walk over to the plane, I am stunned to find out that this plane is actually big enough to have a business class section. Because of all the cancellations, the original plane we were supposed to take has been replaced by a bigger model. I guess I look disappointed, because Chris says, sarcastically, "Now, you *are* hard to please!" I laugh. He is right. I am so mentally prepared to tackle my fears and fly in that small plane that it is almost a letdown.

Once inside I am very happy with all the space. Now I can focus on the view. It is exciting to see the endless jungle through the window, and at long last, I see the sunny shores of the bluest bay of the South China Sea.

# TO THE VILLAGE
## VIETNAM, 2006

Mr. Tan, a very friendly Vietnam Airlines official, meets us at Nha Trang Airport. He takes us straight to a minivan at the back of the airport. He explains we'll be heading to the village of Khánh So'n, where we will spend the night before setting off early the next morning for the mountain.

We haven't been driving for long when we stop to have lunch at a most idyllic spot. A little restaurant on stilts, in the middle of a swamp. We walk over wooden pontoons to get to the entrance. Inside, everything is made of bamboo. *The Deer Hunter* comes to mind. We have octopus as a starter. The unidentified main course is cooked for us at the table, while we get acquainted with our guide.

Mr. Tan is young and upwardly mobile. He is a married lawyer and has two kids. He is the head of the little Vietnam Airlines office in Nha Trang. He climbed the mountain with "Mr. Jack," of whom he speaks very fondly. This is much to Chris's surprise. Chris has not liked Jack's methods at all and expects Mr. Tan to feel the same way.

We continue our drive into the countryside. Chris and I recall how we have grown up with the Vietnam War in the background. Images of rice fields and triangular hats have been etched in our minds. We pass a few villages and stop somewhere to use to nature's bathroom. When we get out of the minivan, we are immediately surrounded by a group of little boys. I smile and wave, but a sense of discomfort comes over me. I remember that awful journey in my "ambulance." Those little children peeping into the van. While answering my call of nature, another flashback hits me: the reddish soil, the ants, and the mosquitoes. It gives me the creeps. Again I wonder what I am setting myself up for. More than anything, I am afraid of becoming afraid.

We continue our drive through endless rice fields in silence. When we finally turn into the mountains, my heartbeat quickens in anticipation. I see the kind of peaks I stared at during those eight long days. After half

an hour, we arrive in Khánh So'n. The village. First we pay a visit to the
uniformed head of the People's Committee. We sit down and have a
ritual cup of tea. I let the Vietnamese language become my background
music. I do the dance but feel no connection with this person. It is
protocol to meet him. Then off we go to the community center. This is
much more exciting. Very déjà vu. The building looks exactly like the
hospital where I had first been treated thirteen years ago, though it is
much better maintained. The people at the center seem to have a warm
interest in us. The atmosphere is upbeat.

They take us to an office. They gesture to sit down on one of the
three couches that have been arranged in a U shape. The two official-
looking men across from us start planning our trip with Chris. Again
everything goes over my head. At the back of the room, three giggling
girls sit behind a desk. Everybody in the room seems to think that I look
very young. They joke that the mountain will be a piece of cake for me.
Thankfully, Chris changes the mood by telling them very seriously that
I have bad feet due to the accident. A handsome man enters. He is taller
than the other men and looks different. He is wearing a crisp white shirt,
which accentuates his darker skin. They introduce him as the person who
first found me. His name is Mr. Cao. They tell him to sit down next to
me and to tell his version of the story. I recognize him vaguely, but I am
not able to give his story the focus it deserves. A lot is lost in translation,
and they are often all talking at the same time. I am overwhelmed by all
the attention, their kindness, and the hilarity of the situation.

Finally, when everything has been discussed, one of the men takes
me by the hand and leads me outside to point out the mountain. Now I
am starting to get excited. I begin to build a new memory from the loose
ends that have remained in my mind.

# FEAR AND GRATIFICATIONS
## VIETNAM

Next, Mr. Tan takes us to my "hospital," now a school. It looks nothing like the dingy place I remember. There is electricity and the stone courtyard is freshly painted. I shake hands with the headmaster, walk around, and smile at the children. They look happy and cute in their school uniforms. Long live progress.

Afterward, the minivan drops us off at the brand-new guesthouse. It has electricity, mosquito nets, and a tiled bathroom. But the shower is not properly installed yet, and there is no hot water. Actually, there is hardly any running water. Still, my room next to the "street" is a palace compared with Chris's quarters. His room upstairs is connected to the one Mr. Tan and his driver share. He almost has to climb over their beds to go to the bathroom. I am very grateful he does all this for my sake!

Evening is falling. Both Chris and I feel like having a drink after this long and eventful day. I have asked Chris to bring some wine so we can celebrate when we get to the top of the mountain. We decide to kill half of the bottle now and have some of my cashew nuts with it. All in style. I have fold-up plastic cocktail glasses from a hiking store in New York. We sit down on the stairs of the guesthouse, overlooking the sandy, unpaved street. We watch the sun setting behind "my mountain." Its conelike shape is so appealing to me that I set out for a little walk to get a closer look. It is beautiful, but also quite threatening; it gives me many second and third thoughts. By the time I walk back to the guesthouse, I am practically shitting in my Patagonia pants.

We have dinner at a neon-lit restaurant where we are the only guests. The owner, an elderly woman, is very emotional when we meet. She remembers everything about me. She was at the hospital at the time and had seen me when I was brought in. She keeps on touching me whenever she serves a course, as if she can't believe I am really here. At first I am moved by her awe, but as the evening progresses, I feel more and more uncomfortable.

Chris's face does not help. He cannot reach his wife on the phone and keeps redialing frantically. I suddenly have a fit. I feel stuck here. It is so dark outside. I want to go back home. Get out of here. Now! *Enough already!* I think in a panic. Chris notices the state I am in and suggests his personal concerns are rubbing off on me. We talk about them, and focusing on his anxieties make mine disappear.

When we get back to the guesthouse, there is a crowd waiting for us. It looks like the whole village has come out to meet us. The entire rescue crew who carried me on bare feet down the mountain and the nurses who peeled off my trousers and cleaned my wounds in the little hospital. Even the doctor who cared for me, the very first one. They are all here! And what a cheery and buoyant ambience.

My rescuers, all seven of them, line up before me as if ready for a military inspection. They look very different from one another. Some look Vietnamese, others more like Native Americans, like Mr. Cao. I recognize some of them, but it is dark outside. We pose for a picture. I am about a head taller than the tallest of them; the smallest comes up to my navel.

"I must have been quite a load for you," I say. Chris translates. They laugh and shake their heads. They show with their hands how skinny I was. I thank them over and over again for carrying me down the way they did. I still have no idea of the enormous effort involved.

When I sit down on the stairs of the guesthouse, everyone crowds around me. The children stare at me from a distance, with big brown eyes. One of the older nurses sits at my feet. She goes straight for my scars; she grabs my ankle and strokes my chin. She remembers exactly where my wounds were. With an intimate gesture, her hand glides under my sleeve and cups my elbow. She turns it toward her and inspects the skin graft. I suddenly remember her touch, and she gives me a toothless smile.

They all have stories to tell. They look truly thrilled to see me. As it turns out, they thought I had died. That I did not make it after all. That was the persistent rumor in Vietnam: I had died in Singapore. Their faces are full of wonder when they pass around photographs of Joosje and Maxi. According to their belief system, to save a life during one's lifetime is a major accomplishment. And then for that saved life to give birth to two more . . . I can't remember how long this blissful reunion lasts, but suddenly they leave, all at the same time, as if by agreement. I am alone again with Chris, Mr. Tan, and his driver. They go upstairs to their room, leaving me in my room at ground level. As I close the wooden shutters and look into the deserted street, it almost feels as if I have dreamt it all.

# DARK NIGHT
## VIETNAM

The wooden shutters dim the streetlight, but not the noise. I wake up at one thirty in the morning to the sound of a barking dog. It is sitting right under my window. My nerves take over.

Thankfully, this time around, I can call Jaime and my mother, my dear mental coaches. Jaime says now I should treat it like an exam, that the adrenaline will take over. My mother tells me not to worry about my lack of sleep and just let my body rest. I try, but at three o'clock I switch on the light to find a column of ants in my bed. They have formed a path all the way to the bathroom. That's it; I won't try to sleep any longer. Better start preparing myself. I "shower" with a bucket of cold water, while balancing on top of the toilet to keep the ants from running up my legs.

While putting on my jungle outfit, I study the scars on my legs and feet, wondering how they will hold up.

I tuck all the provisions and extra clothes into my backpack. I spray my socks with antimosquito spray and get my camera and camcorders ready to roll.

When Mr. Tan knocks on my door at four a.m., I am all geared up. Fifteen minutes later a white van appears in front of the guesthouse. Lit by the dim lanterns in the sandy street, Mr. Tan introduces us to the driver, who drives to the community center in the dark. There we pick up three men of the original crew, two army officials, and a lady to accompany me. Chris notes how cute she is and admires her nice smile. I am impressed that he can be aware of that at this wee hour. I just notice the fast beating of my heart. I am incredibly nervous when we drive off in that little van, now crowded with people, into what I know is going to be that jungle. It is pitch-black outside. No more streetlights. No more streets.

I panic.

"I haven't even had breakfast yet!" I say, sounding whiny to my own ears. Chris reminds me of the energy bars I brought from home. Though I am dying to turn around, I focus on unwrapping and eating the funny-tasting chocolate. I drink from the water bottle I am holding on to for dear life, as I have done through every dire circumstance of the last thirteen years. Chris assures me everything will be much better once dawn breaks. He is right. The moment light appears, everything feels like a "home game" to me. The ferns, the trees glowing in a purple light—it is so achingly beautiful. It has all been worth it. Even without having made it up the mountain yet. Just being here.

# 7

# MY MOUNTAIN

## BOUNCING UP
## VIETNAM, 2006

We start out slowly. We have to cross six rivers before beginning our ascent. I feel slightly pathetic wearing my special gear, and with my backpack filled with more. The rest of the crew is dressed as if we are going for a stroll in a park. Two men are wearing flip-flops, and everyone is wearing jeans. Chris keeps on making fun of me because I am so overly geared up. I answer jokingly that I have to be prepared because he is not; he smokes and has not trained at all for the climb. "You might get a heart attack on that mountain. Good manners would have me stay with you after all you have done for me, and I am not going to get caught ill-equipped on that mountain again!" Or dead, for that matter.

Mr. Cao is carrying my backpack, another man the triple load of bottled water I have begged them to bring. Just in case. The man carries this load in a woven basket with improvised cotton straps. I feel guilty. I secretly agree with Chris: what an entitled princess I am.

We don't use the ski poles I have brought all the way from New York. They seemed such a good idea when my friends urged me to get them, but the bamboo sticks the men make for us are much more effective. The men swiftly cut the twigs and leaves off the stalks with a knife, then they show us how easy it is to adjust the height of our grip on the strong

241

bamboo. Very strong indeed. I must have been tied to a stick like this when I was carried down the mountain.

We have breakfast at the beautiful shore of the sixth and final river. I am able to make my last phone calls to my mental coaches. Our Vietnamese companions prepare sandwiches of canned meat, sliced cucumber, and tomatoes. I am not really hungry, but I think of my previous stay in this jungle and have two of them. As we sit and eat, I marvel at both the beauty and bizarreness of my surroundings.

I specifically study Mr. Cao, who is wearing a green jacket with a bright orange lining. I like watching him. He seems comfortingly familiar. That face. Those particular, strong features, framed by the leaves of the jungle. The way he is sitting . . .

Mr. Tan tells us about his life: he grew up in the countryside and married his high school sweetheart. She is a lawyer now. They have a son and a daughter. He likes his job at Vietnam Airlines, but he is passionate about the jungle. He is extremely worried for its demise and points at the many logs we pass. "That is the beginning of a change in habitat we won't be able to reverse," he says. "And that plastic over there," he adds, pointing at some litter, "it will survive us all." I look at the perfection of the nature around me and sigh.

We walk steadily up the steep mountain. I walk with my senses wide open. I can't believe I am not getting tired.

"The angels will carry you up," my yoga teacher promised. I don't know about angels, but I am definitely bouncing up. Perhaps I am being propelled forward by the thoughts of all my dear ones. Or by the strength of their many amulets. Perhaps I am getting energy from the trees again. I still wonder whether I will be able to make it to the top, but I am thoroughly enjoying my surroundings. And the company. My rescuers are constantly pointing out where and how they carried me thirteen years ago. Mr. Tan is also staying near me, sticking out a helping hand before I know I need it.

The Vietnam Airlines officials and Jack did not exaggerate. The climb is steep and the jungle becomes denser and denser as we proceed. And steaming hot. But somehow five hours pass by without too much sweat on my part. Even when they say we are close to the top, I am still light on my feet and breathing evenly.

It is Chris who seems to be in real distress. He is bathed in sweat and looks ten years older. He is breathing so heavily that I am afraid he will collapse. We have to stop more and more often. I am becoming seriously concerned and insist he eat or drink something. After my fifth suggestion, he spits at me, "I told you! I'll have something at the top!"

I decide it is best to stay clear of him for the moment and quickly move to the front of our group. Mr. Tan stays with Chris, and I find myself climbing with just my original rescuers. Like thirteen years ago, they don't speak a word of English. Just like thirteen years ago, I try to read their hand motions.

Suddenly, we stop. Three of them are talking and gesturing at the same time. Anxiety creeps up. Are we lost? They signal for us to wait.

They sit down in silence until an exhausted Chris and a still-fresh-looking Mr. Tan finally catch up to us.

They converse in Vietnamese, and Mr. Tan explains to me this is

Halfway there, O Kha Mountain, Vietnam, 2006

the very place where we camped that eighth night. I laugh, relieved. Of course they are not lost.

"Can you show me how you managed to put me on that stick to sleep?" I ask. They willingly oblige. They hold a bamboo stick on their shoulders and gesture toward the space underneath. Exactly as I remember it: like a roasting pig. They also joke how I kept on begging for a cigarette, moving two fingers in front of their mouths.

"Thank you for not obliging," I say. "It wouldn't have done my collapsed lung any good."

Finally, we reach the top. Mr. Tan first, then Mr. Cao, then me. I take my last steps with so much anticipation that to describe me as glowing would be an understatement. An equally big disappointment follows. This cannot be it. I don't recognize anything! The slope is even curving the wrong way.

"This is not it!" I say, feeling as disturbed as I possibly can be. "Indeed, it isn't," says Mr. Tan. "We are not there yet. This is the point of the first impact, where the plane lost one wing. You were there." He points at a different mountaintop! "They found you on the next ridge, near the main wreckage."

It is at least a mile away; that is, there is at least a mile between the two peaks. We have to go down and up to get there. And I thought we were done climbing. Chris starts to explain how when a plane loses a wing, it turns into half a missile, and how my plane continued flying after the first impact. Mr. Tan shows me where many trees burned down and never grew back. They keep on talking about the mechanics of the crash—how the plane must have lost speed and flipped over on the next ridge.

*Boy talk*, I think. I am more worried about going down and then up again—on my poor feet!

While Mr. Tan and Chris continue their technical speculation, I turn around and ask the other men to take me to the spot.

# TRAPPED
## VIETNAM, 2006

We walk down the mountain and take a mysterious left. Into the jungliest of jungles. Like in *Apocalypse Now*. So thick it seems to have no beginning or end. I start feeling uncomfortably closed in. We seem to have to cross a gorge to get to the other mountain. We descend carefully, step by step, until we stop dead. We have arrived at a crevasse. I think of my children. *Shouldn't I have done so before undertaking this?* The men are conferring loudly in Vietnamese. They start cutting down a tree and cutting off its branches, all the while screaming loudly at one another. I get it: They are making a bridge! To get us over that frightening chasm. That gap we can disappear into forever!

They place the tree trunk across the crevasse, next to a big rock. One man put his foot out. To feel tentatively whether it will hold him. It does. He slowly starts to move along while holding on to the rock. Everyone is tense. It is like watching a tightrope walker between two buildings. I look up to the bit of sky I can make out through all the leaves, to say a little prayer. We are completely closed in! I look back at the man: he has made it safely to the other side and is already helping the second man cross over, and the third. The fourth one to go is the woman. She walks lightly across like a gymnast on the beam, no help.

I am next. I take a couple deep breaths. Mr. Cao helps me onto the "bridge." I embrace the rock for dear life and slowly shuffle toward the helping hand stretched out on the other side. I am across in three endless minutes. "No sweat." I laugh.

Then it is Chris's turn. He manages, cursing all the way through. A smiling Mr. Tan is last. "Did Jack do *this*?" I ask him, once he is next to me. I can't imagine anyone in his seventies even contemplating a stunt like this. Only after I get back to New York does Jack tell me he was a Himalayan mountaineer. He felt it was better not to tell me, but in mountaineering terms, they called this the worst kind of moment: "When you don't have a rope, but you should really have one."

So Jack had done it. But later I discover that, for some mysterious reason, he was shown a different area for the crash site than the actual site. The area is just a hundred yards short of my spot. That explains why I did not recognize anything in his photos. We actually pass the flag and picture he has left in remembrance of his son and daughter-in-law. The picture has faded, but I can still make out the features of the handsome young couple. We respectfully "think a few thoughts," as Jack would say. He was told they died here. Why?

# (ANTI) CLIMAX, 2006

When we finally arrive at the site, my initial reaction to seeing the spot I made my own during those eight days is one of huge disappointment. It is entirely closed in. There is no open view at all. The view of my mountain, the sun, the moon: it is not there. The plane must have slashed away the trees just before it crashed, creating the open view I remember. Now the trees have grown back. There is still a lot of debris scattered around. No metal, but pieces of blue carpet, plastic, chair covers, an exit sign in Russian, and even a jean jacket on a tree. I check whether it is mine. It is not, though I now recall I had one, a denim jacket with short sleeves. The whole area is much smaller than I remember. I am generally bad at estimating distance, but the bodies, the plane, the remaining wing must have been a whole lot closer together than I experienced them at the time. Also the spot where the orange man must have sat is much closer than I remembered. That's why I was able to make out his face!

I look nearby and find Mr. Cao squatting on top of a rock. The sight of him there gives me a strong feeling of recognition. I become more certain

Window from the plane, O Kha Peak, Vietnam, 2006

when I draw away from the group and settle on my personal spot, about six yards up the hill from where we are going to have lunch. I look down at the group as they are making the preparations. And suddenly I know for sure: it is him! How can I have missed it? He is squatting the same way. Not in plasticky orange this time, but in his crisp, white, button-down shirt. It makes his face look darker. That face! *That beautiful face I thought I had made up all these years. That beautiful, tender man.* He saved my life!

I don't get a chance to tell Chris. When I come down the hill from my spot, he has already opened the wine and asks me to find the camping glasses—to make a toast. I get the glasses from my backpack and quickly screw them together. Our hosts have made a table from logs. We are having the remaining canned meat for lunch.

"To our hosts and to Annette," Chris says, holding up his glass. A bit shy all of a sudden, I make a toast back: to him, to them, and to all who died here so prematurely.

Then Chris turns to my savior and asks, "How and where did you

"It is him!" O Kha Peak, Vietnam, 2006

find her?" *Of course it is him. He was next to me all along! How could I have missed it?*

He starts to giggle as he speaks. He covers his mouth. He seems to look ashamed. Chris translates: "He confessed that when he first saw you, he thought you were a ghost! He had never seen a white person before and had never seen blue eyes," Chris says. "He was just waiting for the ghost to disappear, before getting his friends to help clean up the site." I can't believe my ears.

"*That's* why you didn't answer," I respond directly to my savior. "I was screaming and screaming, and you were just staring and staring!" I turn to Chris in disbelief. After all those years of speculation!

"The mystery of the orange man has been solved!" he says, solemnly.

"I can't believe it!" I almost shout. I let it sink in a minute. Of course I had looked like a ghost. There were all those dead people and this thin, white creature in a blue poncho sitting among them. With blue—and they must have seemed to Mr. Cao extraterrestrial—eyes.

Cheers, laughter, and tears, O Kha Peak, Vietnam, 2006

The man goes on to tell us how afraid he was. He actually looks it! He says he was too afraid to act until I took my hood off. He copies the move. Then he realized I did look somewhat human, and it was only then that he decided to fetch his friends!

Now I am the one staring. So had I not taken that hood off, I would have died a ghost?

# MY MOUNTAIN
## VIETNAM, 2006

The spell from solving the mystery of the orange man is broken by a sudden movement. One of the guys jumps up. He starts to talk nervously to the others. They all leap. In panic. I look at Chris.

"What's happening?" I ask. But before he can answer, I see the object of their dismay. A four-inch-long centipede is walking steadily across our "table." One of the men crushes the poisonous sucker right before our eyes. Chris has already jumped up, but I stay dead calm.

"For you this may be nothing," Chris laughs, "but can you see why the Vietnam Air people said it would be too dangerous to stay overnight?"

I shrug. I really would like to camp out here. Make all that climbing effort worth my while. Spend the night, see the moon. Besides, then we would have time to relax a bit. Now it is almost time to go already;

With Chris, O Kha Peak, Vietnam, 2006

otherwise we won't get back to the van before dark. It takes at least five hours to get down the mountain. I really don't feel like leaving yet. I climb back up to my spot while the men clean the table.

"Why don't you all go ahead and leave me here for a while?" I shout. Perhaps a bit rude of me to ask, but they give me a look of understanding. "I am very happy to make a head start," says Chris, looking his old self, the color back in his face. It must be the victory wine and the cigarette.

I can hear the crew retreating. Their sounds are gradually taken over by the noises of the jungle. I remember that cacophony. Only now do I realize how loud and intense it is. I guess you have to be truly alone to notice.

# TWO ROADS DIVERGED
## VIETNAM, 2006

I sit down on the leaves. And the twigs. How uncomfortable! I look down the mountain through the trees. So many trees. It is so much more claustrophobic than I remember! And not as green. Not as pretty.

I try to look at the leaves for a second, but my eyes are drawn to the bigger picture. *Different mind-set then than now,* I think. It doesn't help that I am surrounded by all those little pieces of debris. Like September 11. I reach for a blue piece of carpet and examine it between my fingers. Too many thoughts are fighting for attention. And those sounds!

I look behind me and try to imagine the fuselage. With Pasje in it. I can think of him now. I should think of him. Here is where his life ended. I have gone on. Moved on. Though never really without him. Strange that I don't feel his presence here. Not stronger than usual, at least. The thirty-six-year-old man who died here was his cocoon. A nice one. Including his personality, which I loved and I liked. And have mourned and missed. Still miss. The personality I admired and got along with so well. What has stayed with me is something else. Something extra. Something more essential. His love. Our love.

I work my way farther up the mountain and stop at a rock. I search in my backpack for the small wooden dolphin and the little white seal I have brought. I place them on the rock.

"Bye, Pasje." I leave them for about a minute. Then I grab the seal and put it back in my pocket. He won't need it. I do. In its place I put down a little Buddha statue. For Hamish and Sylvie. I am glad I can do this for them, for Jack. At the right spot. This is where they really died. How strange they didn't bring Jack here. *Is there something they did not want him to find here?*

Suddenly I hear buzzing. Is it a bee?

"Pappie?" I say out loud. "How nice of you to come." I know the others can't be too far away, but I am feeling quite lonely.

I study my surroundings. There is no doubt I must have been in an altered state of mind, consciousness, awareness—whatever—thirteen years ago. Stuck here for eight bloody days! I take a sip of water. It still helps.

A Buddha for Hamish and Sylvie, O Kha Peak, Vietnam, 2006

I have to pee. I check around. No one. And no painfully broken hips this time. I squat down and see the jungle floor up close again. And the red ants. Like good old neighbors. Charming.

Time to go back. I walk in the direction we came from. Hey, it doesn't lead anywhere! I look at the other path, leading down the mountain.

"Two roads diverged in a wood and—oopsie!—there I stood!" I recite while stepping over the knee-high plants between them. Neither path has been much traveled. No, this one leads too steeply down the mountain: I will fall if I go any farther! Back up. To the other trail. I walk a few yards, but again I only bump into trees. I am lost!

"Yoo-hoo! Is anyone there?"

No answer. Only the jungle sounds. That is just great. "Hello? I am lost!" I can hear the catch in my voice.

I hear rustling, and there is Mr. Tan. Thank God. He has stayed behind while the others went ahead. He has been so discreet to remain at shouting distance. What a hero. I turn back to the site. Take one last look. *Bye, Pasje. Bye, mountain.*

# DOWN TO THE RIVER
## VIETNAM, 2006

Going down the mountain is much more challenging than I expected. The mountain seems much steeper, and there are trees everywhere. Were they that close to one another on the way up too? The men must have done some serious slalom when they carried me down on that big stick! The rain must have made it just as slippery as it is now. I am pondering that when I slip and slide down a few yards on my bottom. And slip again some moments later. And again. By the time we catch up to the others, Mr. Tan has pulled me up at least four times.

I ask them to take a break. I need to change my shoes. My feet really hurt. I have a pair of sneakers in the backpack that Mr. Cao, "the orange man," is still carrying for me. He walks over to me, turns around, and gestures to get them from his back. He waits dutifully while I am digging for the shoes. He does not have to bend his knees, as I am much taller. I change into my sneakers and put my hiking boots in the backpack. All the while, he is standing close by with his back toward me. I suddenly feel a surge of emotion. It is a strange intimacy, as if we are the only two people on that mountain. Again. From then on, he does not leave my side. He makes me a new walking stick and shows me how to go from tree to tree, using them as aids in our descent. He keeps on looking at me with those intense eyes, in which I now discern a warmth I did not notice before.

After four hours of straight descent we come to a flatter area when we are back at the beautiful spot where we had breakfast that morning. I am both exhausted and exhilarated.

I am sitting on the same large stone I sat on at six in the morning. Was that only eleven hours ago? It seems like a lifetime. Again I let the Vietnamese chatter become background music. I let the river run over my scarred and blistered feet. The water comes down rapidly. It is the same river as eleven hours ago, but different water. Like Siddhartha's river—ever changing and ever the same. Like it was different thirteen years ago, but in essence the same as today. The difference in my perspective

With the crew at the bottom of O Kha Mountain, Vietnam, 2006

between this morning—when I was fearing fear more than anything, not knowing what to expect—and now. Different but somehow the same, as I always knew it would be.

I think of the writer's question: "How is going back to Vietnam going to change your life?" It won't and it will. It indeed has been an opening: it has opened up more than I could have hoped for. It fortified my drive to share my story, and now I also want to include Vietnam and these kind people I have connected to into my future.

Wading through the cold water of the six rivers is now bliss for our tired feet. What a relief to finally make out the little van with Mr. Tan's driver leaning against it. We've made it! And it is still light, just about.

We drive back to the community center with the last rays of the afternoon sun painting the countryside orange. I am already nostalgic, filled with emotions and parting from the crew with regret. I do an extra thank-you round to the original crew members, ending with the orange man. "You saved my life," I say.

He smiles, showing me his teeth. For the first time.

# FINALLY, NHA TRANG
## VIETNAM, 2006

We drive back through the mountains in silence. It is dark. We are exhausted. We turn onto Route One to Nha Trang, a road Jack has described as "sheer terror." I don't notice or care. I am finally going to see that jinxed destination, beautifully bordered by jungle and the South China Sea, where Pasje planned our romantic getaway.

At first sight, Nha Trang looks like a typical beach resort. We stop at a rather shoddy-looking hotel, near an intersection filled with rushing cars. Chris immediately protests to Mr. Tan. "This is way too noisy," he says. "It is kind of Vietnam Airlines to invite us, and I appreciate the hospitality, but I could really do with a good night's sleep."

Mr. Tan smiles his customary smile. "No problem," he says, and he drives us to a more upmarket hotel. It has a pool. We check in, enjoy our showers—very much—and meet in the lobby afterward.

We cross the boulevard to the beach. There is a long row of restaurants. The European way. We have dinner in a trendy pizzeria where we can enjoy the sound of the sea on one side and the latest music on the other. We let the cold beer soothe our sore muscles. We talk like both good friends and business associates. The kind of relationship I enjoy and am used to having with men.

But I also feel a bit awkward and guilty to finally be here without Pasje. It is just his kind of place. Instead I am here with a stranger whom I met only through his death.

When we get back to the hotel, Chris can hardly make it up the stairs. I nastily show off by skipping three steps at a time. We are both happy it is over. We say good night. Like shipmates back on shore. Or like two investment bankers who have just closed the biggest deal ever. Both happy and relieved.

It is eerie to see the relics I brought from the mountain when I get back to my room: the pieces of carpet, the exit sign in Russian. The visit to the site already feels like a dream. I wrap up the relics, pack them out of sight in my bag, and go to bed.

I can't sleep. After being awake for twenty hours, eleven of which were brutal physical exercise, I somehow feel too energized. The adrenaline Jaime promised me is still running. Jaime . . . I call him again to say all is well. And that Chris is totally the hero he described. Maxi and Joosje are at school. All is well there too.

I put out the light. Images of the day are running through my head. The jungle, the mountain, the orange man, Chris. It is as if at this moment he embodies all the men I have loved and lost. All the men who have loved me. Pasje, my father, Jaime too. I decide to ask Chris if I can adopt him as my brother.

The next day we meet Mr. Tan for breakfast. He has brought three other Vietnam Airlines officials: one local gentleman, who is acting as if he is Mr. Tan's boss, and two ladies from Hanoi. Mrs. Anh, an executive for corporate affairs, is the one who accompanied Jack but refused to climb the mountain a second time with us. She acts quite cold. Mrs. Mai, international affairs, is married to the former Vietnamese ambassador to the Netherlands. She smiles a lot.

We have a polite meal, exchanging pleasantries about each other's countries, but I can't help feeling resentment underneath. For Pasje, for Hamish, for Jack. For all my wounds.

They turn it into an official ceremony by giving me a gold-plated pin from Vietnam Airlines and a hand-stitched tablecloth. They ask a waiter to take a picture.

"Cheese!" we all say, standing in a line, me holding up the pin.

# BAO DAI'S VILLAS
## VIETNAM, 2006

After the breakfast, Chris and I go to that fateful palace, the hotel Pasje booked thirteen years ago for our romantic vacation.

"Bao Dai's Villas is one of the few remaining examples of French Colonial architecture in Vietnam," my guidebook says. "Built in 1923 as a holiday resort for the last Vietnamese king and queen, it sits on a promontory of 120 thousand square meters of lush vegetation. The villas overlook the South China Sea and its coastal islands, and enjoy sea breeze all year round." In the taxi, Chris tells me how enthusiastic Pasje was about our trip, how worried he was about the plane ride to this place because of my claustrophobia. Worried I would stop him in his tracks on the runway.

Why hadn't I?

Bao Dai's Villas, Nha Trang, Vietnam, 2006

When the taxi drives up the circular driveway, I can't believe my eyes. What an enchanting place! It couldn't be any more romantic. A palace on a cliff with the crispy blue sea crashing at its side. Beautiful gardens. What a perfect combination. *Oh, Pasje, you did such a good job. I wish you could see it with your own eyes.*

I am overcome with a feeling of waste. Tremendous waste. My eyes are burning. I walk away from Chris, who discreetly stays behind, over toward the water. I watch how the water hits the rocks. My favorite sight. Pasje knew.

I pick up some stones and throw them angrily into the sea. *Why? Why him? Why us? What did he do? What did I do?* Tears are rolling down my face. I throw more stones. Almost violently now. Rock after rock. More and more. Waves of anger, frustration, grief. Then I realize what I am doing and start laughing. At myself. It suddenly seems bizarre that, just like thirteen years ago, I kept my act together on that mountain and now I am letting myself go at sea level. Floodgates burst wide open! Like thirteen years ago, when I saw my mother's face, I let go so much I almost died.

I straighten my back and gesture to Chris that I want to check out the buildings. By myself. They are great—not too luxurious, just right. It would have been perfect. Good old Pasje!

I wander back to the sea and sit down on a rock. I see the waves crashing against the cliff. The tears well up again. Now for Jaime. Why can't we overcome our differences and go beyond the opposites? Go beyond our personalities? Embrace the paradox of something being both right and wrong, of someone being strong and loving and also angry and uptight. Of someone being messy and chaotic but also responsible? Will we be able to find the middle? Or meet in the beyond, like we used to?

As long as we live, there will be duality. It is the tension of opposites at work. Too much tension now, but that's how things get created, and how a balance is achieved. Eventually.

We are all like separate waves until we crash and we become equal parts of the ocean again. Waves only appear to be separate for the short period between when they form and when they crash. It is such a short ride, life.

For now, I live happily with what I have. Just as there once was a Pasje and Annette, there has been a Jaime and Annette. Once they were strong together; they just aren't right now. Just like after losing Pasje through death, even if I end up losing Jaime through life, I won't lose him altogether. He has given me too much for that. A love so strong I'll carry it with me. It is there, like Mozart's music, which can still move people even though the artist is long dead. Perhaps at this moment in time, in these earthly frames, Jaime and I cannot be together. But that doesn't make what came before any less meaningful. I take a deep breath, stand up from the rock, and take in the beauty of the waves.

# Reflection: Waves

When I discovered Coldplay, I walked around all day, listening through headphones. And with tears in my eyes.

I thought how Pasje would have liked "Clocks." If only I could call him and let him hear. It was partly for him that I kept up with new music. His eyes used to well up when he found a new sound. He would make me listen. He would look at me with eager eyes, hoping I would be as enthusiastic as he was. But I needed to hear something a couple times to like it. He liked new.

"Old becomes background music," he used to say. "You don't really hear it anymore."

I remember when he discovered U2. Before anyone else knew we had. How he said, "Listen to that voice, that new sound." His eyes were filled with tears and with such tenderness, even for the little boy on the cover. We played U2 at his funeral. Only at the age of forty-something, listening to Coldplay, did I finally understand how he felt.

It still hurts to recall Pasje by listening to his songs. They bring him back so vividly. Bring back his love. Our love. Still there but on a different frequency.

I can bring the old Jaime back too. The way I bring back Pasje.

But it costs me more effort to bring Jaime back. He is alive. And kicking. Alive but not at home. The wound from our gradual separation is open and might stay open. Losing through life can be more painful than losing through death. The grief hits me the same. Unannounced. Like a wave. So I just have to stay still in this one too—let it come over me.

There is much love to live on, both past and present. Past for me. Present for our children. And I can still put on our music, sit on our balcony, look at our restaurants, our opera house, our city. And bring it all back.

I carry it all with me. It is there and it will always be there. Whatever happens.

## *Reflection: Lucky*

Once upon a time, I wanted to go see my fiancé in Vietnam. Lucky. I had to postpone the trip. Unlucky.

I went one month later. Via Hong Kong. Uncharacteristically, I did not miss my flight, even though it left two hours earlier than planned. Lucky. If I had missed it, I might not have been on that domestic flight in Vietnam and I would not have crashed into that mountain. Unlucky.

I survived. Lucky.

My fiancé died. Everyone else did too. Very unlucky.

I found love again. Very lucky. I may be losing it. Unlucky.

I also made lots of money. Lucky. I spent some, lucky enough, but I ended up losing half in 2008 with a bad investor. Unlucky. I got two beautiful children. Very lucky. One turned out to be autistic. Unlucky. He has shown me a depth in human life in a way a typical boy would not have done. How lucky!

So what does that make me? Lucky or unlucky?

# THE HELICOPTER
# VIETNAM, 2006

In the van leaving Nha Trang for the airport, Mr. Tan, Chris, and I talk as if we are about to part as old friends. We all agree it has been an extraordinary experience. We vow to revisit the mountain with our daughters one day. "Once they are old enough and before we are too old," Chris suggests.

"There is one more person I'd like you to meet," Mr. Tan says when we are walking over to his office in the airport building. "Do you remember the helicopter?"

"I am so sorry, I don't," I answer. "Until I got to Vietnam I thought that was just another rumor."

"Oh hell, it wasn't," Chris intervenes. "I heard it taking off! I was called to come to the offices of Vietnam Airlines. When I arrived in the crisis room, people were listening in on headphones. A team of doctors and officials was on the way to the crash site in a military chopper."

Mr. Tan adds, "The daughter of the physician who was on that helicopter works for me now. He and the seven other souls aboard died in that crash."

I have no time to let it sink in. A beautiful young girl walks out. When she sees me, she bursts into tears. I take her in my arms and hug her. She says, sobbing against my chest, "My papa went out to rescue you, and he never came back!"

## Reflection: Taking Loss, Gaining Love

"No pain, no gain," we used to say on Wall Street. Today I am still convinced there is a great yield in taking a loss. When the loss is taken consciously. By facing and defining, not by cutting or denying. After properly taking a loss, there is always some kind of compensation, an expansion even. I now know how much I have gained as a result of my losses.

When I found myself alone in the Vietnamese jungle, I had to accept that reality in order to survive. I remained calm. I stayed still with it. I shifted my focus. I could see the beauty. I surrendered myself unconditionally. And that was when it happened: I felt connected; I had the most heavenly experience on earth. When I lost my fiancé, I was forced to take a loss on the future we had envisioned together. I had to go through the process of grieving thoroughly in order to build another future. I did. And then he stayed with me.

I also had to take a loss on the future I envisioned for my son. Only then could I accept him for who he is. I learned to see what *is* there. Not only do I accept him, I celebrate him daily as a gift.

Taking a loss is not the same as cutting your losses and letting go is not the same as moving on. You have to consciously take your loss in order to integrate what is lost. Stay still with it and let it hurt. Don't deny or reject the situation as if it should not have happened. When you do that, you harden both your heart and your mind, and you cannot be open. In order to stay open, you must stay present. When you stay present, you can see the beauty—the flip side of the loss.

If you know what it's like to be hurt, then you can imagine the pain of another. When you stay open, you can connect to others and so find the beauty in the connection.

When you stay open, every loss of a loved one gives an option to peel away a layer, revealing more love. Like peeling an artichoke, with unconditional love at its heart.

Nothing stays lost forever. Whatever or whomever we have lost becomes an integral part of us and will always be present. As Einstein proved, energy cannot be destroyed; it changes form.

Loss actually brings you closer to the love you had—and still have—than ever before. The bigger the attachment, the bigger the feeling of loss; the bigger the loss, the deeper the love. Grieving equals loving.

We are flying back to Ho Chi Minh City. In a small plane this time. I don't mind. I have not even requested the front row or an aisle seat. I just have to look out the window, see the sea, and see the jungle. I put my purse in the net on the seat before me. LIFE VEST, it says. My eyes search for the exit sign. It is in English. Chris is sitting next to me, reading a paper. He seems eager to get back to his family. He has never been away from them for this long. I am very grateful for the sacrifice. I'll miss him. I still have a few more days to go before I'll see my family, flying back to New York via Singapore and Amsterdam, where I'll stay with my dear mother to tell her the stories.

I have many stories to tell. So many things were not what they had seemed. In a good way. There are many more versions of the truth. But then, isn't the truth multifaceted anyway? In the end, everyone's intentions were pure. Chris, Mr. Tan, the orange man—each one giving without condition.

Getting to the top of my mountain: Was it mind over matter, or was I carried up by those who thought of me? Both, I believe. In the same way, it was all kinds of love that kept me going thirteen years ago—a bed of it, for and from many. That love ultimately enabled me to surrender. To the jungle, to the moment, to life, to death.

We are all physically, mentally, and emotionally much stronger than we think we are. Nobody likes to be tested, but once we are, we realize we are stronger than we ever thought possible, and we come to value and appreciate the test.

Climbing the mountain was all about the process of getting there.

It allowed me to connect to all the people whose lives were touched and intertwined by the airplane crash. We are all instrumental in each other's stories. And everyone's story is instrumental for all of us. Both positively and negatively. Another eight people died rescuing me, leaving that sweet girl—and how many more?—fatherless. My story is about her and everyone else involved.

The jungle has taught me to transcend, to surrender, and to connect vertically, to the universe, to God. It has taught me where to get energy.

Maxi has taught me about compassion, to connect laterally to others. Where to give energy.

That is what I am here for: to connect to people as equals, not to get a kick out of my "higher" self. Besides, my happiest moments have been when I had no self at all.

I look out the window, through my own reflection. The sea is getting more and more distant. How idyllic, I think nostalgically. It must be one of the most beautiful bays in the world. Right underneath us stretches the endless jungle. I try to make out anything specific, but I can't. Just giant patches of green. How big is the nowhere we have been in the middle of—and beautiful.

Objects are visible because of the light that reflects off them.

Myra, Chris, Mr. Cao, Mr. Tan, Numachi, doctors, and nurses. Maxi's teachers, my family, my friends, Jaime, Joosje, and Maxi. I am only a reflection in your eyes.

# AFTERWORD

## By seventeen-year-old Joosje Lupa

Years of slash and burn have transformed O Kha Mountain, thinning the dense jungle into which VN 474 crashed more than twenty years ago.

It was this new O Kha that I saw in August 2014, when my mother's Vietnamese publishers, First News, invited her to Ho Chi Minh City for the press release of the translation of *Turbulence*.

"I won't go without you, of course," my mother told me matter-of-factly. She wanted to show me the place where her life had taken a turn, and for me to meet her rescuers, without whom I would not exist. The publisher agreed, if I would write an afterword from my point of view, as one of the birth children of the story.

Our trip was remarkably appropriate for that month: in Buddhism, the seventh month on the lunar calendar is the ghost month, when the realm of the dead and the realm of the living are thought to be open, and the deceased are believed to visit the living.

## 192 Hours, Ho Chi Minh City Airport, August 9, 2014

Flashing cameras. A poster with the words ANNETTE HERFKENS and an airplane smashed across it. From the horseshoe of people waiting to welcome their loved ones emerges a small crowd, every member equipped with a camera or recording device. I watch as the horde engulfs my mother. Questions start immediately: "How does it feel to be back in Vietnam? What are your emotions at this moment?"

My mother answers with a broad smile; only I can see how surprised she is. "The last time I came to Vietnam, I was fearful, but now I am thrilled to be here." She pulls me forward. "And this time I've brought my daughter!"

A man hands her a large bouquet of flowers wrapped in colorful paper. "Fresh, new," he says with enthusiasm. Another man hands her a translated copy of her book, and a third starts interviewing her for a TV camera. First News representatives step in and warmly guide us to our van. We gape at each other in amazement as the car sets out into bustling traffic, entering the swarm of motorcycles that dominate the streets.

We stay at the Continental Hotel, old-worldly and grand, with wooden panels and broad marble stairs. It feels as if I am walking onto the set of a movie I've watched over and over again; I can see the scenes running in my head. It is the hotel where my father stayed in 1992 when he learned my mother was still alive. I imagine him here with his long hair, his white T-shirt, and his determination. The only person convinced against all odds that she hadn't died. My mother also stayed here in 2006; I imagine her before she went back to the mountain, alone and apprehensive, the climb looming over her. I was at home in New York then, only nine years old and unaware of the huge undertaking she was facing.

We are given no time to settle into our beautiful suite overlooking the colonial opera house surrounded by buzzing traffic. First News has fully scheduled our eight-day trip. After two interviews in the lobby, we are driven to the First News office to meet its president, Mr. Nguyen Phuoc. He sits at the head of a large, wooden table with a cigarette in one hand and a cell phone in the other. A large painting of Ho Chi Minh looms over him. He welcomes us literally with open arms, enthusiastically embracing us both. He explains that the tight schedule is to give as many Vietnamese the opportunity to meet us. He fixes his gaze on my mother:

"We love your story and way of thinking. We want people here to know about you."

## Atonement

Early the next morning is the press conference, marking the official release of the book. It takes place in a large room, decorated with floor-to-ceiling posters of my mother's name and picture coupled with the book's cover and Vietnamese title: *192 Hours*. It is so crowded that people are jostling to stand in the back. Representatives from all the major Vietnamese TV stations and newspapers are in attendance. So is Chris, Pasje's friend who climbed up the mountain with my mother in 2006. Chris's warmth and familiar Dutch sense of humor quickly make him feel like an uncle and puts me at ease. My mother gives a short opening speech, expressing how lucky she feels to be here with me. She ends with: "I have lost a lot in this country, but I have also gained something big: new insight into life and death, and lessons that still help me to this day."

Mr. Phuoc then stands up and introduces the wife of the pilot in command of the rescue helicopter, Mi-8, that crashed searching for my mother. Her name is Ms. Lan. She stands up quickly and rushes toward the front of the room. Short and feminine, with resolute features, she hugs my mother, who, nearly twice her height, embraces her like a child. Ms. Lan remains standing, looking at my mother, as she describes to the journalists the longest weeks of her life. It took a month before her husband's body was found in the jungle. "It felt like a year," she says, her face reddening, tears running down her cheeks. She was twenty-six years old at the time and five months into her first pregnancy. My mother's hand rises to her mouth in horror.

Three more women come forward: the widows of the pilot, the copilot, and the technician on flight VN 474. They look at her with care and also a kind of eagerness. Later they tell me that seeing her and hearing her recollection of the crash brings them closer to their loved ones in their last moments of life.

The wife of the pilot, Ms. Thuy, relates, "Anytime there's a plane crash, we can feel the pain of the victims' families. They must be as lost as we were twenty-two years ago."

Next, journalists line up to interview my mother. A young reporter introduces herself to me and says, "I am amazed by your mom. She was so brave—eight days in the jungle? I wish—I think we all wish—we could be as strong as your mother was."

This is strange. To see my mother accessible to many, to see those same lessons I take for granted affect so many people. I suddenly see my mother as 3-D, as separate from myself, separate from the person who raised me, put me in bed at night, and scolded me for my manners. I see her as the survivor of an airplane crash, the woman who not only struggled for eight days in the jungle to stay alive but also integrated it as a positive experience.

I know my mother's story inside out. It's my "party story," the story I tell people when I am asked for a fun fact. Then editing the manuscript of *Turbulence* the summer before my junior year acquainted me deeply with it. Yet that's all it was for me at the time: a story. Even as I read my mother's own words describing her survival, it seemed as if they described a different person. Moreover, she has the habit of playing down her ordeal.

Now it is real to me. It becomes clear how she has internalized her misfortune but hasn't let it take over her life. She uses what she learns but isn't overcome by it. When I am with her in a crowded subway without water, I see her panic, I see the claustrophobia, the phobia of being without water settle in. I see the thoughts flit with panicky minors across her eyes. But then as I keep watching, I see her recognize the fear, tell me the fear, sit still with it, let it be, and overcome it. She doesn't blame the accident or whine; she remembers and goes on. I now understand how those lessons influenced my upbringing. "You can't control what happens to you," she would tell me when things went awry, "but you can control your reaction."

Now, in Vietnam, seeing readers and reporters line up to meet her, seeing the awe in their eyes, it all comes together. My mother makes them feel empowered when she speaks of her survival and when she tells them they have that same ability within themselves.

## The Flight

The next part of our journey is a trip to Nha Trang, to the base of O Kha Mountain. We are picked up in the lobby at five a.m. the following day. It appears First News has tried to replicate the journey of 1992 as much as possible, for they have booked the exact same Vietnam Airlines flight to Nha Trang as that fateful one nearly twenty-two years ago.

The cameras are on us from the moment our car arrives at the airport, where the widows of the two pilots greet us; they are coming with us to O Kha. Our seats are in the second row on the left of the non–Yak-40 plane, exactly where my mother and Pasje sat twenty-two years ago. But now I sit beside her, not Pasje. Through the window I can see the terrain she flew over—and into.

"Are you afraid?" I ask tentatively.

"No," she responds firmly. "Now I trust." Then she thinks for a moment and adds, kissing me, "And you are here." She always says that fear rests largely on trust.

When we get off the plane, she communicates her memories calmly, almost casually pointing out the spot on the tarmac where she lay on a stretcher. As usual, she has an uncanny ability to make light of things. She compliments a woman's leather jacket as she usually would, normalizing the situation.

Mr. Tan, the Vietnam Airlines official who climbed the mountain with her, is waiting for us. My mother exclaims in delight when she sees him, and the two catch up excitedly. It's strange to see them interact; I have heard and read much about Mr. Tan but have never fully understood the extent to which they relate to each other. I feel like an outsider.

After passing another wall of photographers, we see a big, blue tour van waiting for us. It has 192 HOURS and my mother's name written across both sides. Mr. Tan, my mother, and I sit in the first row, and the rest of our crew—the interpreter, An Dien; the two widows; and various photographers and journalists—fill in the rows behind us.

I look out the window in disbelief as we enter the mountains in the customized van. We are in the very mountain range where my mother crashed! The place of "fortune and misfortune," as she calls it. A distant world I have previously only glimpsed through the pages of *Turbulence*.

During the car ride the usual speculation about the details of my mother's rescue come up. An Dien tells us in a hushed, excited voice the rumors he has heard that the head of the police was seconds away from shooting her after she was found. *Maybe the pressure of a half-dead, white foreigner was more than they could handle after all?* We are intrigued, but as with most rumors, my mother shakes it off. How much can you really know for sure?

We stop to have a snack in a restaurant, where we are met with a great surprise: The owner of establishment turns out to be one of my mother's seven rescuers! His name is Ho Trong Nhung; he is sixty-four years old and slim, with thinning gray hair. My mother greets him joyfully, and he smiles back at her, remembering. An Dien asks him if he would share his side of the story.

Ho Trong Nhung scrunches up his face, remembering the horrible smell of the bodies—a smell that, so many years later, has stayed with him. He recalls the persistent leeches on my mother's body. He is a little shy for cameras but tells his story strongly and confidently: How he carried her down for five hours. How they fed her only rice water, no rice. How she begged for a smoke, which he laughingly imitates, putting two fingers to his lips. He remembers how my mother waved at them, how he initially mistook her for a monkey. *First a ghost, now a monkey? Nice, Mother . . . charming.*

## *The Orange Man*

The orange man is the definite climax in my party story. My mother has always spoken about him with tenderness and enthusiasm. In a way, he gave her life, and in turn gave life to my brother and me. Meeting him is also the anticipated climax of our trip, the part I am most looking forward to. We follow An Dien down a dirt path into breathtaking scenery. *As if I have a breath to take!* My heart is pounding at the prospect of meeting the man I have heard so much about. Low, green mountains provide the idyllic backdrop for endless short yellow-green grass with sparse trees and a few cattle grazing calmly.

There he is. A slim man in green, high-waisted trousers and a tucked-in pale yellow shirt standing beneath a tree. Cao Van Hanh. The moment my mother sees him, she drops her bag and runs toward him. As they embrace, she seems like a giant in comparison. They join hands and look into each other's eyes. All he can see is her, and all she can see is him. They don't notice the swarm of cameras that surge out of the bushes and trees behind them, all trying to capture the moment.

I step forward. The moment Cao and I make eye contact, the clicking cameras and the immense heat fade away. I see tears glistening on his cheeks and I am taken aback by the tangible emotion in the air. I reach for his hands, and he lets me hold them. I ask the translator to please thank him on behalf of me and my brother for saving our mother.

Cao comes with us in the van a short ride to the foot of O Kha. Before us is a large, open space, with a small stream running through it. The widows separate to perform the worship ceremony for their husbands. They hold smoking sticks of incense in their hands as they stand with bowed heads. The mountain is a constant presence over us. I imagine my young mother, alone amid those trees and in the shadow of that mountain. Then I look beside me, where she stands staring at the same spot. I see the scars on her arms and legs that have been familiar to me since I was a toddler.

A few feet away, the orange man is also gazing at O Kha Mountain. Three very different yet deeply connected people thinking the same thoughts.

We walk back to the car together in shared silence.

At lunch in the community center in To Hap, Cao tells us through An Dien that he was born in Ba Cum Bac village in 1959 and is from the Raglai ethnic group. He was drafted into the army at age fifteen, where he served from '73 to '79 as a nurse; he was never involved in the fighting. After he was dispatched from the army, he met his wife in her hometown, To Hap, in 1980, and they married the same year. Together they have five children and two grandchildren.

He seems to recall the day he found my mother clearly. The morning of the plane crash, he was having breakfast with his family at home; it was raining. Suddenly, he heard a big explosion but didn't know what it was. He was told the next day that it was a civilian crash and was mobilized by the military to look for the wreckage. He just kept looking until he found it. He describes how the paths were much rougher in 1992, and much denser, how deforestation has changed the landscape. It is almost a different mountain now. As he speaks, I note the sincerity in his eyes, the sharp, defined bone structure of his cheeks, and the energy that makes him almost like a little boy, while his face shows the strain of his sixty-five years. Then, he shocks us with the news that he had been the head of the police at the time, and in charge of the rescue mission. *Wait!?* Didn't An Dien tell us it was the head of the police who had wanted to shoot my mother in the first place? *That does not fit our heroic image of him at all!* Was our hero also crying because he had luckily changed his mind?

## An American and a Vietnamese Daughter

Back at Ho Chi Minh City Airport, more photographers and selfie requests await us. A small-framed, quiet-looking girl with glasses approaches me and in perfect English introduces herself as Ms. Lan's daughter, Bao. She is able to translate some thoughts that perhaps her mother feels more comfortable translating through her daughter than through An Dien. "My mom is truly happy that your mom survived. She does not have any hard feelings toward her. My mom is grateful to your mom, and feels a mutual understanding as a fellow widow." Ms. Lan stands beside Bao as she speaks, enthusiastically nodding her head. "I was still in my mother's womb when my dad died," Bao shares. "I never met him."

Then Bao turns and hands me a large frame. It is a hand-embroidered screen with a clock skillfully incorporated into it, delicate little stitches indicating each hour. On the back is written "To Joosje, from Bao." The embroidery depicts a young girl sitting on the ground and looking thoughtfully into the distance.

"That's you," Bao tells me.

I am stunned. I expected Bao to resent me; her father died looking for my mother. Instead, she is open and kind. She has even put thought, care, and a lot of effort into a gift for me.

## The American War: Củ Chi Tunnels

We are given one "vacation day" in Ho Chi Minh City. No interviews, no calls, no signings, no public appearances. *Finally!* I thought *The star needs to rest!*

We decide to use this day to take a tour offered by the Hotel Continental of the Củ Chi tunnels, a vast network of underground tunnels that were used by the Vietcong during the Vietnam War, and their base of operations for the Tết Offensive in 1968. A chance to learn more about the military history that was an irreplaceable part of Vietnam's history. Coming out of a year of AP US History in school, I have learned in depth about the war between the United States and

Vietnam. The "Vietnam War" as I had been used to hearing in class, but the "American War" to the Vietnamese, as our guide referred to it.

The morning of our free day we awake early to meet our guide in the lobby promptly at seven thirty. She is a young, small-framed woman, both a student and, as she excitedly tells us, an entrepreneur who created an antimosquito mixture. Talking with her is easy during our ride to the tunnels, and we quickly grow to like her.

Throughout the tour, she constantly refers to "the enemy." Not the Americans, only the enemy. Having grown up in the United States, I feel a partial responsibility for the destruction and ignorance it released upon this country. Yet I can still hear and see in my head the American veterans of this war, the war of *two* sides, like any war. I see and hear them say, "I am a veteran of the Vietnam War," with pleading eyes. I see the Vietnam Veterans Memorial before me, from a class trip to DC in eighth grade. I see the 58,307 names inscribed upon it. The enemy. Our guide proudly describes the array of devices displayed from wartime— these traps were used to trip the enemy, to make them fall, capture them, puncture them, spear them in their "big fat bellies." I think of young American boys in a country whose culture could not be further from their own, boys who had no idea what they were drafted into.

We walk through the forest, largely unchanged since the war. My mother even comments on the similarity of the light coming through the trees to her jungle. Suddenly, guns go off in the distance. It makes me shiver. A mock shooting field near the site of the tunnels for gun aficionados where they can practice shooting targets in a realistic environment. *Call of Duty* in action. Here, of all places! But we can't see that. All we see is nature in all directions. The fact that civilization is quite nearby completely exits the mind, and the sounds of those bullets fills and overcrowds the air. It gives me a small taste of what it must have been like during that brutal war. How must the soldiers have felt as they trampled through these woods? The Americans weighed down with equipment, terrified and utterly unsure of the way, and the Vietnamese, more familiar with the terrain but horrified by the American equipment and attitude? Both charged with the fear of bumping into the enemy.

Then there were the tunnels themselves. Just ten seconds within one is enough to shoot off countless what-if scenarios in my head. Not to mention the claustrophobia.

*What if the ceiling collapses? What if water floods? What if I suffocate? What if, what if?* It takes my life of hearing my mother protest what-if thinking to calm myself down. What's more, during the war all those what-ifs that for me are silly, self-indulgent, panic scenarios were actual, real possibilities. The anxiety alone is unimaginable.

## Readers' Questions

The same day we arrive back in Ho Chi Minh City from Nha Trang, we have a meet-and-greet with readers in Fahasa, the biggest bookstore chain in Vietnam. It is raining so hard it seems as if no one will come, but we don't realize how regular the rain is. Every afternoon, the sky opens up and lays all its woes onto Ho Chi Minh City. It pours with dense, thick drops. Yet the area Fahasa has set up in the front of the store fills up completely; people are standing in the back due to the lack of seating.

The audience is charged with excited energy. The journey to Nha Trang has been a tiring one, yet despite her exhaustion, my mother gives her introductory speech smoothly and with heart. Now it is time for questions.

After satisfying the usual curiosities, a lady from the back raises her hand enthusiastically.

"How do you stop yourself from crying?" she asks.

My mother clearly enjoys this refreshing question and takes a moment to think. "You have to shift your focus," she answers. "It's practice, I guess. As a trader on Wall Street, crying was not an option. I learned to choose my moments."

The lady laughs and contently concludes, "So it is not about not crying, but knowing when to cry."

"And knowing when to fight and when to surrender," my mother adds, moving the attention to the second half of her book, the part about autism. [Autism is a delicate subject in Vietnam, where disabled children are seen as a punishment for their mothers' bad karma. Their parents hide them out of shame.]

"Other than being in a plane crash, or being stuck for days, one of my greatest fears was having a child with autism. That fear also came true. Once I learned to accept him, I could see the beauty in him. He became my Buddha, and I celebrate him every day."

## Mr. 601

Pasje's "Mr. Fix-It-All," Mr. Hung, has invited us for a drink at the Norfolk Hotel, where Pasje used to live. Both meeting him and seeing the hotel are a first for my mother in almost twenty-two years.

A large group awaits us at a table in the lobby: Mr. Hung and his wife, managers of the hotel, and two lovely women who worked there in 1992. The women recount how kind Pasje was, how he always took the time to speak to those working at the front desk. They tenderly called him Mr. 601, after his room number. The general manager of the hotel offers us more than a drink. "We also invite you both to stay the night in his renovated suite," he says.

"Thank you, but no thank you," my mother politely refuses, slightly embarrassed. "But we would be delighted to see the room."

Our group crowds into the small, mirrored elevator. Everyone is constantly taking pictures with their phones. The manager opens the door to the suite and suddenly the breath is knocked out of me. *I feel Pasje in this room!* Odd. I have never met him. Then again, perhaps I have met him: through my mother's descriptions, through the way my mother's family and friends still talk about him, through the pictures I have seen. Through *Turbulence*. I look at my mother and see she feels the same presence.

She escapes out onto the balcony where she took the last-ever picture of Pasje. I watch her from inside, from the room where she spent her last night before the crash, the final night of her "old life." I join her on the balcony, and she hugs me tightly.

I think of the question a journalist asked me: how did it make me feel to honor the life of the man who, had he not died, would have prevented the union of my parents? I do not think of Pasje that way. He is permanently on one side of the divide that the crash created in my mother's life. I know how much she loved him, and from what I know of him, I think he was worthy of her love. But I also know the love my parents had for each other. For many years, they complemented each other perfectly, in work and in life. They were the most dynamic of all duos. Their love led to my existence, and that of the most important person in the world to me: my brother, the person who taught me how to see past limits.

My mother has had two big loves. On the surface, it looks like she has lost both of them, one through death, one through life (my parents are unfortunately now divorced). But I believe my mother never really *lost* them; love knows no labels or limits. Pasje has stayed with her. And Jaime is my father, my brother's father. They are still united in their love for us.

## Ripples

The accident happened more than twenty years ago, and it may have been a stone in the water, but stones create waves. The waves of the crash in 1992 have had an impact on Vietnamese families, the families of Willem, Jack Emmerson, the Swedes who cremated Pasje, and on both my mother and her family.

Eventually waves turn into ripples. The ripples of the crash now affect the next generation, daughters unborn at the time, daughters who would not be alive without the stone, daughters of Vietnam Airlines crew members, the granddaughter of Jack Emmerson, who reached out to my mother through e-mail. She was reading the book to her grandfather. This summer in Vietnam, I saw how *Turbulence* brings the ripple effect to its readers. It disseminates the message of one event, one stone. The ripples connect us.

Mr. Tan has linked me to his daughter on Facebook, and as he put it when I met him, "No more past; the future." Life goes on; generations keep being born. Although the event, the stone, becomes a distant memory, its lessons keep living. We must take what we have learned and share it. Internalize the past and move forward with the ripples as they expand.

# ACKNOWLEDGMENTS

For me, creation is an exchange with other people. It is in the air, like a third entity. Like a tennis ball, hanging in the air between two players, as Joseph Campbell said. This is the 189th version of *Turbulence*, and I am happy to say that every single version has been an interactive and collective effort. Every word, idea, and clipped sentence has been discussed with or reviewed by others: my generous friends around the world in different time zones, who, in endless phone conversations and email exchanges, had the stamina to keep on chewing on its content and discussing life's big questions. And when they woke up to the latest version in their mailbox, they read it, again. And again.

Without the daily presence of Julie Roelvink, *Turbulence* would not have existed at all. For a whole long year, I would write two pages in the very early morning, send them off to her in London, and get them back with cheer, red edits, and suggestions. I would work them out in the afternoon and send the result back at the end of my night. The next day, with comforting predictability, I would find an edited version in my mailbox. She virtually held my hand throughout the whole process.

As always, everything I do with more than a little help from my friends: the biggest direct efforts were made by Dorine Hermans and Caroline Noordhoek Hegt, but the endless philosophizing with Jane Bischoff, Rosario Conde, and Susan Le Picart also shaped the book's content

Michiel Hupkes, Costas Michalopoulos, Caroline Binsbergen, Inge Jonckheer, Regina Monticone, and Greg Alessandro were the emergency editors. Many thanks to the interactive readers: Christina Heinl, Ian Fentan, Ray van Mourik, Reinout Albers, Connie Lippert, Eveline Herfkens, Laetitia Lindgren, Doug and Monica Taylor, Ann Keller, Noami Baeza, Titia Deurvorst, Annetine Gelijns, and the whole of Jackson Taylor's writing group, from whom I have learned so much more than writing. Thanks to Sue Rosen for referring me to Jackson. Thanks to Michael Denneny not only for his edits, but also for believing in me as a writer and putting the publishing world in perspective. When publishers declined to include Maxi because "autism was a turn off," I decided to self-publish with the help of Marc Corsey of Eclipse Publishing Services, Lisa Weinert, and Tyson Cornell, Archer.

*Turbulence* was published with success in Vietnam. Thanks to Meulenhoff /De Boekerij. *Turbulence* became a bestseller in The Netherlands, which in turn secured French, German, and Portuguese editions. I was delighted when Regan Arts acquired and produced this version with the tireless aid of Zainab Choudhry. I have admired Judith Regan ever since she interviewed Joosje and me on her radio show. Also thanks to Kathryn Huck and F. Mauricio Artavia.

I thank all the contributors who wrote their perspectives. And Jack, who guided me up the mountain with our many phone conversations and emails. When I visited him in Glasgow, he was waiting at the train station, holding a picture of me attached to a stick.

I also want to say thanks to and for Joosje Lupa: for being a sixteen-, seventeen-, and eighteen-year-old daughter who is willing and grown-up enough to edit her own mother's life.

And thanks to all the other posses I could not live and love without, in any dimension. Both earthly and ethereal.